Miracles

PHILOSOPHICAL TOPICS

Paul Edwards, General Editor

Miracles

Edited, with an Introduction by

RICHARD SWINBURNE

OXFORD UNIVERSITY

Macmillan Publishing Company
New York

Collier Macmillan Publishers
London

Macmillan Publishing Company
866 Third Avenue, New York, New York 10022

Collier Macmillan Canada, Inc.

Library of Congress Cataloging-in-Publication Data

Miracles.

(Philosophical topics)
Bibliography: p.
1. Miracles. I. Swinburne, Richard. II. Series:
Philosophical topics (New York, N.Y.)
BL487.M57   1989   210   88-5121
ISBN 0-02-418731-3

Printing: 1 2 3 4 5 6 7   Year: 9 0 1 2 3 4 5

CONTENTS

Miracles

1

INTRODUCTION

THIS BOOK IS about miracles—what they are, what would count as evidence that they have occurred, and whether it matters whether or not they have occurred.[1] It is not primarily concerned with historical evidence about whether certain particular miracles (such as Christ rising from the dead or walking on water) have occurred, but it is primarily concerned with whether historical evidence could show anything about such things and whether it matters if it can. It is concerned with the framework within which a historical debate must be conducted. It contains a selection of writings written from different viewpoints by philosophers, classical and modern. The reader is left to form his or her own view on who wins the argument.

At the end is a bibliography of important, relevant writings not contained in this volume. Numbers in square brackets, both in this introduction and in the extracts in the volume, refer to the items so numbered herein ([2] to [16]) or listed in the bibliography (items [17] onward).

---

1. Some of the material in this Introduction comes from Chapters 1 and 2 of my book *The Concept of Miracle*. (London: Macmillann Publishers Ltd., 1970). Chapter 3 of that book is used as [8] in this collection, and Chapter 4 as [13]. I am grateful to Macmillan Publishers Ltd. for permission to reuse this material in this form.

What Is a Miracle?

Many people understand by a *miracle* (and by words normally so translated into English) an event of an extraordinary kind brought about by a god and of religious significance. But some of the terms in this definition can be interpreted in various ways, which we must now distinguish. Further, *miracle* is sometimes used in a wider or a narrower sense than any of the senses that result from giving a precise meaning to some of the vague terms of this initial definition. These we must clarify.

"An Event of an Extraordinary Kind"

What counts as "of an extraordinary kind" depends on what is one's understanding of what happens ordinarily. Thus, on the view of Aristotle inherited by most medieval thinkers, each object belonged to a kind, and objects of each kind had natures specific to objects of that kind. An object's nature determined how it behaved naturally—that is, when not acted upon by another object. Thus it belonged to the nature of a plant to take in nourishment, grow, and subsequently decay, and its doing these things was natural behavior for it. Other objects, however, in virtue of their natures could make an object do what it would not do naturally (when that behavior of the latter object was its moving, that motion was said to be violent motion). A plant could not by its nature move across the Earth, but a human being could carry it across the Earth, thereby subjecting it to violent motion. A human's nature was such that he or she had the power of producing such motion in the plant. So the occurrences in the world, that is, the changes of state of objects, were either occurrences that were natural behaviors of the objects concerned or were produced by other objects who by nature had the power to produce such occurrences. On the medieval view in general, objects had no option but to exercise their power in certain circumstances (plants will thrive in a favorable climate, and raindrops cannot but fall from the sky), but some objects (rational agents such as men or women) often have a choice whether or not to exercise their powers.

St. Thomas Aquinas (c. 1225 – 74) claimed that to be a miracle an event had to be such as to be beyond the natural power of any created thing to produce. (For his account see [2] in this volume.) It was in consequence of this understanding of "extraordinary" that Aquinas held that God, as alone uncreated, could alone work miracles. Others, however, and especially Pope Benedict XIV (1675–1758), whose work *De Miraculis* forms a standard statement of Roman Catholic doctrine, more naturally allow that something is a miracle whose production exceeds "the power of visible and corporeal nature only" [18] 1.1.12). Hence, on Benedict's view angels could work miracles. He further held that humans could work miracles if they were for an instant given powers (by an agent able to bestow such powers) beyond their nature.

However, talk about objects having natures in virtue of which they exercise certain powers is talk that belongs to ancient rather than modern science. Since the seventeenth century we have come to think of the behavior of things as governed not by their nature or by other objects in virtue of their nature but by laws of nature, or natural laws, which declare which events must or must probably follow other events. (This new way of talking is not one forced on people by any new scientific discovery, but is simply a different and sometimes more convenient way of setting forth our knowledge of the behavior of things.)

Natural laws may be universal or statistical in form. Universal laws are of the form "so-and-sos necessarily do (or are) such-and-such"; statistical laws are of the form "so-and-sos do (or are) such-and-such with such-and-such probability." Universal laws state what must happen; statistical laws state what has a certain in-built probability (in the sense of propensity) of happening in a particular case. Paradigm examples of universal laws are Newton's three laws of motion and his law of gravitation, which together state how bodies of different masses having certain initial arrangements and velocities subsequently have certain other arrangements and velocities. Since the eighteenth century many people, especially scientists, have believed that natural laws governed all events of all kinds. From the eighteenth to the beginning of the twentieth century most people believed that all natural laws were universal, so that the preceding state of the universe invariably determined in all its detail what its subsequent state was to be. This view may be called physical determinism. Yet since the development of quantum theory in this century, many scientists have come to hold that the fundamental natural laws are statistical. These are the laws governing the behavior of the fundamental particles, such as photons, electrons, and mesons, out of which the ordinary familiar objects that surround us are composed. It is a consequence of such laws, for example, that all photons approaching a potential barrier of a certain kind have a certain probability of passing through it and a certain probability of being reflected. There is no necessity about what an individual photon will do. However, although the probability of some small-scale event is often not especially close to one or zero, probabilities on the small scale often produce near-necessities on the large scale. So although one is far from certain what an individual fundamental particle will do, idiosyncrasies cancel out, and one can be pretty near certain to within a minute margin of error what a large number of such particles will do—which is why the behavior of ordinary size objects is in general so consistent (just as it follows that if it is equally probable that a coin will fall heads or tails on any one occasion, then in a million throws very nearly half of the throws will be heads and very nearly half will be tails).

Given talk of natural laws, an event that goes against them or "violates" them would seem to be an event "of an extraordinary kind." (This notion of "violation" is examined in more detail later on.) If the laws are universal, such an event would be one whose nonoccurrence is predicted by the laws. If the laws are statistical, an event whose occurrence the laws rendered as highly improbable would seem to be an event of "an extraordinary kind." These seem to be the most natural modern equivalents of an event whose production exceeds the power of visible and corporeal nature. Many have certainly understood an event of this kind to be well on the way to being a miracle.

It is possible, of course, that people may think that L is a law of nature when it is not, and so may wrongly suppose that an event that violates L is a violation of a law of nature. Putting the matter in Aquinas's terminology of the powers of objects, he comments that the ignorant may not realize that it is within the natural power of a magnet to attract iron ([2] 102.1). And because of the progress of science, even the scientifically educated of a period in history may think that some apparent regularity is a law of nature when really it is not, and so they would suppose that some event E violates natural laws when it does not. Because of the difficulty sometimes involved in discerning whether an event is a violation of a law of nature, some have thought that what matters is whether an event seemed to those involved to be such a violation, not whether it really was. The fact that it appears thus, given perhaps that other conditions are also fulfilled, makes an event a miracle. Yet although the term is occasionally used in such a subjective sense, I do not think that this use is in fact at all common. For if something previously believed to be a violation of natural laws and for that reason a miracle is shown in fact to be in accord with natural laws, we are apt to say that it was not a miracle after all, not that it is now no longer a miracle.

However, there are other events that occur in perfect accord with natural laws, and yet are so "extraordinary" that many might consider them candidates for being miracles. These are extraordinary coincidences. Even given determinism, what happens is not solely a function of which laws operate. Laws state the subsequent effect of certain initial conditions, and what happens is a function as much of the initial conditions as of the laws. The state of the world today, given determinism, is a consequence of its state yesterday, and its state yesterday a consequence of its state the day before, and so on. (If there was an initial moment of the universe, then its subsequent state is, given the laws, a consequence of its initial state.) Now in any period of history, events of certain kinds are very frequent and events of other kinds very rare, and which are frequent and which are rare are, for any given set of natural laws, a consequence of a past state of the universe (which will not itself have been determined solely by the laws, but by yet earlier states, if such there were). Whereas the laws alone determine which event succeeds which, their coincidence (which event happens at the same time as which other event) depend also on initial states. Some coincidences will be normal, some abnormal or extraordinary. Some philosophers and theologians have wanted to allow the extraordinary coincidence as an event of an extraordinary kind, which was a candidate for being a miracle, and ordinary talk would seem to allow this usage. In [6] in this volume, R.F. Holland distinguishes the coincidence miracle from what I have called the "violation" miracle and describes an example of a coincidence that we might wish to call miraculous.

"An Event Brought About by a god"

The second condition stated in my original definition was that to be a miracle an event must be brought about by a god. I understand by a god a nonembodied rational agent of great power. By a rational agent I mean someone who has beliefs and acts intentionally (that is, for reasons). By saying the agent is "nonembodied" I mean that (except perhaps temporarily and by their own choice) the agent has no body; that is, there is no one material object through which alone the agent can act on the world and acquire justified beliefs about it. By the agent being of great power I mean that he or she can produce effects far beyond the normal powers of humans.

This second condition may be made more tight or more loose. On a tighter definition an event would be a miracle only if brought about by God, not by any god. By God I mean the God of the Christians, Jews, and Moslems. (Since the defining properties by which Christians, Jews, and Moslems pick out the object of their worship are very similar—omnipotence, omniscience, perfect goodness, and so on—it is natural to say that Christians, Jews, and Moslems worship the same God. They do, of course, differ in their beliefs about what other properties that God has: Christians, unlike Moslems, for instance, believe that he is three "persons" in one "substance," and that he redeemed the world through Christ.) By Aquinas's definition of "miracle," only God can work miracles.

The second condition can be made looser by allowing any agent, not necessarily a god, to work miracles. It does not seem obviously self-contradictory to suppose that some embodied rational agent such as a human being worked a miracle. Benedict allowed that a human could work a miracle if temporarily given superhuman power.

"An Event of Religious Significance"

The third requirement in my definition for an event being a miracle is that it should have religious significance. If a god intervened in the natural order to make a feather land here rather than there for no deep ultimate purpose, or to upset a child's box of toys just for spite, these events would not naturally be described as miracles. To be a miracle an event must contribute significantly toward a holy divine purpose for the world.

On a wide understanding of religious significance, an event will have religious significance if it is a good event and a contribution to or foretaste of the ultimate destiny of the world. Thus the healing of a sick person will, by the Christian view, be of religious significance, since the world's ultimate destiny is, according to the Christian view, a state where evil, including sickness, is no more. But narrower views of religious significance are possible. For Benedict XIV, it is required of miracles "that they serve to confirm The Catholic Faith, or to demonstrate the sanctity of some man" ([18] 1.4.6). One way in which an extraordinary event could "confirm" a doctrine would be if it occurred in answer to prayer asking for confirmation of the doctrine as, if it occurred, did Elijah's purported miracle on Mount Carmel (1 Kings 18).

Elijah challenged the prophets of Baal: "Call ye on the name of your god, and I will call on the name of the Lord: and the god that answereth by fire let him be God." The prayer of the prophets of Baal got no response, but in answer to Elijah's prayer "the fire of the Lord fell, and consumed the burnt offering, and the wood, and the stones, and the dust," soaked in water, "and licked up the water that was in the trench." Another way in which an extraordinary event could confirm a doctrine could be by symbolizing it. If Jesus fed the five thousand in the wilderness with the five loaves and two fishes (see John 6:1–14), he was repeating on a larger scale an event believed to have been performed by Elisha (2 Kings 4:42 ff.), and thus, by the Jewish understanding, symbolizing his being a new and greater Elisha.

So then, religious significance can be understood in a wider or narrower sense. But in order to be a miracle, an event must surely have religious significance in some sense. Extraordinary events lacking religious significance are more appropriately characterized as magical or psychic phenomena rather than as miracles. It is for this reason that many ancient writers on miracles have written that a miracle is not an event contrary to nature but an event beyond nature. The point of this remark is that whereas an event that is a miracle is not in accordance with the nature of the objects involved in it, it is nevertheless in accordance with the divinely ordained natural order as a whole. It is indeed, Aquinas would argue, contrary to the nature of the sea that it "open up and offer a way through which people may pass," but its doing so at the time of the Israelite exodus from Egypt was part of the divine plan for the human race, and so in a sense it was very much a natural event. Miracles are events with a point in the overall scheme of things, and so in a sense are very much regular.

For a few modern writers any event of great religious significance is, as such, a miracle. It is not necessary for them that it be an event of an extraordinary kind brought about by a god or a human using abnormal powers (in the senses earlier described). A definition of this kind is offered by the Protestant theologian Paul Tillich (1886–1965).

(See [7] in this volume.) But although one may have good reason for recommending that *miracle* be used in this sense in the future, it is important to note that it is not the traditional sense; and if used in this new sense, *miracle* would take over a job often done previously by the word *sign* (or words so translated into English). When Ezekiel joined two sticks (Ezekiel 37:15–28) to show that God would unite into one people the tribes of Israel and Judah, there was nothing above nature in his physical movements, although his action had great religious significance. By a Tillichian definition, Ezekiel would have done a miracle, but it seems more natural to say that he performed a sign, although there was nothing miraculous in what he did.

As well as being used in the ways described above, the word *miracle* is sometimes used by people who do not wish to make any religious point. "It was a miracle" may sometimes mean simply that the event was highly unexpected and highly desirable. This use of *miracle* seems very much a derivative one, and is of no interest for the philosophy of religion.

By our initial definition, a miracle is an event of an extraordinary kind, brought about by a god, and of religious significance. We have seen how these conditions in our definition may be understood in narrower or wider ways, and how one or more of these conditions may be dropped, so that different senses of *miracle* result. The concepts of "extraordinary coincidence" or "religious significance" do not seem to raise any philosophical problems peculiar to the topic of miracles. The notion of a coincidence is perfectly comprehensible, and, given a religious system established on good grounds, the concept of religious significance seems perfectly comprehensible and applicable. (To examine the grounds for postulating such a system would be to go beyond the narrow confines set for this book, but some readings on this topic are listed in the Bibliography.) The main philosophical problems arise with the other concepts to which we have referred.

For the rest of this introduction, I shall understand a miracle in the sense of a *violation of a law of nature by a god*. I say this because all the philosophical problems peculiar to the topic of miracles arise with this definition, and because when we rightly add that a miracle has to be "of religious significance," we do get what is, I think, the most common understanding of this notion in the major religions over the past two millennia. In particular, Christians have generally claimed that from time to time God brings about miracles in this sense, and that evidence of violations in circumstances where God might be expected to bring them about is evidence (among other evidence) that God exists. The importance for Christian apologetic of the occurrence of miracles in this way made the Scottish philosopher David Hume (1711–76) understand *miracle* in just such a sense. Hume wrote that "a miracle may be accurately defined, as a transgression of a law of nature by a particular volition of the Deity, or by the interposition of some invisible agent" [3] p. 28, n. 3).

As we shall see, Hume argued that it is most unlikely that there can be good evidence for the occurrence of miracles in this sense.

The Coherence of the Definition

Recent philosophical writing has produced two separate challenges to the coherence of this definition of a miracle—as a violation of a law of nature by a god—suggesting that it contains some internal inconsistency, so that there could not possibly be such a thing as a miracle. The first challenge states that the notion of a "violation" of a law of nature (at any rate of a universal law) is incoherent. For a purported universal law of nature allegedly states what necessarily (and so always) happens, and if there was exception to a purported law, it would not really be a law at all. Discovering a body that levitated (rose upward despite being made of matter that normally in that environment fell downward) would show that the "law" of gravity was not a law, and so it had not been violated. (This argument does not show that there cannot be a "violation" of a statistical law, for statistical laws do allow occasional improbable events to occur.) In [5] Alastair McKinnon presents this objection very forcefully. The notion of a "violation" requires careful definition to avoid such an objection. In [8] I try to meet this objection by understanding a "violation" of a law of nature as a "nonrepeatable counterinstance" to it, i.e., an exception that would not be repeated under similar circumstances. (In this I follow Ninian Smart [32] and I then spell out an understanding of the "necessity" of a law of nature that rules out the occurrence only of repeatable, not of nonrepeatable exceptions to it.) If the levitation would not automatically occur again under similar circumstances, it would violate the law of gravity, without showing that it is not a law—on my suggested understanding of the "necessity" of a law of nature. This gives us a coherent and applicable sense of *miracle*.

The second challenge to the coherence of our definition arises from the consideration that to say that a miracle was (among other things) an event caused by a god is to say that it has a cause. In citing its cause, we explain its occurrence. But, the objection goes, explaining anything at all consists of showing that its occurrence was in accordance with some law of nature. So whatever can be explained is no violation of a law; and there cannot be such a thing as a caused violation. In [27] Patrick Nowell-Smith argued against an opponent on these lines:

> Let him consider the meaning of the word "explanation" and let him ask himself whether this notion does not involve that of a law or hypothesis capable of predictive expansion. And then let him ask himself whether such an explanation would not be natural, in whatever terms it was couched, and how the notion of "the supernatural" could play any part in it.

The defender of the coherence of our definition must claim that there is a way of explaining events other than the "scientific" way in terms of initial conditions and laws of nature. The defender must say that when we explain the results of intentional actions in terms of the purposes or intentions of agents, their beliefs, and capacities, we are using a quite different pattern of explanation from the scientific. When we explain the motion of my hand by my moving it, seeking to execute a purpose (to wave goodbye), in virtue of a belief (that you would see my hand moving and interpret it as such a wave) and a capacity (to cause the motion of my hand), we do seem to be using a very different pattern of explanation from the scientific, and yet one that really does explain why my hand moved. Whether such a "personal explanation" is quite different from a scientific explanation is, however, a controversial issue in the philosophy of mind. A simple defense is given in [11] of the view that personal explanation, and so causality by a personal agent ("agent causality"), is different in kind from the scientific. If it isn't, there could not be a violation of a law of nature, caused by some agent.

Historical Evidence for the Occurrence of Miracles

If our definition of *miracle* survives these challenges to its coherence, the next question is whether there could be good historical evidence that a miracle had occurred. All modern discussion of this matter takes off from the famous Section 10 of Hume's *Enquiry Concerning Human Understanding* ([3] in this volume).

Part 1 of Section 10 is devoted to showing on philosophical grounds that the evidence against the occurrence of any purported miracle is normally likely to be extremely strong and to outweigh by far the evidence in favor of the occurrence. When he is conducting any enquiry, Hume claims, and, in particular, any historical inquiry "a wise man . . . proportions his belief to the evidence" ([3] p. 24). If it be claimed that some particular event *E* happened, an investigator will weigh the evidence in favor of *E* having happened against the evidence that *E* did not happen. The evidence will include memories, the testimony of witnesses, and our experience of what generally happens. Thus a judge or detective will weigh the evidence of one witness that Jones robbed the safe against the evidence of two witnesses that he was not in the vicinity at the time in question and evidence that Jones had never robbed a safe before. The more unusual the alleged event, the heavier is the evidence against it having happened. This is so because it is a basic principle of reasoning about matters of fact (often called by philosophers inductive reasoning) that the more often an event of a certain type *A* has been followed by an event of some type *B*, the more reason we have for expecting that the next event of type *A* will be followed by an event of type *B*. And the more often an event of type *A* has not been followed by an event of type *B*, the less reason we have to expect that the next one will be. Hence, the more often Jones is known in certain circumstances to have robbed safes, the more reasonable it is to assume that in similar circumstances he robbed another one. The more often rods of a certain constitution have broken when subjected to a certain strain, the more reasonable it is to expect that another one will. The evidence of what usually happens counts heavily against the testimony of witnesses that something abnormal did occur. A fortiori, if we have evidence that on all other known occasions an event of type *A* has been followed by an event of type *B*, then the evidence is very heavy against the claim that on one particular occasion an event of type *A* was not followed by an event of type *B*. Evidence of very many such particular observations establishes those general and apparently invariable correlations that we term laws of nature. Consequently, all such observations count against a claim that there has been one exception to this pattern. And it would take a great deal of evidence on the other side, the testimony of many reliable witnesses, to overcome this weight.

Thus very many astronomical and mechanical data that have been observed are instances of Newton's laws of motion. It is a consequence of Newton's laws that, given the present and past positions of sun and planets, the sun (relative to the Earth) never stays still. Consequently, the innumerable observations that substantiate Newton's laws are counter evidence to the claim in the Book of Joshua that for one day, while the Israelites conquered the Amorites, the sun stayed still (Joshua 10:13).

The question of a violation of a law of nature arises only when we suppose that we have actually got a law of nature. All the evidence that L is a law of nature is evidence against the claim that it was violated on a particular occasion. Because of the vast amount of evidence needed to establish L as a law of nature, it is most unlikely, Hume is in effect arguing, that there will be enough detailed historical evidence to outweigh it and to show that on a particular occasion an event E occurred, which L predicted would not occur. And if there were evidence to show that L did not operate on more than one occasion, that will suggest that L is not a law of nature at all.

Hume's argument is a powerful one; there is a useful modern commentary and development of it in a selection from J.L. Mackie [9]. Whether we accept it depends on the principles for weighing the evidence of what normally happens (itself established by historical evidence) against historical evidence of what did happen on a particular occasion. Historical evidence may include one's own apparent memories, the testimony of many witnesses, and traces. One may apparently remember having seen E occur. More usually, a number of witnesses may report having seen E occur. And sometimes there may be traces, that is, the physical effects that would have been caused by E if E did, in fact, occur. Thus there may be a photograph of what happened, or footprints and fingerprints may corroborate testimony. Hume's official position is that, although historical evidence could outweigh the evidence of what normally happens to produce a balance of evidence in favor of the occurrence of a miracle, this is most unlikely. The only kind of historical evidence that Hume considered was testimony, and he claimed that "no testimony is sufficient to establish a miracle, unless the testimony be of such a kind that its falsehood would be more miraculous" (i.e., more improbable) "than the fact, which it endeavours to establish, and even in that case there is a mutual destruction of arguments, and the superior only gives us an assurance suitable to that degree of force, which remains, after deducting the inferior." But although this is his official position, it seems that when Hume, in Part II of Section 10, comes to consider some particular cases, his standards are so high that no historical evidence could ever outweigh the evidence of what normally happens, to establish the occurrence of a miracle.

Discussion of Hume's argument is unfortunately complicated by an aspect of it that I have so far not brought up. For reasons arising from other parts of his philosophy (see his *Enquiry Concerning Human Understanding*, Sections 4, 5, and 7), Hume regarded laws of nature merely as true statements about what always happens, not as statements about what happens with physical "necessity" or probability. But there is a difference between what always happens and what necessarily happens—it may be a mere coincidence that all *A*'s are *B*, rather than it being a necessity in nature that *A*'s have to be *B*. But the more evidence we have that some regularity (e.g., *A*'s being *B*) holds in very many diverse circumstances, that is evidence that it is a law of nature that *A*'s are *B*, that being A causes something to be *B*, and so evidence that that regularity will operate in any other circumstances. In [10] Antony Flew argues that Hume's failure to recognize this distinction makes his argument less compelling than it should be, and that taking account of the distinction shows us that no historical evidence of what happened on one occasion could ever outweigh the scientific evidence from a well-established law of nature as to what must have happened on that occasion. In [13] I discuss the principles for weighing conflicting evidence and dispute this conclusion of Flew. (The discussion in [6] is also relevant to this issue.)

The calculus of probability is a valuable tool for analyzing weight of evidence. In [12] David Owen applies a well-known theorem of that calculus, Bayes' theorem, to bring out very clearly the principles involved in weighing evidence that a law of nature held on some occasion against the testimony of one witness that it did not. He concludes that if the witness is to be believed, "the reliability of the witness must be greater than the probability that the law of nature holds." He then asks, not unreasonably, "what witness is so reliable?" He does not, however, consider in detail the difference made if there are a number of independent witnesses whose testimony agrees, nor does he consider kinds of historical evidence other than testimony.

Background Evidence From an Overall World View

Laws of nature determine what necessarily happens (or happens with high physical probability). If some law fails to operate on some isolated occasion (i.e., there is a nonrepeatable counterinstance to it), that can only be because its operation has been suspended. But if there is no God or gods,[2] laws of nature are the ultimate determinants of what happens, and the sudden failure of a law of nature to operate merely through chance, to allow a nonrepeatable exception to it to occur, is hardly to be expected. The "necessity" involved in natural laws is a physical push that will virtually invariably force things to conform to the law.

Violations are most unlikely to occur unless they are miracles. Any evidence that there is no God would give even stronger reason to believe that on a given occasion there was no violation of natural laws. A very considerable amount of detailed historical evidence would be needed in order to substantiate the conclusion that a violation occurred, in the face of such opposing evidence. (But if there were such evidence, it would show that the laws of nature were not omnideterminant and so would give grounds for believing that there is a God.)

If there is a God, then ex hypothesi, it is God who keeps in operation the laws of nature. They are not the ultimate determinants of what happens. God can suspend their operation, i.e., violate them, and intervene in the natural order if and when he chooses. Any evidence that there is a God, and any grounds for thinking that God would be expected to intervene in the natural order in certain circumstances such as those in which some reported violation E occurs, will be evidence that E occurred. Less will be needed by way of detailed historical evidence to overcome the evidence of what normally happens. Background evidence from one's overall world view rightly conditions one's judgment about particular cases. As I have noted, the force of other evidence for and against the existence of God can-

2. Henceforward I ignore the possible existence of gods other than God, in order to keep the exposition simpler. Taking account of the possible existence of lesser gods will not significantly affect the main line of argument.

not be discussed here; suffice it to have shown its relevance. If there is a God, then by definition he will have the power to intervene in the natural order. But is it at all likely that God will do so? After all, why should he intervene in an order of things that he has himself created presumably exactly as he wished to create it?

Tillich and many others have argued that God would not intervene in his created order, and hence they preferred a definition of *miracle* such as that given in [7], which allowed there to be instances of miracles, despite natural laws never being violated. More conservative religious believers have held that God does intervene in his created order from time to time, to respond to human needs or prayers, to which it is good that he should be sensitive as they occur. A violation in such circumstances would be "of religious significance."

Two kinds of circumstances in particular have seemed to be suited for a divine intervention. God might be expected to intervene to put his seal on the testimony of some particular prophet, to confirm a doctrine in other words. If a violation occurs, which some prophet predicts that God will bring about and which forwards the recognition of his doctrine, that would put God's seal on that doctrine. For God alone can bring about a violation of natural laws. If he does so, as predicted by a prophet so as to forward the recognition of that prophet's doctrine, God is reasonably taken (in the absence of counterevidence) to be giving his blessing to that doctrine and so declaring it true. Unless God is to violate natural laws, how can humans know whether some doctrine is true except by the natural light of their own reason, and is that going to be good enough to discover deep metaphysical truths? Christians have normally claimed that the miracles reported in connection with the life and death of Jesus Christ, and above all the reported miracle of his Resurrection, have this function of showing that Christ was God's special messenger and that what he said was true. That background evidence of the existence of God is crucial for the assessment of historical evidence, and that God might be expected to bring about miracles to confirm a revelation such as that of Christ was argued against Hume by William Paley (1743–1805) ([4] in this volume).

Religious believers have also held that God might be expected to intervene in the natural order in answer to petitionary prayer. If God is to take humans seriously, he must interact with them and that involves changing things in the world in response to their requests.

Eleonore Stump argues this in [15]. But if petitionary prayer is something to which God responds by interfering in nature, does not this imply that miracles would have to occur rather more frequently than there is any evidence to suppose that they do? This issue is considered by Terence Penelhum in [14].

Do Miracles Occur?

This volume is concerned with how arguments for or against the occurrence of a particular miracle ought to go. But in order to bring the discussion down to earth a bit, it does contain one passage that claims that there is good evidence from history to suppose that miracles do occur and another that claims that there is good reason to suppose that they do not.

The first passage [16] is the defense by Richard Purtill of the plausibility of Christian claims for the occurrences of the miracles reported in the New Testament. The other passage is Part II of Hume's Section 10, where he produces four arguments designed to show that "there never was a miraculous event established" in the way that he argued in Part I would be needed to show the occurrence of a miracle. Hume claims that "there is not to be found, in all history, any miracle attested by a sufficient number of men, of such unquestioned good sense, education, and learning, as to secure us against all delusion in themselves" [3] p. 29). Secondly, he observes that people in general love to gossip about the marvelous and surprising, and that religious people do not hesitate to tell falsehoods to propagate what they believe to be basically true. Thirdly, Hume also claims that "it forms a strong presumption against all supernatural and miraculous relations, that they are observed chiefly to abound among ignorant and barbarous nations" ([3] p. 31).

These three points are purported factual claims and no one would dispute that in so far as they are correct, they tend to diminish the worth of tales of miracles. Whether they are correct is an issue beyond the main focus of this book, but it is important to note that whether they are correct or not depends, sometimes crucially, on how Hume's terms are to be understood, e.g., what is to count as "sufficient" men, "unquestioned" good sense, and an "ignorant and barbarous nation"? Nations ignorant and barbarous in some respects are often very cultured, learned, and morally sensitive in other respects.

Hume's fourth argument in Part II is an important one. He points out that miracles are reported in the context of many different religious systems, and he then goes on to claim that a report of a miracle in one such context counts against the occurrence of a miracle in a different context. The argument is that if a miracle of ancient Greco-Roman religion occurred as described, that is evidence that the gods of the Greeks and Romans exist, and if a Christian miracle occurred as described, that is evidence that the God of Christians exists. But if the gods of the Greeks and Romans exist, the God of the Christians does not, and conversely. Therefore the evidence in favor of a Greco-Roman miracle is evidence against the existence of the God of the Christians, and hence evidence against the occurrence of Christian miracles, and conversely. And so, generally, reports of miracles, Hume claims, tend to cancel out each other's evidential force. Whether Hume is right in this claim depends on two empirical considerations. First, it must be that the miracles "wrought in each religion" would be if they occurred, evidence for theological propositions of each religion incompatible with those of the other religion. Some reported miracles are certainly of this kind. The Resurrection of Christ, if it occurred as predicted by Christ, apparently setting a seal on his teaching, does support some detailed doctrine. Some equally striking violation of a natural law in response to a prayer that it happen to prove that Christ was not sent by God would indeed, if it occurred, fit the Humean pattern of conflict. But miracles that would be merely answers to individual prayers for help, rather than confirmations of doctrine, do not seem to fit the Humean pattern. If most alleged miracles occurred as reported, they would show at most the power of a god or gods and their concern for the needs of humans, and little more specific in the way of doctrine, which would weaken the force of Hume's point considerably.

Secondly, it must be the case that those miracles wrought in the context of different religious systems, which do give support to incompatible doctrines, have similar support from historical evidence. It may be claimed, as, for example, by Purtill, that Christian miracles of this type (and above all "the" Christian miracle of the Resurrection) are well authenticated, to an extent in which doctrine-supporting miracles of other religions are not. At that point the argument about miracles must move to details of history. The point of a volume such as this, however, is to help an investigator become clear in his or her own mind about just what the force of various pieces of documented historical evidence would be, if they were discovered.

2

ST. THOMAS AQUINAS*

Miracles

NOW, IF SOMEONE says that, since God did implant [a natural
order of causes and effects] in things, the production in things   3.99.9
of an effect independently of its proper causes, and apart from
the order established by Him, could not be done without a change
in this order, this objection can be refuted by the very nature of things.
For the order imposed on things by God is based on what usually
occurs, *in most cases*, in things, but not on what is always so. In fact,
many natural causes produce their effects in the same way, but not
always. Sometimes, indeed, though rarely, an event occurs in a different way, either due to a defect in the power of an agent, or to the
unsuitable condition of the matter, or to an agent with greater
strength—as when nature gives rise to a sixth finger on a man. But
the order of providence does not fail, or suffer change, because of
such an event. Indeed, the very fact that the natural order, which
is based on things that happen in most cases, does fail at times is subject to divine providence. So, if by means of a created power it can

*St. Thomas Aquinas (1225–1274) was the most important philosopher in the history
of Western philosophy from Aristotle in the fourth century BC until Descartes in the seventeenth century A.D. He developed a systematic Christian philosophy, sensitive to pagan
philosophy and science, supported by thorough detailed argumentation. This selection is
from *Summa Contra Gentiles*, translated by Vernon J. Bourke under the title *On the Truth
of the Catholic Faith*, (New York: Doubleday and Co., 1956).

happen that the natural order is changed from what is usually so to what occurs rarely—without any change of divine providence—then it is more certain that divine power can sometimes produce an effect, without prejudice to its providence, apart from the order implanted in natural things by God. In fact, He does this at times to manifest His power. For it can be manifested in no better way, that the whole of nature is subject to the divine will, than by the fact that sometimes He does something outside the order of nature. Indeed, this makes it evident that the order of things has proceeded from Him, not by natural necessity, but by free will.

3.100.1 However, it seems that we should keep in mind that, though God at times does something apart from the order implanted in things, He does nothing contrary to nature.

3.100.6 Furthermore, all creatures are related to God as art products are to an artist, . . . Consequently, the whole of nature is like an artifact of the divine artistic mind. But it is not contrary to the essential character of an artist if he should work in a different way on his product, even after he has given it its first form. Neither, then, is it against nature if God does something to natural things in a different way from that to which the course of nature is accustomed.

3.101.1 Things that are at times divinely accomplished, apart from the generally established order in things, are customarily called *miracles*; for we *admire* with some astonishment a certain event when we observe the effect but do not know its cause. And since one and the same cause is at times known to some people and unknown to others, the result is that, of several who see an effect at the same time, some are moved to admiring astonishment, while others are not. For instance, the astronomer is not astonished when he sees an eclipse of the sun, for he knows its cause, but the person who is ignorant of this science must be amazed, for he ignores the cause. And so, a certain event is wondrous to one person, but not so to another. So, a thing that has a completely hidden cause is wondrous in an unqualified way, and this the name, *miracle*, suggests; namely, what *is of itself filled with admirable wonder*, not simply in relation to one person or another. Now, absolutely speaking, the cause hidden from every man is God. In fact, we proved above [1] that no man in the present state of life can grasp His essence intellectually. Therefore,

---

[1] This is a reference to *Summa Contra Gentiles* 3.47.

those things must properly be called miraculous which are done by divine power apart from the order generally followed in things.

Now, there are various degrees and orders of these miracles. Indeed, the highest rank among miracles is held by those events   3.101.2 in which something is done by God which nature never could do. For example, that two bodies should be coincident; that the sun reverse its course, or stand still; that the sea open up and offer a way through which people may pass. And even among these an order may be observed. For the greater the things that God does are, and the more they are removed from the capacity of nature, the greater the miracle is. Thus, it is more miraculous for the sun to reverse its course than for the sea to be divided.

Then, the second degree among miracles is held by those events in which God does something which nature can do, but not   3.101.3 in this order. It is a work of nature for an animal to live, to see, and to walk; but for it to live after death, to see after becoming blind, to walk after paralysis of the limbs, this nature cannot do— but God at times does such works miraculously. Even among this degree of miracles a gradation is evident, according as what is done is more removed from the capacity of nature.

Now, the third degree of miracles occurs when God does what is usually done by the working of nature, but without the   3.101.4 operation of the principles of nature. For example, a person may be cured by divine power from a fever which could be cured naturally, and it may rain independently of the working of the principles of nature.

It can be shown from the foregoing that God alone can work   3.102.1 miracles.

In fact, whatever is completely confined under a certain order cannot work above that order. But every creature is established   3.102.2 under the order which God has put in things. So, no creature can operate above this order; but that is what it means to work miracles.

Again, when any finite power produces the proper effect to which it is determined, this is not a miracle, though it may   3.102.3 be a matter of wonder for some person who does not understand that power. For example, it may seem astonishing to ignorant people that a magnet attracts iron or that some little fish might hold back a ship. But the potency of every creature is limited to some definite effect or to certain effects. So, whatever is done by the power of any creature cannot be called a miracle properly, even though it may be astonishing to one who does not comprehend the power of this creature. But what is done by divine power, which, being infinite, is incomprehensible in itself, is truly miraculous.

3

DAVID HUME

❧

Of Miracles

❧

PART I

Bread & body
Blood & wine of communion
(PROTESTANT)

THERE IS, IN Dr. Tillotson's writings, an argument against the _real presence_, which is as concise, and elegant, and strong as any argument can possibly be supposed against a doctrine, so little worthy of a serious refutation. It is acknowledged on all hands, says that learned prelate, that the authority, either of the scripture or of tradition, is founded merely in the testimony of the apostles, who were eye-witnesses to those miracles of our Savior, by which he proved his divine mission. Our evidence, then, for the truth of the *Christian* religion is less than the evidence for the truth of our senses; because, even in the first authors of our religion, it was no greater; and it is evident it must diminish in passing from them to their disciples; nor can any one rest such confidence in their testimony, as in the immediate object of his senses. But a weaker evidence can never destroy a stronger; and therefore, were the doctrine of the real presence ever so clearly revealed in scripture, it were directly contrary to the rules of just reasoning to give our assent to it. It contradicts sense, though

---

* David Hume (1711–76) was the most influential philosopher in the Empiricist tradition, which has dominated the philosophy of the English-speaking world during the past three hundred years. He lived in Edinburgh. This selection is Section 10 of his *Enquiry Concerning Human Understanding*, first published in 1748.

both the scripture and tradition, on which it is supposed to be built, carry not such evidence with them as sense; when they are considered merely as external evidences, and are not brought home to every one's breast, by the immediate operation of the Holy Spirit.

Nothing is so convenient as a decisive argument of this kind, which must at least *silence* the most arrogant bigotry and superstition, and free us from their impertinent solicitations. I flatter myself, that I have discovered an argument of a like nature, which, if just, will, with the wise and learned, be an everlasting check to all kinds of superstitious delusion, and consequently, will be useful as long as the world endures. For so long, I presume, will the accounts of miracles and prodigies be found in all history, sacred and profane.

Though experience be our only guide in reasoning concerning matters of fact; it must be acknowledged, that this guide is not altogether infallible, but in some cases is apt to lead us into errors. One, who in our climate, should expect better weather in any week of June than in one of December, would reason justly, and conformably to experience; but it is certain, that he may happen, in the event, to find himself mistaken. However, we may observe, that, in such a case, he would have no cause to complain of experience; because it commonly informs us beforehand of the uncertainty, by that contrariety of events, which we may learn from a diligent observation. All effects follow not with like certainty from their supposed causes. Some events are found, in all countries and all ages, to have been constantly conjoined together. Others are found to have been more variable, and sometimes to disappoint our expectations; so that, in our reasonings concerning matter of fact, there are all imaginable degrees of assurance, from the highest certainty to the lowest species of moral evidence.

A wise man, therefore, proportions his belief to the evidence. In such conclusions as are founded on an infallible experience, he expects the event with the last degree of assurance, and regards his past experience as a full *proof* of the future existence of that event. In other cases, he proceeds with more caution: He weighs the opposite experiments: He considers which side is supported by the greater number of experiments: to that side he inclines, with doubt and hesitation; and when at last he fixed his judgment, the evidence exceeds not what we properly call *probability*. All probability, then, supposes an opposition of experiments and observations, where the one side is found to overbalance the other, and to produce a degree of evidence, proportioned to the superiority. A hundred instances or experiments on one side, and fifty on another, afford a doubtful expectation of any event; though a hundred uniform experiments, with only one that is contradictory, reasonably begets a pretty strong degree of assurance. In all cases, we must balance the opposite experiments, where they are opposite, and deduct the *smaller number* from the greater, in order to know the exact force of the superior evidence.

To apply these principles to a particular instance; we may observe, that there is no species of reasoning more common, more useful, and even necessary to human life, than that which is derived from the testimony of men, and the reports of eye-witnesses and spectators. This species of reasoning, perhaps, one may deny to be founded on the relation of cause and effect. I shall not dispute about a word. It will be sufficient to observe that our assurance in any argument of this kind is derived from no other principle than our observation of the veracity of human testimony, and of the usual conformity of facts to the reports of witnesses. It being a general maxim, that no objects have any discoverable connexion together, and that all the inferences, which we can draw from one to another, are founded merely on our experience of their constant and regular conjunction; it is evident, that we ought not to make an exception to this maxim in favor of human testimony, whose connexion with any event seems, in itself, as little necessary as any other. Were not the memory tenacious to a certain degree; had not men commonly an inclination to truth and a principle of probity, were they not sensible to shame, when detected in a falsehood: Were not these, I say, discovered by *experience* to be qualities, inherent in human nature, we should never repose the least confidence in human testimony. A man delirious, or noted for falsehood and villany, has no manner of authority with us.

And as the evidence, derived from witnesses and human testimony, is founded on past experience, so it varies with the experience, and is regarded either as *proof* or a *probability*, according as the conjunction between any particular kind of report and any kind of object has been found to be constant or variable. There are a number of circumstances to be taken into consideration in all judgments of this kind; and the ultimate standard, by which we determine all disputes, that may arise concerning them, is always derived from experience and observation. Where this experience is not entirely uniform on any side, it is attended with an unavoidable contrariety in our judgments, and with the same opposition and mutual destruction of argument as in every other kind of evidence. We frequently hesitate concerning the reports of others. We balance the opposite circumstances, which cause any doubt or uncertainty; and when we discover a superiority on one side, we incline to it; but still with a diminution of assurance, in proportion to the force of its antagonist.

This contrariety of evidence, in the present case, may be derived from several different causes; from the opposition of contrary testimony; from the character or number of the witnesses; from the manner of their delivering their testimony; or from the union of all these circumstances. We entertain a suspicion concerning any matter of fact, when the witnesses contradict each other; when they are but few, or of a doutbful character; when they have an interest in what they affirm; when they deliver their testimony with hesitation, or, on the contrary, with too violent asseverations. There are many other particulars of the same kind, which may diminish or destroy the force of any argument, derived from human testimony.

Suppose, for instance, that the fact, which the testimony endeavors to establish, partakes of the extraordinary and the marvelous; in that case, the evidence, resulting from the testimony, admits of a diminution, greater or less, in proportion as the fact is more or less unusual. The reason why we place any credit in witnesses and historians is not derived from any *connexion*, which we perceive *a priori*, between testimony and reality, but because we are accustomed to find a conformity between them. But when the fact attested is such a one as has seldom fallen under our observation, here is a contest of two opposite experiences; of which the one destroys the other, as far as its force goes, and the superior can only operate on the mind by the force which remains. The very same principle of experience, which gives us a certain degree of assurance in the testimony of witnesses, gives us also, in this case, another degree of assurance against the fact, which they endeavor to establish; from which contradiction there necessarily arises a counterpoize, and mutual destruction of belief and authority.

I should not believe such a story were it told me by Cato, was a proverbial saying in Rome, even during the lifetime of that philosophical patriot.[1] The incredibility of a fact, it was allowed, might invalidate so great an authority.

1. Plutarch, in vita Catonis.

The Indian prince, who refused to believe the first relations concerning the effects of frost, reasoned justly; and it naturally required very strong testimony to engage his assent to facts, that arose from a state of nature, with which he was unacquainted, and which bore so little analogy to those events, of which he had had constant and uniform experience. Though they were not contrary to his experience, they were not conformable to it.[2]

But in order to encrease the probability against the testimony of witnesses, let us suppose, that the fact, which they affirm, instead of being only marvelous, is really miraculous; and suppose also, that the testimony considered apart and in itself, amounts to an entire proof; in that case, there is proof against proof, of which the strongest must prevail, but still with a diminution of its force, in proportion to that of its antagonist.

A miracle is a violation of the laws of nature; and as a firm and unalterable experience has established these laws, the proof against a miracle, from the very nature of the fact, is as entire as any argument from experience can possibly be imagined. Why is it more than probable, that all men must die; that lead cannot, of itself, remain suspended in the air; that fire consumes wood, and is extinguished by water; unless it be, that these events are found agreeable to the laws of nature, and there is required a violation of these laws, or in other words, a miracle to prevent them? Nothing is esteemed a miracle, if it ever happen in the common course of nature. It is no miracle, if it ever happen in the common course of nature. It is no miracle that a man, seemingly in good health, should die of a sud-

2. No Indian, it is evident, could have experience that water did not freeze in cold climates. This is placing nature in a situation quite unknown to him; and it is impossible for him to tell *a priori* what will result from it. It is making a new experiment, the consequence of which is always uncertain. One may sometimes conjecture from analogy what will follow; but still this is but conjecture. And it must be confessed, that, in the present case of freezing, the event follows contrary to the rules of analogy, and is such as a rational Indian would not look for. The operations of cold upon water are not gradual, according to the degrees of cold; but whenever it comes to the freezing point, the water passes in a moment, from the utmost liquidity to perfect hardness. Such an event, therefore, may be denominated *extraordinary*, and requires a pretty strong testimony, to render it credible to people in a warm climate: But still it is not *miraculous*, nor contrary to uniform experience of the course of nature in cases where all the circumstances are the same. The inhabitants of Sumatra have always seen water fluid in their own climate, and the freezing of their rivers ought to be deemed a prodigy: But they never saw water in Muscovy during the winter; and therefore they cannot reasonably be positive what would there be the consequence.

other, has yet been frequently observed to happen. But it is a miracle, that a dead man should come to life; because that has never been observed in any age or country. There must, therefore, be a uniform experience against every miraculous event, otherwise the event would not merit that appellation. And as a uniform experience amounts to a proof, there is here a direct and full *proof*, from the nature of the fact, against the existence of any miracle; nor can such a proof be destroyed, or the miracle rendered credible, but by an opposite proof, which is superior.[3]

The plain consequence is (and it is a general maxim worthy of our attention), "That no testimony is sufficient to establish a miracle, unless the testimony be of such a kind, that its falsehood would be more miraculous, than the fact, which it endeavors to establish; and even in that case there is a mutual destruction of arguments, and the superior only gives us an assurance suitable to that degree of force, which remains, after deducting the inferior." When anyone tells me, that he saw a dead man restored to life, I immediately consider with myself, whether it be more probable, that this person should either deceive or be deceived, or that the fact, which he relates, should really have happened. I weigh the one miracle against the other; and according to the superiority, which I discover, I pronounce my decision, and always reject the greater miracle. If the falsehood of his testimony would be more miraculous, than the event which he relates; then, and not till then, can he pretend to command my belief or opinion.

---

3. Sometimes an event may not, *in itself*, *seem* to be contrary to the laws of nature, and yet, if it were real, it might, by reason of some circumstances, be denominated a miracle; because, *in fact*, it is contrary to these laws. Thus if a person, claiming a divine authority, should command a sick person to be well, a healthful man to fall down dead, the clouds to pour rain, the winds to blow, in short, should order many natural events, which immediately follow upon his command; these might justly be esteemed miracles, because they are really, in this case, contrary to the laws of nature. For if any suspicion remain, that the event and command concurred by accident, there is no miracle and no transgression of the laws of nature. If this suspicion be removed, there is evidently a miracle, and a transgression of these laws; because nothing can be more contrary to nature than that the voice or command of a man should have such an influence. A miracle may be accurately defined, *a transgression of a law of nature by a particular volition of the Deity, or by the interposition of some invisible agent.* A miracle may either be discoverable by men or not. This alters not its nature and essence. The raising of a house or ship into the air is a visible miracle. The raising of a feather, when the wind wants ever so little of a force requisite for that purpose, is as real a miracle, though not so sensible with regard to us.

PART II

In the foregoing reasoning we have supposed, that the testimony, upon which a miracle is founded, may possibly amount to an entire proof, and that the falsehood of that testimony would be a real prodigy: But it is easy to show, that we have been a great deal too liberal in our concession, and that there never was a miraculous event established on so full an evidence.

For *first*, there is not to be found, in all history, any miracle attested by a sufficient number of men, of such unquestioned good sense, education, and learning, as to secure us against all delusion in themselves; of such undoubted integrity, as to place them beyond all suspicion of any design to deceive others; of such credit and reputation in the eyes of mankind, as to have a great deal to lose in case of their being detected in any falsehood; and at the same time, attesting facts performed in such a public manner and in so celebrated a part of the world, as to render the detection unavoidable: All which circumstances are requisite to give us a full assurance in the testimony of men.

Secondly. We may observe in human nature a principle which, if strictly examined, will be found to diminish extremely the assurance, which we might, from human testimony, have, in any kind of prodigy. The maxim, by which we commonly conduct ourselves in our reasonings, is, that the objects, of which we have no experience, resemble those, of which we have; that what we have found to be most usual is always most probable; and that where there is an opposition of arguments, we ought to give the preference to such as are founded on the greatest number of past observations. But though, in proceeding by this rule, we readily reject any fact which is unusual and incredible in an ordinary degree; yet in advancing farther, the mind observes not always the same rule; but when anything is affirmed utterly absurd and miraculous, it rather the more readily admits of such a fact, upon account of that very circumstance, which ought to destroy all its authority. The passion of *surprise* and *wonder*, arising from miracles, being an agreeable emotion, gives a sensible tendency towards the belief of those events, from which it is derived. And this goes so far, that even those who cannot enjoy this pleasure immediately, nor can believe those miraculous events, of which they are informed, yet love to partake of the satisfaction at second-hand or by rebound, and place a pride and delight in exciting the admiration of others.

With what greediness are the miraculous accounts of travelers received, their descriptions of sea and land monsters, their relations of wonderful adventures, strange men, and uncouth manners? But if the spirit of religion join itself to the love of wonder, there is an end of common sense; and human testimony, in these circumstances, loses all pretensions to authority. A religionist may be an enthusiast, and imagine he sees what has no reality: he may know his narrative to be false, and yet persevere in it, with the best intentions in the world, for the sake of promoting so holy a cause: or even where this delusion has not place, vanity, excited by so strong a temptation, operates on him more powerfully than on the rest of mankind in any other circumstances; and self-interest with equal force. His auditors may not have, and commonly have not, sufficient judgment to canvass his evidence: what judgment they have, they renounce by principle, in these sublime and mysterious subjects: or if they were ever so willing to employ it, passion and a heated imagination disturb the regularity of its operations. Their credulity increases his impudence: and his impudence overpowers their credulity.

Eloquence, when at its highest pitch, leaves little room for reason or reflection; but addressing itself entirely to the fancy or the affections, captivates the willing hearers, and subdues their understanding. Happily, this pitch it seldom attains. But what a Tully or a Demosthenes could scarcely effect over a Roman or Athenian audience, every *Capuchin*, every itinerant or stationary teacher can perform over the generality of mankind, and in a higher degree, by touching such gross and vulgar passions.

The many instances of forged miracles, and prophecies, and supernatural events, which, in all ages, have either been detected by contrary evidence, or which detect themselves by their absurdity, prove sufficiently the strong propensity of mankind to the extraordinary and the marvelous, and ought reasonably to beget a suspicion against all relations of this kind. This is our natural way of thinking, even with regard to the most common and most credible events. For instance: There is no kind of report which rises so easily, and spreads so quickly, especially in country places and provincial towns, as those concerning marriages; insomuch that two young persons of equal condition never see each other twice, but the whole neighborhood immediately join them together. The pleasure of telling a piece of news so interesting, of propagating it, and of being the first reporters of it, spreads the intelligence. And this is so well known, that no man of sense gives attention to these reports, till he find them confirmed by some greater evidence. Do not the same passions, and others still stronger, incline the generality of mankind to believe and report, with the greatest vehemence and assurance, all religious miracles?

Thirdly. It forms a strong presumption against all supernatural and miraculous relations, that they are observed chiefly to abound among ignorant and barbarous nations; or if a civilized people has ever given admission to any of them, that people will be found to have received them from ignorant and barbarous ancestors, who transmitted them with that inviolable sanction and authority, which always attend received opinions. When we peruse the first histories of all nations, we are apt to imagine ourselves transported into some new world; where the whole frame of nature is disjointed, and every element performs its operations in a different manner, from what it does at present. Battles, revolutions, pestilence, famine and death, are never the effect of those natural causes, which we experience. Prodigies, omens, oracles, judgments, quite obscure the few natural events, that are intermingled with them. But as the former grow thinner every page, in proportion as we advance nearer the enlightened ages, we soon learn, that there is nothing mysterious or supernatural in the case, but that all proceeds from the usual propensity of mankind towards the marvelous, and that, though this inclination may at intervals receive a check from sense and learning, it can never be thoroughly extirpated from human nature.

It is strange, a judicious reader is apt to say, upon the perusal of these wonderful historians, *that such prodigious events never happen in our days.* But it is nothing strange, I hope, that men should lie in all ages. You must surely have seen instances enough of that frailty. You have yourself heard many such marvelous relations started, which, being treated with scorn by all the wise and judicious, have at last been abandoned even by the vulgar. Be assured, that those renowned lies, which have spread and flourished to such a monstrous height, arose from like beginnings; but being sown in a more proper soil, shot up at last into prodigies almost equal to those which they relate.

It was a wise policy in that false prophet, Alexander, who though

now forgotten, was once so famous, to lay the first scene of his impostures in Paphlagonia, where, as Lucian tells us, the people were
extremely ignorant and stupid, and ready to swallow even the grossest
delusion. People at a distance, who are weak enough to think the matter at all worth enquiry, have no opportunity of receiving better information. The stories come magnified to them by a hundred circumstances. Fools are industrious in propagating the imposture; while
the wise and learned are contented, in general, to deride its absurdity, without informing themselves of the particular facts, by which
it may be distinctly refuted. And thus the impostor above mentioned was enabled to proceed, from his ignorant Paphlagonians, to the
enlisting of votaries, even among the Grecian philosophers, and men
of the most eminent rank and distinction in Rome: nay, could engage
the attention of that sage emperor Marcus Aurelius; so far as to make
him trust the success of a military expedition to his delusive prophecies.

The advantages are so great, of starting an imposture among an
ignorant people, that, even though the delusion should be too gross
to impose on the generality of them (*which, though seldom, is
sometimes the case*) it has a much better chance for succeeding in
remote countries, than if the first scene had been laid in a city renowned for arts and knowledge. The most ignorant and barbarous
of these barbarians carry the report abroad. None of their countrymen
have a large correspondence, or sufficient credit and authority to contradict and beat down the delusion. Men's inclination to the marvelous
has full opportunity to display itself. And thus a story, which is universally exploded in the place where it was first started, shall pass for
certain at a thousand miles distance. But had Alexander fixed his
residence at Athens, the philosophers of that renowned mart of learning had immediately spread, throughout the whole Roman empire,
their sense of the matter; which, being supported by so great authority,
and displayed by all the force of reason and eloquence, had entirely
opened the eyes of mankind. It is true; Lucian, passing by chance
through Paphlagonia, had an opportunity of performing this good
office. But, though much to be wished, it does not always happen,
that every Alexander meets with Lucian, ready to expose and detect
his impostures.

I may add as a *fourth* reason, which diminishes the authority of
prodigies, that there is no testimony for any, even those which have
not been expressly detected, that is not opposed by an infinite number

of witnesses; so that not only the miracle destroys the credit of testimony, but the testimony destroys itself. To make this the better understood, let us consider, that, in matters of religion, whatever is different is contrary; and that it is impossible the religions of ancient Rome, of Turkey, of Siam, and of China should, all of them, be established on any solid foundation. Every miracle, therefore, pretended to have been wrought in any of these religions (and all of them abound in miracles), as its direct scope is to establish the particular system to which it is attributed; so has it the same force, though more indirectly, to overthrow every other system. In destroying a rival system, it likewise destroys the credit of those miracles, on which that system was established; so that all the prodigies of different religions are to be regarded as contrary facts; and the evidences of these prodigies, whether weak or strong, as opposite to each other. According to this method of reasoning, when we believe any miracle of Mahomet or his successors, we have for our warrant the testimony of a few barbarous Arabians: And on the other hand, we are to regard the authority of Titus Livius, Plutarch, Tacitus, and, in short, of all the authors and witnesses, Grecian, Chinese, and Roman Catholic, who have related any miracle in their particular religion; I say, we are to regard their testimony in the same light as if they had mentioned that Mahometan miracle, and had in express terms contradicted it, with the same certainty as they have for the miracle they relate. This argument may appear over subtile and refined; but is not in reality different from the reasoning of a judge, who supposes, that the credit of two witnesses, maintaining a crime against any one, is destroyed by the testimony of two others, who affirm him to have been two hundred leagues distant, at the same instant when the crime is said to have been committed.

One of the best attested miracles in all profane history, is that which Tacitus reports of Vespasian, who cured a blind man in Alexandria, by means of his spittle, and a lame man by the mere touch of his foot; in obedience to a vision of the god Serapis, who had enjoined them to have recourse to the Emperor, for these miraculous cures. The story may be seen in that fine historian;[4] where every circumstance seems to add weight to the testimony, and might be displayed at large with all the force of argument and eloquence, if any one were now con-

4. Hist. lib. v. cap. 8. Suetonius gives nearly the same account *in vita* Vesp.

cerned to enforce the evidence of that exploded and idolatrous superstition. The gravity, solidity, age, and probity of so great an emperor, who, through the whole course of his life, conversed in a familiar manner with his friends and courtiers, and never affected those extraordinary airs of divinity assumed by Alexander and Demetrius. The historian, a contemporary writer, noted for candor and veracity, and withal, the greatest and most penetrating genius, perhaps, of all antiquity; and so free from any tendency to credulity, that he even lies under the contrary imputation, of atheism and profaneness: The persons, from whose authority he related the miracle, of established character for judgment and veracity, as we may well presume; eye-witnesses of the fact, and confirming their testimony, after the Flavian family was despoiled of the empire, and could no longer give any reward, as the price of a lie. *Utrumque, qui interfuere, nunc quoque memorant, postquam nullum mendacio pretium.* To which if we add the public nature of the facts, as related, it will appear, that no evidence can well be supposed stronger for so gross and so palpable a falsehood.

There is also a memorable story related by Cardinal de Retz, which may well deserve our consideration. When that intriguing politician fled into Spain, to avoid the persecution of his enemies, he passed through Saragossa, the capital of Arragon, where he was shown, in the cathedral, a man, who had served seven years as a doorkeeper, and was well known to everybody in town, that had ever paid his devotions at that church. He had been seen, for so long a time, wanting a leg; but recovered that limb by the rubbing of holy oil upon the stump; and the cardinal assures us that he saw him with two legs. This miracle was vouched by all the canons of the church; and the whole company in town were appealed to for a confirmation of the fact: whom the cardinal found, by their zealous devotion, to be thorough believers of the miracle. Here the relater was also contemporary to the supposed prodigy, of an incredulous and libertine character, as well as of great genius; the miracle of so *singular* a nature as could scarcely admit of a counterfeit, and the witnesses very numerous, and all of them, in a manner, spectators of the fact, to which they gave their testimony. And what adds mightily to the force of the evidence, and may double our surprise on this occasion, is, that the cardinal himself, who relates the story, seems not to give any credit to it, and consequently cannot be suspected of any concurrence in the holy fraud. He considered justly, that it was not requisite, in order to reject a fact of this nature, to be able accurately to disprove the testimony, and to trace its falsehood, through all the circumstances of knavery and credulity which produced it. He knew, that, as this was commonly altogether impossible at any small distance of time and place; so was it extremely difficult, even where one was immediately present, by reason of the bigotry, ignorance, cunning, and roguery of a great part of mankind. He therefore concluded, like a just reasoner, that such an evidence carried falsehood upon the very face of it, and that a miracle, supported by any human testimony, was more properly a subject of derision than of argument.

There surely never was a greater number of miracles ascribed to one person, than those, which were lately said to have been wrought in France upon the tomb of Abbé Paris, the famous Jansenist, with whose sanctity the people were so long deluded. The curing of the sick, giving hearing to the deaf, and sight to the blind, were every where talked of as the usual effects of that holy sepulchre. But what is more extraordinary; many of the miracles were immediately proved upon the spot, before judges of unquestioned integrity, attested by witnesses of credit and distinction, in a learned age, and on the most eminent theatre that is now in the world. Nor is this all: a relation of them was published and dispersed everywhere; nor were the *Jesuits*, though a learned body, supported by the civil magistrate, and determined enemies to those opinions, in whose favor the miracles were said to have been wrought, ever able distinctly to refute or detect them. Where shall we find such a number of circumstances, agreeing to the corroboration of one fact? And what have we to oppose to such a cloud of witnesses, but the absolute impossibility or miraculous nature of the events, which they relate? And this surely, in the eyes of all reasonable people, will alone be regarded as a sufficient refutation.

Is the consequence just, because some human testimony has the utmost force and authority in some cases, when it relates the battle of Philippi or Pharsalia for instance; that therefore all kinds of testimony must, in all cases, have equal force and authority? Suppose that the Caesarean and Pompeian factions had, each of them, claimed the victory in these battles, and that the historians of each party had uniformly ascribed the advantage to their own side; how could mankind at this distance, have been able to determine between them? The contrariety is equally strong between the miracles related by Herodotus or Plutarch, and those delivered by Mariana, Bede, or any monkish historian.

The wise lend a very academic faith to every report which favors the passion of the reporter; whether it magnifies his country, his family, or himself, or in any other way strikes in with his natural inclinations and propensities. But what greater temptation than to appear a missionary, a prophet, an ambassador from heaven? Who would not encounter many dangers and difficulties, in order to attain so sublime a character? Or if, by the help of vanity and a heated imagination, a man has first made a convert of himself, and entered seriously into the delusion; who ever scruples to make use of pious frauds, in support of so holy and meritorious a cause?

The smallest spark may here kindle into the greatest flame; because the materials are always prepared for it. The *avidum genus auricularum*,[5] the gazing populace, receive greedily, without examination, whatever soothes superstition, and promotes wonder.

How many stories of this nature have, in all ages, been detected and exploded in their infancy? How many more have been celebrated for a time, and have afterwards sunk into neglect and oblivion? Where such reports, therefore, fly about, the solution of the phenomenon is obvious; and we judge in conformity to regular experience and observation, when we account for it by the known and natural principles of credulity and delusion. And shall we, rather than have a recourse to so natural a solution, allow of a miraculous violation of the most established laws of nature?

I need not mention the difficulty of detecting a falsehood in any private or even public history, at the place, where it is said to happen; much more when the scene is removed to ever so small a distance. Even a court of judicature, with all the authority, accuracy, and judgment, which they can employ, find themselves often at a loss to distinguish between truth and falsehood in the most recent actions. But the matter never comes to any issue, if trusted to the common method of altercations and debate and flying rumors; especially when men's passions have taken part on either side.

In the infancy of new religions, the wise and learned commonly esteem the matter too inconsiderable to deserve their attention or

5. Lucret.

regard. And when afterwards they would willingly detect the cheat, in order to undeceive the deluded multitude, the season is now past, and the records and witnesses, which might clear up the matter, have perished beyond recovery.

No means of detection remain, but those which must be drawn from the very testimony itself of the reporters: and these, though always sufficient with the judicious and knowing, are commonly too fine to fall under the comprehension of the vulgar.

Upon the whole, then, it appears, that no testimony for any kind of miracle has ever amounted to a probability, much less to a proof; and that, even supposing it amounted to a proof, it would be opposed by another proof; derived from the very nature of the fact, which it would endeavor to establish. It is experience only, which gives authority to human testimony; and it is the same experience, which assures us of the laws of nature. When, therefore, these two kinds of experience are contrary, we have nothing to do but substract the one from the other, and embrace an opinion, either on one side or the other, with that assurance which arises from the remainder. But according to the principle here explained, this substraction, with regard to all popular religions, amounts to an entire annihilation; and therefore we may establish it as a maxim, that no human testimony can have such force as to prove a miracle, and make it a just foundation for any such system of religion.

I beg the limitations here made may be remarked, when I say, that a miracle can never be proved, so as to be the foundation of a system of religion. For I own, that otherwise, there may possibly be miracles, or violations of the usual course of nature, of such a kind as to admit of proof from human testimony, though, perhaps, it will be impossible to find any such in all the records of history. Thus, suppose, all authors, in all languages, agree, that, from the first of January 1600, there was a total darkness over the whole earth for eight days: suppose that the tradition of this extraordinary event is still strong and lively among the people: that all travelers, who return from foreign countries, bring us accounts of the same tradition, without the least variation or contradiction: it is evident, that our present philosophers, instead of doubting the fact, ought to receive it as certain, and ought to search for the causes whence it might be derived. The decay, corruption, and dissolution of nature, is an event rendered probable by so many analogies, that any phenomenon, which seems to have a tendency towards that catastrophe, comes within the reach of human testimony, if that testimony be very extensive and uniform.

But suppose, that all the historians who treat of England, should agree, that, on the first of January 1600, Queen Elizabeth died; that both before and after her death she was seen by her physicians and the whole court, as is usual with persons of her rank; that her successor was acknowledged and proclaimed by the Parliament; and that, after being interred a month, she again appeared, resumed the throne, and governed England for three years: I must confess that I should be surprised at the concurrence of so many odd circumstances, but should not have the least inclination to believe so miraculous an event. I should not doubt of her pretended death, and of those other public circumstances that followed it: I should only assert it to have been pretended, and that it neither was, nor possibly could be real. You would in vain object to me the difficulty, and almost impossibility of deceiving the world in an affair of such consequence; the wisdom and solid judgment of that renowned queen; with the little or no advantage which she could reap from so poor an artifice: All this might astonish me; but I would still reply, that the knavery and folly of men are such common phenomena, that I should rather believe the most extraordinary events to arise from their concurrence, than admit of so signal a violation of the laws of nature.

But should this miracle be ascribed to any new system of religion; men, in all ages, have been so much imposed on by ridiculous stories of that kind, that this very circumstance would be a full proof of a cheat, and sufficient, with all men of sense, not only to make them reject the fact, but even reject it without farther examination. Though the Being to whom the miracle is ascribed, be, in this case, Almighty, it does not, upon that account, become a whit more probable; since it is impossible for us to know the attributes or actions of such a Being, otherwise than from the experience which we have of his productions, in the usual course of nature. This still reduces us to past observation, and obliges us to compare the instances of the violation of truth in the testimony of men, with those of the violation of the laws of nature by miracles, in order to judge which of them is most likely and probable. As the violations of truth are more common in the testimony concerning religious miracles, than in that concerning any other matter of fact; this must diminish very much the authority of the former testimony, and make us form a general resolution, never to lend any attention to it, with whatever specious pretence it may be covered.

Lord Bacon seems to have embraced the same principles of reasoning. "We ought," says he, "to make a collection or particular history of all monsters and prodigious births or productions, and in a word of every thing new, rare, and extraordinary in nature. But this must be done with the most severe scrutiny, lest we depart from truth. Above all, every relation must be considered as suspicious, which depends in any degree upon religion, as the prodigies of Livy: And no less so, every thing that is to be found in the writers of natural magic or alchimy, or such authors, who seem, all of them, to have an unconquerable appetite for falsehood and fable.[6]

I am the better pleased with the method of reasoning here delivered, as I think it may serve to confound those dangerous friends or disguised enemies to the *Christian Religion*, who have undertaken to defend it by the principles of human reason. Our most holy religion is founded on *Faith*, not on reason; and it is a sure method of exposing it to put it to such a trial as it is, by no means, fitted to endure. To make this more evident, let us examine those miracles, related in scripture; and not to lose ourselves in too wide a field, let us confine ourselves to such as we find in the *Pentateuch*, which we shall examine, according to the principles of these pretended Christians, not as the word or testimony of God himself, but as the production of a mere human writer and historian. Here then we are first to consider a book, presented to us by a barbarous and ignorant people, written in an age when they were still more barbarous, and in all probability long after the facts which it relates, corroborated by no concurring testimony, and resembling those fabulous accounts, which every nation gives of its origin. Upon reading this book, we find it full of prodigies and miracles. It gives an account of a state of the world and of human nature entirely different from the present: Of our fall from that state: Of the age of man, extended to near a thousand years: Of the destruction of the world by a deluge: Of the arbitrary choice of one people, as the favorites of heaven; and that people the countrymen of the author: Of their deliverance from bondage by prodigies the most astonishing imaginable: I desire any one to lay his hand upon his heart, and after a serious consideration declare,

6. Nov. Org. lib. ii. aph. 29.

whether he thinks that the falsehood of such a book, supported by such a testimony, would be more extraordinary and miraculous than all the miracles it relates; which is, however, necessary to make it be received, according to the measures of probability above established.

What we have said of miracles may be applied, without any variation, to prophecies; and indeed, all prophecies are real miracles, and as such only, can be admitted as proofs of any revelation. If it did not exceed the capacity of human nature to foretell future events, it would be absurd to employ any prophecy as an argument for a divine mission or authority from heaven. So that, upon the whole, we may conclude, that the *Christian Religion* not only was at first attended with miracles, but even at this day cannot be believed by any reasonable person without one. Mere reason is insufficient to convince us of its veracity: And whoever is moved by *Faith* to assent to it, is conscious of a continued miracle in his own person, which subverts all the principles of his understanding, and gives him a determination to believe what is most contrary to custom and experience.

4

WILLIAM PALEY*

Evidences of Christianity—
Preparatory Considerations

I DEEM IT unnecessary to prove that mankind stood in need of a revelation, because I have met with no serious person who thinks that, even under the Christian revelation, we have too much light, or any degree of assurance which is superfluous. I desire moreover, that, in judging of Christianity, it may be remembered, that the question lies between this religion and none: for, if the Christian religion be not credible, no one, with whom we have to do, will support the pretensions of any other.

Suppose, then, the world we live in to have had a Creator; suppose it to appear, from the predominant aim and tendency of the provisions and contrivances observable in the universe, that the Diety, when he formed it, consulted for the happiness of his sensitive creation; suppose the disposition which dictated this counsel to continue; suppose a part of the creation to have received faculties from their Maker, by which they are capable of rendering a moral obedience to his will, and of voluntarily pursuing any end for which he has designed them; suppose the Creator to intend for these, his rational and accountable agents, a second state of existence, in which their

* William Paley (1743–1805) was Archdeacon of Carlisle. His *Natural Theology* and *Evidences of Christianity*, providing a systematic defense of Christian Theology, were widely influential in the nineteenth century. This selection is the 'Preparatory Considerations' to *Evidences of Christianity*, published in 1794.

situation will be regulated by their behavior in the first state, by which supposition (and by no other) the objection to the divine government in not putting a difference between the good and the bad, and the inconsistency of this confusion with the care and benevolence discoverable in the works of the Deity is done away; suppose it to be of the utmost importance to the subjects of this dispensation to know what is intended for them, that is, suppose the knowledge of it to be highly conducive to the happiness of the species, a purpose which so many provisions of nature are calculated to promote: suppose, nevertheless, almost the whole race, either by the imperfection of their faculties, the misfortune of their situation, or by the loss of some prior revelation, to want this knowledge, and not to be likely, without the aid of a new revelation, to attain it: under these circumstances, is it improbable that a revelation should be made? Is it incredible that God should interpose for such a purpose? Suppose him to design for mankind a future state; is it unlikely that he should acquaint him with it?

Now in what way can a revelation be made, but by miracles? In none which we are able to conceive. Consequently, in whatever degree it is probable, or not very improbable, that a revelation should be communicated to mankind at all; in the same degree is it probable, or not very improbable, that miracles should be wrought. Therefore, when miracles are related to have been wrought in the promulgating of a revelation manifestly wanted, and, if true, of inestimable value, the improbability which arises from the miraculous nature of the things related, is not greater than the original improbability that such a revelation should be imparted by God.

I wish it, however, to be correctly understood, in what manner, and to what extent, this argument is alleged. We do not assume the attributes of the Deity, or the existence of a future state, in order to *prove* the reality of miracles. That reality always must be proved by evidence. We assert only, that in miracles adduced in support of revelation, there is not any such antecedent improbability as no testimony can surmount. And for the purpose of maintaining this assertion, we contend, that the incredibility of miracles related to have been wrought in attestation of a message from God, conveying intelligence of a future state of rewards and punishments, and teaching mankind how to prepare themselves for that state, is not in itself greater than the event, call it either probable or improbable, of the two following propositions being true: namely, first, that a future state of existence should be destined by God for his human creation; and, secondly, that, being so destined, he should acquaint them with it. It is not necessary for our purpose, that these propositions be capable of proof, or even that, by arguments drawn from the light of nature, they can be made out to be probable; it is enough that we are able to say concerning them, that they are not so violently improbable, so contradictory to what we already believe of the divine power and character, that either the propositions themselves, or facts strictly connected with the propositions (and therefore no farther improbable than they are improbable) ought to be rejected at first sight, and to be rejected by whatever strength or complication of evidence they be attested.

This is the prejudication we would resist. For to this length does a modern objection to miracles go, *viz.* that no human testimony can in any case render them credible. I think the reflection above stated, that, if there be a revelation, there must be miracles, and that, under the circumstances in which the human species are placed, a revelation is not improbable, or not improbable in any great degree, to be a fair answer to the whole objection.

But since it is an objection which stands in the very threshold of our argument, and, if admitted, is a bar to every proof, and to all future reasoning upon the subject, it may be necessary, before we proceed farther, to examine the principle upon which it professes to be founded; which principle is concisely this, "That it is contrary to experience that a miracle should be true, but not contrary to experience that testimony should be false."

Now there appears a small ambiguity in the term "experience," and in the phrases "contrary to experience," or "contradicting experience," which it may be necessary to remove in the first place. Strictly speaking, the narrative of a fact is *then* only contrary to experience, when the fact is related to have existed at a time and place, at which time and place we being present did not perceive it to exist; as if it should be asserted, that in a particular room, and at a particular hour of a certain day, a man was raised from the dead, in which room, and at the time specified, we, being present and looking on, perceived no such event to have taken place. Here the assertion is contrary to experience properly so called: and this is a contrariety which no evidence can surmount. It matters nothing, whether the fact be of a miraculous nature, or not. But although this be the experience, and the contrariety, which archbishop Tillotson alleged in the quotation with which Mr. Hume opens his Essay, it is certainly not that experience, nor that contrariety, which Mr. Hume himself intended to object. And, short of this, I know no intelligible signification which can be affixed to the term "contrary to experience," but one, *viz.* that of not having ourselves experienced any thing similar to the thing related, or such things not being generally experienced by others. I say "not generally": for to state concerning the fact in question, that no such thing was *ever* experienced, or that *universal* experience is against it, is to assume the subject of the controversy.

Now the improbability which arises from the want (for this properly is a want, not a contradiction) of experience, is only equal to the probability there is, that, if the thing were true, we should experience things similar to it, or that such things would be generally experienced. Suppose it then to be true that miracles were wrought on the first promulgation of Christianity, when nothing but miracles could decide its authority, is it certain that such miracles would be repeated so often, and in so many places, as to become objects of general experience? Is it a probability approaching to certainty? Is it a probability of any great strength or force? Is it such as no evidence can encounter? And yet this probability is the exact *converse*, and therefore, the exact measure, of the improbability which arises from the want of experience, and which Mr. Hume represents as invincible by human testimony.

It is not like alleging a new law of nature, or a new experiment in natural philosophy; because, when these are related, it is expected that, under the same circumstances, the same effect will follow universally; and in proportion as this expectation is justly entertained, the want of a corresponding experience negatives the history. But to expect concerning a miracle, that it should succeed upon a repetition, is to expect that which would make it cease to be a miracle, which is contrary to its nature as such, and would totally destroy the use and purpose for which it was wrought.

The force of experience as an objection to miracles, is founded in the presumption, either that the course of nature is invariable, or that, if it be ever varied, variations will be frequent and general. Has the necessity of this alternative been demonstrated? Permit us to call the course of nature the agency of an intelligent Being; and is there any good reason for judging this state of the case to be probable? Ought we not rather to expect that such a Being, on occasions of peculiar importance, may interrupt the order which he had appointed, yet, that such occasions should return seldom; that these interruptions consequently should be confined to the experience of a few; that the want of it, therefore, in many, should be matter neither of surprise nor objection?

But as a continuation of the argument from experience, it is said, that, when we advance accounts of miracles, we assign effects without causes, or we attribute effects to causes inadequate to the purpose, or to causes, of the operation of which we have no experience. Of what causes, we may ask, and of what effects does the objection speak? If it be answered that, when we ascribe the cure of the palsy to a touch, of blindness to the anointing of the eyes with clay, or the raising of the dead to a word, we lay ourselves open to this imputation; we reply, that we ascribe no such effects to such causes. We perceive no virtue or energy in these things more than in other things of the same kind. They are merely signs to connect the miracle with its end. The effect we ascribe simply to the volition of the Deity; of whose existence and power, not to say of whose presence and agency, we have previous and independent proof. We have, therefore, all we seek for in the works of rational agents—a sufficient power and an adequate motive. In a word, once believe that there is a God, and miracles are not incredible.

Mr. Hume states the case of miracles to be a contest of opposite improbabilities, that is to say, a question whether it be more improbable that the miracle should be true, or the testimony false: and this I think a fair account of the controversy. But herein I remark a want of argumentative justice, that, in describing the improbability of miracles, he suppresses all those circumstances of extenuation, which result from our knowledge of the existence, power, and disposition, of the Deity; his concern in the creation, the end answered by the miracle, the importance of that end, and its subserviency to the plan pursued in the work of nature. As Mr. Hume has represented the question, miracles are alike incredible to him who is previously assured of the constant agency of a Divine Being, and to him who believes that no such Being exists in the universe. They are equally incredible, whether related to have been wrought upon occasions the most deserving, and for purposes the most beneficial, or for no assignable end whatever, or for an end confessedly trifling or pernicious. This surely cannot be a correct statement. In adjusting also the other side of the balance, the strength and weight of testimony, this author has provided an answer to every possible accumulation of historical proof by telling us, that we are not obliged to explain how the story of the evidence arose. Now I think that we *are* obliged; not, perhaps, to show by positive accounts how it did, but by a probable hypothesis how it might so happen. The existence of the testimony is a phenomenon; the truth of the fact solves the phenomenon. If we reject this solution, we ought to have some other to rest in; and none, even by our adversaries, can be admitted, which is not inconsistent with the principles that regulate human affairs and human conduct at present, or which makes men *then* to have been a different kind of beings from what they are now.

But the short consideration which, independently of every other, convinces me that there is no solid foundation in Mr. Hume's conclusion is the following. When a theorem is proposed to a mathematician, the first thing he does with it is to try it upon a simple case, and if it produce a false result, he is sure that there must be some mistake in the demonstration. Now to proceed in this way with what may be called Mr. Hume's theorem. If twelve men, whose probity and good sense I had long known, should seriously and circumstantially relate to me an account of a miracle wrought before their eyes, and in which it was impossible that they should be deceived; if the governor of the country, hearing a rumor of this account, should call these men into his presence, and offer them a short proposal, either to confess the imposture, or submit to be tied up to a gibbet; if they should refuse with one voice to acknowledge that there existed any falsehood or imposture in the case; if this threat were communicated to them separately, yet with no different effect; if it was at last executed; if I myself saw them, one after another, consenting to be racked, burnt, or strangled, rather than give up the truth of their account;—still, if Mr. Hume's rule be my guide, I am not to believe them. Now I undertake to say that there exists not a skeptic in the world who would not believe them, or who would defend such incredulity.

Instances of spurious miracles supported by strong apparent testimony, undoubtedly demand examination; Mr. Hume has endeavored to fortify his argument by some examples of this kind. I hope in a proper place to show that none of them reach the strength or circumstances of the Christian evidence. In these, however, consist the weight of his objection: in the principle itself, I am persuaded, there is none.

5

ALASTAIR McKINNON*

Miracle

THERE ARE TWO main supernaturalist senses of *miracle*. They are: (1) an event involving the suspension of natural law, and (2) an event conflicting with our understanding of nature. We begin with the first of these senses.

The core of our objection is quite simple: the idea of a suspension of natural law is self-contradictory. This follows from the meaning of the term. Natural law is not, as has been widely supposed, a kind of code for nature having legislative and, perhaps particularly, prohibitive force. This is an outdated, untenable, and completely unscientific view. Natural laws bear no similarities to civil codes and they do not in any way constrain the course of nature. They exert no opposition or resistance to anything, not even to the odd or exceptional. They are simply highly generalized shorthand descriptions of how things do in fact happen. (This is misleading but will do for the moment.) Hence there can be no suspensions of natural law rightly understood. Or, as here defined, *miracle* contains a contradiction in terms.

Once we understand natural law in this proper sense we see that such law, as distinct from our conception of it, is inherently inviolable. Hence anything which happens, even an apparent miracle, happens

* From of "'Miracle' and 'Paradox,'" *American Philosophical Quarterly*, 1967, 4: 309.

according to law. Or, negatively, no actual event could possibly violate a law of nature. Hence there can be no miracles in that sense of the term with which we are now concerned. Or, less misleadingly, it is in the nature of the case impossible that there should be an event which could be properly described by this term.

This contradiction may stand out more clearly if for *natural law* we substitute the expression *the actual course of events*. *Miracle* would then be defined as "an event involving the suspension of the actual course of events." And someone who insisted upon describing an event as a miracle would be in the rather odd position of claiming that its occurrence was contrary to the actual course of events.

But miracle (1) is not merely a contradiction in terms. It is also what might be called a contradiction in use. We see this in the plight of one confronted with an event conceived as a miracle. Such a person is faced with a dilemma. He can affirm the reality of this event and repudiate the "laws" which it violates. Or he can affirm these "laws" and repudiate the event. What he cannot do is to affirm both the event and the "laws" of which it is a violation. And this is to say that he cannot affirm that the event is both real and miraculous.

This can be put in a slightly different way. Belief in an event is belief that it happened. Belief that an event is a miracle is belief that it violates natural law. But, as already seen, such violations are impossible. Hence in respect of any alleged event we must choose between believing that it was actual and that it was not even possible. What we cannot believe, what it makes no sense to believe, is that any real or alleged event is a miracle in this sense. This, of course, is not to legislate for the course of events in the empirical world: it is simply to draw out the consequences of the self-contradictory nature of this concept.

So much for sense (1). What now of the more sophisticated (2) ("an event conflicting with our understanding of nature")? The clash posited by this sense is not within nature, as in (1), but rather between an event and our conception of nature. The idea of such a clash is not contradictory. Nor are such clashes either infrequent or always illusory. Hence there might be occasions on which *miracle* could be legitimately used in this sense. For example, I might use "x is a miracle (2)" to mean "x baffles me" or "I know no laws which could account for x." And if this was all I wanted to say, if my only concern was to register my lack of comprehension, then I would be as invulnerable as when I describe my dog as brown. But there are two relevant points. The original statement, so intended, deals not with the event as such but rather with my reaction to it; here the term *miracle* is being used expressively rather than descriptively. Secondly, in fact people do not use this term merely in this limited way. They do not use it simply to say that they do not know the appropriate law: they use it also to express their belief that there is no such law. They use it not merely to indicate their lack of comprehension but at the same time to insinuate their belief that the event cannot, perhaps should not, be comprehended. And if they did not so use it, it would be difficult to see how this term could have any distinctive meaning, much less the peculiar "religious" force it obviously has.

Though innocent when used expressively, this sense is contradictory when used to describe an event. One who so uses it implicitly affirms a conception of nature with which this is at variance. But he cannot believe both that the event happened and that the conception of nature with which it conflicts is adequate. In attempting to do so he necessarily contradicts himself. He is like the man who says, "Yes, this cat is white" then blandly adds, ". . . but I still hold that all cats are black."

Such a person may reasonably be asked to surrender either the historicity of the event or the conception of nature with which it conflicts. But as the proponent of an allegedly historical event he cannot well do the former. Nor, if the evidence was ever adequate, should he do so. He must therefore admit the inadequacy of the conception of nature with which he has been working. To do this is to put brackets around it, to withdraw it from circulation; it is to void or cancel the check. But in so doing he has cut the thread by which the whole structure was suspended and has repudiated the ground upon which he originally urged this description. The moral is clear: to affirm the historicity of an event is to destroy the ground for regarding it as a miracle.

Of course there is one other move open to our victim. Instead of surrendering his conception of nature as inadequate he might instead proclaim it a true and faithful copy. In so doing he locates the clash once again within the sphere of nature. But this brings him back to sense (1) and the impossible contradictions with which it is afflicted.

It appears then that one who insists upon describing an event as a miracle is faced with two equally impossible alternatives. If he attempts to represent the event as an instance of (2) he is forced by the logic of his position to withdraw the term completely. If he attempts instead to represent it as a case of (1) he forces himself to say that the event in question both is and is not a part of the actual course of events. Such a person is like a fly in a spider's web, he has ways around but no way out.

The conclusion of this matter can be stated "paradoxically": all the properly descriptive senses of *miracle* are logically improper.

6

R. F. HOLLAND*

⤷⤶

The Miraculous

⤶⤷

MOST PEOPLE THINK of a miracle as a violation of natural law; and a good many of those who regard the miraculous in this way incline to the idea that miracles are impossible and that "science" tells us this (the more sophisticated might say that what tells us this is an unconfused *conception* of science). I shall argue that the conception of the miraculous as a violation of natural law is an inadequate conception because it is unduly restrictive, though there is also a sense in which it is not restrictive enough. To qualify for being accounted a miracle an occurrence does not have to be characterizable as a violation of natural law. However, though I do not take the conception of miracles as violations of natural law to be an adequate conception of the miraculous, I shall maintain that occurrences are conceivable in respect to which it could be said that some law or laws of nature had been violated—or it could be said equally that there was a contradiction in our experience: and if the surrounding circumstances were appropriate it would be possible for such occurrences to have a kind of human significance and hence intelligible for them to be hailed as miracles. I see no philosophical reason against this.

But consider first the following example. A child riding his toy motor car strays on to an unguarded railway crossing near his house

*American Philosophical Quarterly, 1965, 2: 43–51.

and a wheel of his car gets stuck down the side of one of the rails. An express train is due to pass with the signals in its favor and a curve in the track makes it impossible for the driver to stop his train in time to avoid any obstruction he might encounter on the crossing. The mother coming out of the house to look for her child sees him on the crossing and hears the train approaching. She runs forward shouting and waving. The little boy remains seated in his car looking downward, engrossed in the task of pedaling it free. The brakes of the train are applied and it comes to rest a few feet from the child. The mother thanks God for the miracle; which she never ceases to think of as such although, as she in due course learns, there was nothing supernatural about the manner in which the brakes of the train came to be applied. The driver had fainted, for a reason that had nothing to do with the presence of the child on the line, and the brakes were applied automatically as his hand ceased to exert pressure on the control lever. He fainted on this particular afternoon because his blood pressure had risen after an exceptionally heavy lunch during which he had quarreled with a colleague, and the change in blood pressure caused a clot of blood to be dislodged and circulate. He fainted at the time when he did on the afternoon in question because this was the time at which the coagulation in his bloodstream reached the brain.

Thus the stopping of the train and the fact that it stopped when it did have a natural explanation. I do not say a *scientific* explanation, for it does not seem to me that the explanation here as a whole is of this kind (in order for something to be unsusceptible of scientific explanation it does not have to be anything so queer and grandiose as a miracle). The form of explanation in the present case, I would say, is *historical*; and the considerations that enter into it are various. They include medical factors, for instance, and had these constituted the whole extent of the matter the explanation could have been called scientific. But as it is, the medical considerations, though obviously important, are only one aspect of a complex story, alongside other considerations of a practical and social kind; and in addition there is a reference to mechanical considerations. All of these enter into the explanation of, or story behind, the stopping of the train. And just as there is an explanatory story behind the train's stopping when and where it did, so there is an explanatory story behind the presence of the child on the line at the time when, and in the place where, he was. But these two explanations or histories are independent of each other. They are about as disconnected as the history of the steam loom is from the history of the Ming dynasty. The spaciotemporal coincidence, I mean the fact that the child was on the line at the time when the train approached and the train stopped a few feet short of the place where he was, is exactly what I have just called it, a coincidence—something which a chronicle of events can merely record, like the fact that the Ming dynasty was in power at the same time as the house of Lancaster.

But unlike the coincidence between the rise of the Ming dynasty and the arrival of the dynasty of Lancaster, the coincidence of the child's presence on the line with the arrival and then the stopping of the train is impressive, significant; not because it is very unusual for trains to be halted in the way this one was, but because the life of a child was imperiled and then, against expectation, preserved. The significance of some coincidences as opposed to others arises from their relation to human needs and hopes and fears, their effects for good or ill upon our lives. So we speak of our luck (fortune, fate, etc.). And the kind of thing that, outside religion, we call luck is in religious parlance the grace of God or a miracle of God. But while the reference here is the same, the meaning is different. The meaning is different in that whatever happens by God's grace or by a miracle is something for which God is thanked or thankable, something which has been or could have been prayed for, something which can be regarded with awe and be taken as a sign or made the subject of a vow (e.g., to go on a pilgrimage), all of which can only take place against the background of a religious tradition. Whereas what happens by a stroke of luck is something in regard to which one just seizes one's opportunity or feels glad about or feels relieved about, something for which one may thank one's lucky stars. To say that one thanks one's lucky stars is simply to express one's relief or to emphasize the intensity of the relief: if it signifies anything more than this it signifies a superstition (*cf.* touching wood).

But although a coincidence can be taken religiously as a sign and called a miracle and made the subject of a vow, it cannot without confusion be taken as a sign of divine interference with the natural order. If someone protests that it is no part of the natural order that an express train should stop for a child on the line whom the driver cannot see then in *protesting* this he misses the point. What he says has been agreed to be perfectly true in the sense that there is no natural order relating the train's motion to the child which could be either preserved or interfered with. The concept of the miraculous which we have so far been considering is distinct therefore from the concept exemplified in the biblical stories of the turning of water into wine and the feeding of five thousand people on a very few loaves and fishes. Let us call the former the contingency concept and the latter the violation concept.

To establish the contingency concept of the miraculous as a possible concept it seems to me enough to point out (1) that *pace* Spinoza, Leibniz, and others, there are genuine contingencies in the world, and (2) that certain of these contingencies can be, and are in fact, regarded religiously in the manner I have indicated. If you assent to this and still express a doubt—"But are they really miracles?"— then you must now be questioning whether people are right to react to contingencies in this way, questioning whether you ought yourself to go along with them. Why not just stick to talking of luck? When you think this you are somewhat in the position of one who watches others fall in love and as an outsider thinks it unreasonable, hyperbolical, ridiculous (surely friendship should suffice).

To turn now to the concept of the miraculous as a violation of natural law: I am aware of two arguments which, if they were correct, would show that this concept were not a possible concept. The first can be found in chapter ten of Hume's *Enquiry Concerning Human Understanding*:

> Nothing is esteemed a miracle, if it ever happen in the common course of nature. It is no miracle that a man, seemingly in good health, should die on a sudden: because such a kind of death, though more unusual than any other, has yet been frequently observed to happen. But it is a miracle, that a dead man should come to life; because that has never been observed in any age or country. There must, therefore, be a uniform experience against every miraculous event, otherwise the event would not merit that appellation. And as a uniform experience amounts to a proof, there is here a direct and full *proof*, from the nature of the fact, against the existence of any miracle; nor can such a proof be destroyed, or the miracle rendered credible, but by an opposite proof, which is superior.
>
> The plain consequence is (and it is a general maxim worthy of our attention), "That no testimony is sufficient to establish a miracle, unless the testimony be of such a kind, that its falsehood would be

more miraculous, than the fact, which it endeavours to establish; and even in that case there is a mutual destruction of arguments, and the superior only gives us an assurance suitable to that degree of force, which remains, after deducting the inferior." When anyone tells me, that he saw a dead man restored to life, I immediately consider with myself, whether it be more probable, that this person should either deceive or be deceived, or that the fact, which he relates, should really have happened. I weigh the one miracle against the other; and according to the superiority, which I discover, I pronounce my decision, and always reject the greater miracle. If the falsehood of his testimony would be more miraculous, than the event which he relates; then, and not till then, can he pretent to command my belief or opinion ([3] pp. 27f of this volume).

Hume's concern in the chapter from which I have just quoted is ostensibly with the problem of assessing the *testimony of others* in regard to the allegedly miraculous. This is not the same problem as that which arises for the man who has to decide whether or not he himself has witnessed a miracle. Hume gives an inadequate account of the considerations which would influence one's decision to accept or reject the insistence of another person that something has happened which one finds it extremely hard to believe could have happened. The character and temperament of the witness, the kind of person he is and the kind of understanding one has of him, the closeness or distance of one's personal relationship with him are obviously important here, whereas Hume suggests that if we give credence to some witnesses rather than others the reason must be simply that we are accustomed to find in their case a conformity between testimony and reality. Maybe the weakness of Hume's account of the nature of our trust or lack of trust in witnesses is connected with the fact that in some way he intended his treatment of the problem of witness concerning the miraculous to have a more general application—as if he were trying to cut across the distinction between the case where we are ourselves confronted with a miracle (or something we may be inclined to call one) and the case where other people intervene, and wanting us to consider it all as fundamentally a single problem of evidence, a problem of witness in which it would make no difference whether what were doing the witnessing were a person other than oneself, or oneself in the role of a witness to oneself, or one's senses as witnesses to oneself. This anyway is the view I am going to take of his intention here.

I can imagine it being contended that, while Hume has produced a strong argument against the possibility of our ever having certitude or even very good evidence that a miracle has occurred, his thesis does not amount to an argument against the possibility of miracles as such. But I think this would be a misunderstanding. For if Hume is right, the situation is not just that we do not happen as a matter of fact to have certitude or even good evidence for the occurrence of any miracle, but rather that *nothing can count* as good evidence: the logic of testimony precludes this. And in precluding this it must, so far as I can see, preclude equally our having *poor* evidence for the occurrence of any miracle, since a contrast between good evidence and poor evidence is necessary if there is to be sense in speaking of either. Equally it must follow that there can be no such thing as (because nothing is being allowed to count as) discovering, recognizing, becoming aware, etc., that a miracle has occurred; and if there be no such thing as finding out or being aware (etc.) that a miracle has occurred, there can be no such thing as failing to find out or failing to be aware that a miracle has occurred either; no such thing as a discovered or an undiscovered miracle . . . *en fin*, no such thing as a miracle. So Hume's argument is, after all, an argument against the very possibility of miracles. I do not think his argument is cogent either on the interpretation I have just put upon it or on the interpretation according to which it would be an argument merely against the possibility of our having good evidence for a miracle. But before giving my reason I would like first to mention the only other line of argument which I can at present envisage against the conception of the miraculous as a violation of natural law.

Consider the proposition that a criminal is a violator of the laws of the state. With this proposition in mind you will start to wonder, when someone says that a miracle is a violation of the laws of nature, if he is not confusing a law of nature with a judicial law as laid down by some legal authority. A judicial law is obviously something which can be violated. The laws of the state prescribe and their prescriptions can be flouted. But are the laws of nature in any sense prescriptions? Maybe they are in the sense that they prescribe to us what we are to expect, but since *we* formulated the laws this is really a matter of our offering prescriptions or recipes to ourselves. And we can certainly fail to act on these prescriptions. But the occurrences which the laws are about are not prescribed to: they are simply *des*cribed.

And if anything should happen of which we are inclined to say that it goes counter to a law of nature, what this must mean is that the description we have framed has been, not flouted or violated, but falsified. We have encountered something that the description does not fit and we must therefore withdraw or modify our description. The law was wrong; we framed it wrongly: or rather what we framed has turned out not to have been a law. The relation between an occurrence and a law of nature is different then from a man's relation to a law of the state, for when the latter is deviated from we do not, save in exceptional circumstances, say that the law is wrong but rather that the man is wrong—he is a criminal. To suggest that an occurrence which has falsified a law of nature is *wrong* would be an absurdity: and it would be just as absurd to suggest that the law has been violated. Nothing can be conceived to be a violation of natural law, and if that is how the miraculous is conceived there can be no such thing as the miraculous. Laws of nature can be formulated or reformulated to cope with any eventuality, and would-be miracles are transformed automatically into natural occurrences the moment science gets on the track of them.

But there is an objection to this line of argument. If we say that a law of nature is a description, what exactly are we taking it to be a description of? A description of what has happened up to now or is actually happening now? Suppose we have a law to the effect that all unsupported bodies fall. From this I can deduce that if the pen now in my hand were unsupported it *would* fall and that when in a moment I withdraw from it the support it now has it *will* fall. But if the law were simply a description of what has happened up to now or is happening now and no more, these deductions would be impossible. So it looks as if the law must somehow describe the future as well as the past and present. "A description of the future." But what on earth is that? For until the future ceases to be the future and becomes actual there are no events for the description to describe— over and above those that either have already taken place or are at this moment taking place.

It seems that if we are to continue to maintain that a natural law is nothing but a description then we must say that the description covers not only the actual but also the possible and is every bit as much a description of the one as it is of the other. And this only amounts to a pleonastic way of saying that the law tells us, defines for us, what is and is not *possible* in regard to the behavior of unsupported bodies. At which point we might just as well drop the talk about describing altogether and admit that the law does not just describe—it stipulates: stipulates that it is impossible for an unsupported body to do anything other than fall. Laws of nature and legal laws, though they may not resemble each other in other respects, are at least alike in this: that they both stipulate something. Moreover the stipulations which we call laws of nature are in many cases so solidly founded and knitted together with other stipulations, other laws, that they come to be something in the nature of a framework through which we look at the world and which to a considerable degree dictates our ways of describing phenomena.

Notice, however, that insofar as we resist in this way the second of the two arguments for the impossibility of the violation concept of the miraculous and insofar as we object to the suggestion that it is possible for our laws of nature to be dropped or reformulated in a sort of *ad hoc* manner to accommodate any would-be miracle, we seem to be making the first argument—the Humean argument against the miraculous—all the stronger. For if we take a law of nature to be more than a generalized description of what has happened up to now, and if at the same time we upgrade the mere probability or belief to which Hume thought we were confined here into certainty and real knowledge, then surely it must seem that our reluctance to throw overboard a whole nexus of well-established, mutually supporting laws and theories must be so great as to justify us in rejecting out of hand, and not being prepared to assign even a degree of probability to, any testimony to an occurrence which our system of natural law decisively rules out; and surely we shall be justified in classifying as illusory any experience which purports to be the experience of such an occurrence.

The truth is that this position is not at all justified, and we should only be landed in inconsistency if we adopted it. For if it were granted that there can be no certainty in regard to the individual case, if there can be no real knowledge that a particular event has occurred in exactly the way that it has, how could our system of laws have got established in the first place?

On Hume's view, the empirical in general was synonymous with the probable. No law of nature could have more than a degree of probability, and neither for that matter could the occurrence of any particular event. This is what gave point to the idea of a balance of probabilities and hence to his thesis about the impossibility of ever establishing a miracle. But while in the one case, that of the general law, he was prepared (in the passage from which I quoted) to allow that the probability could have the status of a proof, in the other case he was curiously reluctant to allow this.

Now if in the interest of good conceptual sense we upgrade the probability of natural laws into certainty, so as to be able to distinguish a well-established law from a more or less tenable hypothesis, it is equally in the interest of good conceptual sense that we should upgrade in a comparable fashion the probability attaching to particular events and states of affairs, so as to allow that some of these, as opposed to others, can be certain and really known to be what they are. Otherwise a distinction gets blurred which is at least as important as the distinction between a law and a hypothesis—namely the distinction between a hypothesis and a fact. The distinction between a hypothesis and a fact is for instance the distinction between my saying when I come upon an infant who is screaming and writhing and holding his ear "he's got an abscess" and my making this statement again after looking into the ear, whether by means of an instrument or without, and actually seeing, coming upon, the abscess. Or again it is the difference between the statement "it is snowing" when made by me now as I sit here and the same statement uttered as I go outside the building into the snow and get snowed on. The second statement, unlike the first, is uttered directly in the face of the circumstance which makes it true. I can be as certain in that situation that it is snowing as I can be of anything. And if there weren't things of this kind of which we can be certain, we wouldn't be able to be uncertain of anything either.

If it were remarked here that our senses are capable of deceiving us, I should reply that it does not follow from this that there are not occasions when we know perfectly well that we are not being deceived. And this is one of them. I submit that nothing would persuade you—or if it would it shouldn't—that you are not at this moment in the familiar surroundings of your university and that in what you see as you look around this room you are subject to an illusion. And if something very strange were to happen, such as one of us bursting into flame, you'd soon know it for what it was; and of course you'd expect the natural cause to be duly discovered (the smoldering pipe which set fire to the matches or whatever it might be).

But then suppose you failed to discover any cause. Or suppose that something happened which was truly bizarre, like my rising slowly and steadily three feet into the air and staying there. You could *know* that this happened if it did, and probably you would laugh and presume there must be some natural explanation: a rod behind, a disguised support beneath, a thin wire above. Or could it even be done by air pressure in some way? Or by a tremendously powerful magnet on the next floor, attracting metal in my clothing? Or if not by magnetic attraction then by magnetic repulsion? I rise in the air then, and since it is no magician's demonstration you can and do search under me, over me, and around me. But suppose you find nothing, nothing on me and nothing in the room or above, below, or around it. You cannot think it is the effect of an anti-gravity device (even if there be sense in that idea) because there just is no device. And you know that, excluding phenomena like tornadoes, it is impossible for a physical body in free air to behave thus in the absence of a special device. So does it not come to this: that if I were to rise in the air now, you could be completely certain of two incompatible things: (1) that it is impossible, and (2) that it has happened?

Now against what I have just said I envisage two objections. The first is that my rising three feet into the air in the absence of some special cause can only be held to be an impossibility by someone who is ignorant of the statistical basis of modern physics. For example, the water in a kettle comprises a vast number of atoms in motion and anything I do to the kettle, such as tilting it or heating it, will affect the movements of these atoms. But there is no way of determining what the effect will be in the case of any single atom. It is no more within the power of physicists to predict that a particular atom will change its position in such and such a way, or even at all, than it is within the power of insurance actuaries to predict that a certain man will die next week in a road accident, or die at all. However, reliable statistical statements can be made by actuaries about the life prospects of large numbers of people taken together and somewhat similarly, statistical laws are framed by physicists about the behavior of atoms in large numbers. Statistical laws are laws of probability and it gets argued that, since this is the kind of law on which the behavior of water in a heated vessel ultimately rests, there can be no *certainty* that the kettle on the hob will boil however fierce the fire, no certainty that it will boil absolutely *every* time, because there is always the probability—infinitesimally small admittedly, but still a definite probability—that enough of the constituent atoms in their molecules will move in a way that is incompatible with its doing so. Vessels of water and rubber balls seem to be the most frequently used examples when this argument is deployed, but the suggestion has been made to me that it (or some similar argument) could be applied to the behavior of an unsupported body near the surface of the earth, in respect of which it could be maintained that there is a certain probability, albeit a very low one, in favor of the body's having its state of rest three feet above the ground.

However, it seems to me that any such argument must rest on the kind of confusion that Eddington fell into when he said, mentioning facts about atoms as the reason, that his table was not solid but consisted largely of empty space. If you add to this that your table is in a continuous vibratory motion and that the laws governing its behavior are laws of probability only you are continuing in the same vein. To make the confusion more symmetrical you might perhaps go on to say that the movements of tables in space are only predictable even with probability when tables get together in large numbers (which accounts for the existence of warehouses). Anyway my point is that, using words in their ordinary senses, it is about as certain and as much a matter of common understanding that my kettle, when put on a fierce fire, will boil or that I shall not next moment float three feet in the air as it is certain and a matter of common understanding that my desk is solid and will continue for some time to be so. The validity of my statement about the desk is not impugned by any assertion about the behavior of atoms whether singly or in the aggregate; neither is the validity of the corresponding statements about the kettle and my inability to float in the air impugned by any assertion about the statistical basis of modern science.

The second objection grants the impossibility of a body's rising three feet into the air in the absence of a special cause and grants my certitude of this. But what I can never be certain of, the objection runs, is that all the special causes and devices that accomplish this are absent. So I am entirely unjustified in asserting the outright impossibility of the phenomenon—especially when I think to do so in the very teeth of its occurrence. My saying that it is impossible could only have the force here of an ejaculation like "Struth!" *Ab esse ad posse valet consequentia.* Supposing the thing to have occurred, our response as ungullible people should be to maintain confidence in the existence of a natural cause, to persist indefinitely in searching for one and to classify the occurrence in the meantime as an unsolved problem. So runs the second objection.

However, the idea that one cannot establish the absence of a natural cause is not to my mind the unassailable piece of logic it might seem at first glance to be. Both our common understanding and our scientific understanding include conceptions of the sort of thing that can and cannot happen, and of the sort of thing that has to take place to bring about some other sort of thing. These conceptions are presupposed to our arguing in such patterns as "A will do such and such unless Y," or "If Z happens it can only be from this, that or the other (kind of) cause," or "If W cannot be done in this way or that way it cannot be done at all." An example of the first pattern is "The horse will die if it gets no food." My rising steadily three feet in the air is a subject for argument according to the second pattern. The second pattern presents the surface appearance of being more complicated than the first, but logically it is not. Let us turn our attention to the example of the first pattern.

Suppose that a horse, which has been normally born and reared, and is now deprived of all nourishment (we could be completely certain of this)—suppose that, instead of dying, this horse goes on thriving (which again is something we could be completely certain about). A series of thorough examinations reveals no abnormality in the horse's condition: its digestive system is always found to be working and to be at every moment in more or less the state it would have been in if the horse had eaten a meal an hour or two before. This is utterly inconsistent with our whole conception of the needs and capacities of horses; and because it is an impossibility in the light of our prevailing conception, my objector, in the event of its happening, would expect us to abandon the conception—as though we had to have consistency at any price. Whereas the position I advocate is that the price is too high and it would be better to be left with the inconsistency; and that in any event the prevailing conception has a logical status not altogether unlike that of a necessary truth and cannot be simply thrown away as a mistake—not when it rests on the experience of generations, not when all the other horses in the world are continuing to behave as horses have always done, and especially not when one considers the way our conception of the needs and capacities of horses interlocks with conceptions of the needs and capacities of other living things and with a conception of the difference between animate and inanimate behavior quite generally. These conceptions form part of a common understanding that is well established and with us to stay. Any number of discoveries remains to be made by zoologists and plenty of scope exists for conceptual revision in biological theory, but it is a confusion to think it follows from this that we are less than well enough acquainted with, and might have serious misconceptions about, what is and is not possible in the behavior under familiar conditions of common objects with which we have a long history of practical dealings. Similarly with the relation between common understanding and physical discoveries, physical theories: what has been said about the self-sustaining horse seems to me applicable *mutatis mutandis* to the levitation example also. Not that my thesis about the miraculous rests on the acceptance of this particular example. The objector who thinks there is a loophole in it for natural explanation strikes me as lacking a sense of the absurd but can keep his opinion for the moment, since he will (I hope) be shown the loophole being closed in a further example with which I shall conclude.

I did not in any case mean to suggest that if I rose in the air now in the absence of any device it would be at all proper for a religious person to hail this as a miracle. Far from it. From a religious point of view it would either signify nothing at all or else be regarded as a sign of devilry; and if the phenomenon persisted I should think that a religious person might well have recourse to exorcism, if that figured among the institutions of his religion. Suppose, however, that by rising into the air I were to avoid an otherwise certain death: then it would (against a religious background) become possible to speak of a miracle, just as it would in what I called the contingency case. Or the phenomenon could be a miracle although nothing at all were achieved by it, provided I were a religiously significant figure, one of whom prophets had spoken, or at least an exceptionally holy man.

My thesis then in regard to the violation concept of the miraculous, by contrast with the contingency concept, which we have seen to be also a possible concept, is that a conflict of certainties is a necessary though not a sufficient condition of the miraculous. In other words a miracle, though it cannot only be this, must at least be something the occurrence of which can be categorized at one and the same time as empirically certain and conceptually impossible. If it were less than conceptually impossible it would reduce merely to a very unusual occurrence such as could be treated (because of the empirical certainty) in the manner of a decisive experiment and result in a modification to the prevailing conception of natural law; while if it were less than empirically certain nothing more would be called for in regard to it than a suspension of judgment. So if there is to be a type of the miraculous other than the contingency kind it must offend against the principle *ab esse ad posse valet consequentia*. And since the violation concept of the miraculous does seem to me to be a possible concept I therefore reject that time honored logical principle.

I know that my suggestion that something could be at one and the same time empirically certain and conceptually impossible will sound to many people ridiculous. Must not the actual occurrence of something show that it *was* conceptually possible after all? And if I contend, as I do, that the fact that something has occurred might *not* necessarily show that it was conceptually possible; or to put it the other way round—if I contend, as I do, that the fact that something is conceptually impossible does not necessarily preclude its occurrence, then am I not opening the door to the instantiation of round squares, female fathers, and similar paradigms of senselessness? The answer is that the door is being opened only as far as is needed and no farther; certainly not to instantiations of the *self*-contradictory. There is more than one kind of conceptual impossibility.

Let me illustrate my meaning finally by reference to the New Testament story of the turning of water into wine. I am not assuming that this story is true, but I think that it logically could be. Hence if anyone chooses to maintain its truth as a matter of faith I see no philosophical objection to his doing so. A number of people could have been quite sure, could have had the fullest empirical certainty, that a vessel contained water at one moment and wine a moment later—good wine, as St. John says—without any device having been applied to it in the intervening time. Not that this last really needs to be added; for that any device should have existed *then* at least is inconceivable, even if it might just be argued to be a conceptual possibility now. I have in mind the very remote possibility of a liquid chemically indistinguishable from say mature claret being produced by means of atomic and molecular transformations. The device would have to be conceived as something enormously complicated, requiring a large supply of power. Anything less thorough-going would hardly meet the case, for those who are alleged to have drunk the wine were practiced wine-bibbers, capable of detecting at once the difference between a true wine and a concocted variety in the "British Wine, Ruby Type" category. However, that water could conceivably have been turned into wine in the first century A.D. by means of a device is ruled out of court at once by common understanding; and though the verdict is supported by scientific knowledge, common understanding has no need of this support.

In the case of my previous example of a man, myself for instance, rising three feet into the air and remaining there unsupported, it was difficult to deal with the objection that we could not be certain there wasn't some special cause operating, *some* explanation even though we had searched to the utmost of our ability and had found none. And I imagined the objector trying to lay it down as axiomatic that while there is such a thing as not knowing what the cause or explanation of a phenomenon might be there can be no such thing as establishing the absence of a cause. The example of water being turned into wine is stronger, and I would think decisive, here. At one moment, let us suppose, there was water and at another moment wine, in the same vessel, although nobody had emptied out the water and poured in the wine. This is something that could conceivably have been established with certainty. What is not conceivable is that it could have been done by a device. Nor is it conceivable that there could have been a natural cause of it. For this would have had to be the natural cause of the water's becoming wine. And water's becoming wine is not the description of any conceivable natural process. It is conceptually impossible that the wine could have been got naturally from water, save in the very strained sense that moisture is needed to nourish the vines from which the grapes are taken, and this very strained sense is irrelevant here.

"But can we not still escape from the necessity to assert that one and the same thing is both empirically certain and conceptually impossible? For what has been said to be conceptually impossible is the turning of water into wine. However, when allusion is made to the alleged miracle, all the expression 'turned into' can signify is that at one moment there was water and at a moment later wine. This is what could have been empirically certain: whereas what is conceptually impossible is that water should have been turned into wine if one really *means* turned into. It is not conceptually impossible that at one moment water should have been found and at another moment wine in the same vessel, even though nobody had emptied out the water and poured in the wine." So someone might try to argue. But I cannot see that it does any good. To the suggestion that the thing is conceivable so long as we refrain from saying that the water *turned into* the wine I would reply: either the water turns into the wine or else it disappears and wine springs into existence in its place. But water cannot *conceivably* disappear like that without going anywhere, and wine cannot *conceivably* spring into existence from nowhere. Look at it in terms of transformation, or look at it in terms of "coming into being and passing away"—or just look at it. Whatever you do, you cannot make sense of it: on all accounts it is inconceivable. So I keep to the position that the New Testament story of the turning of water into wine is the story of something that could have been known empirically to have occurred, and it is also the story of the occurrence of something which is conceptually impossible. It has to be both in order to be the miracle-story which, whether true or false, it is.

That expression "the occurrence of something which is conceptually impossible" was used deliberately just then. And it will be objected, no doubt, that to speak of something which is conceptually impossible is to speak of a nullity. To ask for an example of something that is conceptually impossible is not (I shall be told) like asking for a sample of a substance and you cannot in order to comply with this request produce anything visible or tangible, you cannot point to an occurrence. Indeed you cannot, strictly speaking, offer a description either: you can only utter a form of words. What I have been arguing in effect is that there is a contradiction in St. John's "description" of the water-into-wine episode. But if so, then nothing has really been described; or alternatively something has been—one should not say mis-described but rather garbled—since a conceptual impossibility is *ex vi termini* one of which sense cannot be made.

I would reply to this that sense can certainly be made of a conceptual impossibility in the respect that one can see often enough that there *is* a conceptual impossibility there and also, often enough, what kind of a conceptual impossibility it is and how it arises. We can see there is an inconsistency; and words, moreover, are not the only things in which we can see inconsistency. Human actions can be pointed to here quite obviously. And I am maintaining that there is also such a thing as making sense, and failing to make sense, of *events*. If the objector holds that in the case of events, unlike the case of human actions, sense must always be there although one perhaps fails to find it, I ask: how does he know? Why the *must*? It is not part of my case that to regard a sequence of events as senseless or miraculous is to construe it as if it were a sort of action, or to see the invisible hand of a super-person at work in it. I have contended that there are circumstances in respect to which the expression "occurrence of something which is conceptually impossible" would have a natural enough use, and I have offered three examples. I think the expression "violation of a law of nature" could also be introduced quite naturally in this connection; we could even speak of "a contradiction in our experience."

7

PAUL TILLICH*

Revelation and Miracle

THE WORD "MIRACLE" according to the ordinary definition, designates a happening that contradicts the laws of nature. This definition and the innumerable unverified miracle stories in all religions have rendered the term misleading and dangerous for theological use. But a word which expresses a genuine experience can only be dropped if a substitute is at hand, and it does not seem that such a substitute has been found. The New Testament often uses the Greek word *sēmeion*, "sign," pointing to the religious meaning of the miracles. But the word "sign" without a qualifying addition cannot express this religious meaning. It would be more accurate to add the word "event" to "sign" and to speak of *sign-events*. The original meaning of miracle, "that which produces astonishment," is quite adequate for describing the "giving side" of a revelatory experience. But this connotation has been swallowed by the bad connotation of a supranatural interference which destroys the natural structure of events. The bad connotation is avoided in the word "sign" and the phrase "sign-event."

While the original naïve religious consciousness accepts astounding stories in connection with divine manifestations without

*Paul Tillich (1886–1965) was an influential German-American theologian in the modern German tradition of theology. This selection is from *Systematic Theology*, vol. 1 (Chicago: University of Chicago Press, 1951), pp. 115–18.

elaborating a supranaturalistic theory of miracles, rationalistic periods make the negation of natural laws the main point in miracle stories. A kind of irrationalist rationalism develops in which the degree of absurdity in a miracle story becomes the measure of its religious value. The more impossible, the more revelatory! Already in the New Testament one can observe that, the later the tradition, the more the antinatural element is emphasized over against the sign element. In the post-apostolic period, when the apocryphal Gospels were produced, there were no checks against absurdity. Pagans and Christians alike were not so much interested in the presence of the divine in shaking and sign-giving events as they were in the sensation produced in their rationalistic minds by antirational happenings. This rationalistic antirationalism infected later Christianity, and it is still a burden for the life of the church and for theology.

The manifestation of the mystery of being does not destroy the structure of being in which it becomes manifest. The ecstasy in which the mystery is received does not destroy the rational structure of the mind by which it is received. The sign-event which gives the mystery of revelation does not destroy the rational structure of the reality in which it appears. If these criteria are applied, a meaningful doctrine of sign-events or miracles can be stated.

One should not use the word "miracle" for events which create astonishment for a certain time, such as scientific discoveries, technical creations, impressive works of art or politics, personal achievements, etc. These cease to produce astonishment after one has become accustomed to them, although a profound admiration of them may remain and even increase. Nor are the structures of reality, the *Gestalten*, the qualities, the inner *teloi* of things miracles, although they always will be objects of admiration. There is an element of astonishment in admiration, but it is not a numinous astonishment; it does not point to a miracle.

As ecstasy presupposes the shock of nonbeing in the mind, so sign-events presuppose the stigma of nonbeing in the reality. In shock and stigma, which are strictly correlated, the negative side of the mystery of being appears. The word "stigma" points to marks of disgrace, for example, in the case of a criminal, and to marks of grace, for example, in the case of a saint; in both instances, however, it indicates something negative. There is a stigma that appears on everything, the stigma of finitude, or implicit and inescapable nonbeing. It is striking that in many miracle stories there is a description of the "numinous" dread which grasps those who participate in the miraculous events. There is the feeling that the solid ground of ordinary reality is taken "out from under" their feet. The correlative experience of the stigma of nonbeing in the reality and the shock of nonbeing in the mind produces this feeling, which, although not revelatory in itself, accompanies every genuine revelatory experience.

Miracles cannot be interpreted in terms of a supranatural interference in natural processes. If such an interpretation were true, the manifestation of the ground of being would destroy the structure of being; God would be split within himself, as religious dualism has asserted. It would be more adequate to call such a miracle "demonic," not because it is produced by "demons," but because it discloses a "structure of destruction." It corresponds with the state of "being possessed" in the mind and could be called "sorcery." The supranaturalistic theory of miracles makes God a sorcerer and a cause of "possession": it confuses God with demonic structures in the mind and in reality. There are such structures, based on a distortion of genuine manifestations of the mystery of being. A supranaturalistic theology which employs patterns derived from the structure of possession and sorcery for the sake of describing the nature of revelation in terms of the destruction of the subjective as well as of objective reason is certainly intolerable.

The sign-events in which the mystery of being gives itself consist in special constellations of elements of reality in correlation with special constellations of elements of the mind. A genuine miracle is first of all an event which is astonishing, unusual, shaking, without contradicting the rational structure of reality. In the second place, it is an event which points to the mystery of being, expressing its relation to us in a definite way. In the third place, it is an occurrence which is received as a sign-event in an ecstatic experience. Only if these three conditions are fulfilled can one speak of a genuine miracle. That which does not shake one by its astonishing character has no revelatory power. That which shakes one without pointing to the mystery of being is not miracle but sorcery. That which is not received in ecstasy is a report about the belief in a miracle, not an actual miracle. This is emphasized in the synoptic records of the miracles of Jesus. Miracles are given only to those for whom they are sign-events, to those who receive them in faith. Jesus refuses to perform "objective" miracles. They are a contradiction in terms. This strict correlation makes it possible to exchange the words describing miracles and those describing ecstasy. One can say that ecstasy is the miracle of the mind and that miracle is the ecstasy of reality.

Since neither ecstasy nor miracle destroys the structure of cognitive reason, scientific analysis, psychological and physical, as well as historical investigation are possible and necessary. Research can and must proceed without restriction. It can undercut the superstitions and demonic interpretations of revelation, ecstasy, and miracle. Science, psychology, and history are allies of theology in the fight against the supranaturalistic distortions of genuine revelation. Scientific explanation and historical criticism protect revelation; they cannot dissolve it, for revelation belongs to a dimension of reality for which scientific and historical analysis are inadequate. Revelation is the manifestation of the depth of reason and the ground of being. It points to the mystery of existence and to our ultimate concern. It is independent of what science and history say about the conditions in which it appears; and it cannot make science and history dependent on itself. No conflict between different dimensions of reality is possible. Reason receives revelation in ecstasy and miracles; but reason is not destroyed by revelation, just as revelation is not emptied by reason.

8

RICHARD SWINBURNE*

Violation of a Law of Nature

Laws of Nature

THE TASK OF the theoretical scientist is to set forth the laws of nature (which may be physical, chemical, biological or psychological laws, or laws of any other science). In any field he will have a number of observational results. He seeks the most natural generalization or extrapolation of those results, or, as I shall put it, the simplest formula from which the past results can be deduced.

In a primitive way ordinary people generalize their observations in the most natural or simple way to obtain general statements about how things behave, from which they can deduce how things will behave in future. Thus, to take a well-worn example, suppose that swans had not previously been observed and then we observe in different parts of England a number of swans and find them all to be white. We might set forward a hypothesis "all swans are white." This allows us to infer of each past swan observed that it was white, and predicts of each future swan which will be observed that it will be white. We might set forward a hypothesis "all swans are white." This allows us to infer of each past swan observed that it was white, and but elsewhere are black." Yet this would never be seriously proposed because it is so obviously less simple than, a less natural extrapolation from the data than, the alternative formula.

*Chapter 3 of my book, *The Concept of Miracle*. London: Macmillan and Co., 1970.

The task of the scientist may thus be compared to that of a man finding a formula governing the occurrence of points on a graph. Compatible with any finite set of data, there will always be an infinite number of possible formulae from which the data can be predicted. We can rule out many by further tests, but however many tests we make we shall still have only a finite number of data and hence an infinite number of formulae compatible with them. Yet some of these formulae will be highly complex relative to the data so that no scientist would consider that the data provided evidence that those formulae were laws of nature. Others are very simple formulae such that the data can be said to provide evidence that they are laws of nature. Thus suppose the scientist finds marks at $(1,1)$, $(2,2)$, $(3,3)$, and $(4,4)$, the first number of each pair being the x-coordinate and the second the y-coordinate. One formula which would predict these marks is $x = y$. Another one is $(x - 1) (x - 2) (x - 3) (x - 4) + x = y$. But clearly we would not regard the data as supporting the second formula. It is too clumsy a formula to explain four observations. Among simple formulae supported by the data, the simplest is the best supported and regarded, provisionally, as correct. If the formula survives further tests, that increases the evidence in its favor as a law.

What counts as a formula of sufficient simplicity to be adopted as a law and so used for prediction in the absence of simpler formulae is a matter of the quantity and variety of the data on the basis of which it is constructed. While

$$(x - 1) (x - 2) (x - 3) (x - 4) + x = y$$

would not do if supported only by the four cited data, it could reasonably be put forward on the basis of four hundred data. Einstein's field equations of General Relativity could hardly be put forward solely on the basis of observations of the movement of Mercury's perihelion (observations compatible with those equations) but could be put forward on the basis of an enormous number of terrestrial and planetary motions and of optical phenomena, previously accounted for by Newtonian mechanics or the Special Theory of Relativity, and of certain further phenomena (such as the movement of Mercury's perihelion) not compatible with the latter theories.

Often, unlike in my two initial examples, a number of different formulae of similar simplicity (no one clearly simpler than the rest) are equally compatible with past data, yet, being different formulae, make different predictions for the future. An artificial example of this would be if we had a number of points on a graph which could be fitted on to hyperbolic curves of different eccentricity but not on to any simpler curves (e.g. a straight line). More complicated real-life examples are provided by current cosmological theories, e.g., "big bang" and "steady state" theories. They all take account of the same data of astronomy and mechanics, yet integrate these in different ways so as to get different predictions. Yet many of them seem equally simple, no one a more natural extrapolation from the data than the others. In such cases, in so far as he can, a scientist will test between conflicting predictions and reject those formulae which yield incorrect predictions. If he can do this and is left with only one formula compatible with the data of observation, then he will adopt that.

Sometimes the scientist will be able to see no simple formula, that is formula of sufficient simplicity, compatible with a collection of data in some field, and in that case will not feel justified in adopting any one formula and making predictions on the basis of it. If in our studies of swans we had observed in England several white, several black, and several red ones with no obvious pattern of geographical distribution, we would not be able to produce any simple formula covering these data which would enable us to predict the colors of future swans. In so far as a formula is simple and the simplest known formula compatible with observations, we regard it—provisionally—as a law of nature. Any proposed law of nature will be corrigible—that is, future observations could show the proposed law not to be a true law. But in so far as a formula survives further tests, that increases the evidence in its favor as a true law.

Another example of these points is provided by Kepler's work on planetary motion. Studying the positions of planets observed during the previous thirty years, Kepler sought formulae from which those results could be deduced. But not any formulae would do; the formulae would have to be formulae of fairly simple curves, describing each planet as having traveled along a curve of that type, in order for us to be justified in supposing that the formulae described the future as well as the past behavior of planets. If the formulae were simply records of past positions with unrelated predictions attached, we would not, despite the fact that they accurately recorded past positions, think ourselves justified in believing the future predictions yielded by them. Only if they were the formulae of simple curves which fitted the past positions would we think that we could predict from them. Kepler eventually fitted the positions of each planet on to an ellipse, having the Sun at one focus. The neat fit of the past positions on to this curve justified men in supposing that planets in future would travel in elliptical paths.

The general points of the last few pages would, I believe—with qualifications and additions—be accepted by most philosophers of science. Philosophers of science today are very concerned to bring out clearly and explicitly the criteria for choosing between alternative theories equally compatible with observations obtained so far, criteria which, in common with many philosophers of science, I have termed criteria of simplicity. But although philosophers may still disagree about exactly what those criteria are, they agree that such criteria operate, and they agree in many particular cases when two different theories equally compatible with observations obtained to date are constructed which of the two is to be preferred.

The upshot of all this is that—against McKinnon—(see [5]) laws of nature do not just describe what happens ("the actual course of events"). They describe what happens in a regular and predictable way. When what happens is entirely irregular and unpredictable, its occurrence is not something describable by natural laws.

Meaning of "Violation of a Law of Nature"

Given this understanding of a law of nature, what is meant by a violation of a law of nature? I think that those who, like Hume, have used this or a similar expression have intended to mean by it an occurence of a non-repeatable counter-instance to a law of nature (this useful definition is provided by Professor Ninian Smart in his discussion of Hume's account of miracles [32]). The use of the definiens and of the definiendum, violation of a law of nature, both assume that the operation of a law of nature is logically compatible with the occurrence of an exception to its operation. This point will be developed below.

Clearly, as we have noted, events contrary to predictions of formulae which we had good reason to believe to be laws of nature often occur. But if we have good reason to believe that they have occurred and good reason to believe that similar events would occur in similar circumstances, then undoubtedly we have good reason to believe that the formulae which we previously believed to be the laws of nature were not in fact such laws. For then the real laws of nature will, we can best suppose, be the old purported laws with a modification for the circumstances in question. There cannot be repeatable counter-instances to genuine laws of nature, that is, counter-instances which would be repeated in similar circumstances. Repeatable counter-instances to purported laws only show those purported laws not to be genuine laws.

But what are we to say if we have good reason to believe that an event E has occurred contrary to predictions of a formula L which otherwise we have good reason to believe to a law of nature, and we have good reason to believe that events similar to E would not occur in circumstances as similar as we like in any respect to those of the occurrence of E? E would then be a non-repeatable counter-instance to L. In this case we could say *either* (as before) that L cannot be the law of nature operative in the field, since an exception to its operation has occurred, *or* that L is the law of nature operative in the field, but that an exceptional non-repeatable counter-instance to its occurrence has occurred. The advantage of saying the former is particularly obvious where universal laws are involved. As a universal law has the form "so-and-sos always do such and such," it seems formally incompatible with a couner-instance reported by "this is a so-and-so, and did not do such-and-such," Both statements cannot be true together, the argument goes; evidence in favor of the exception is evidence against the purported law. The advantage of saying the latter is however this. The evidence shows that we cannot replace L by a more successful law allowing us to predict E as well as other phenomena supporting L. For any modified formula which allowed us to predict E would allow us to predict similar events in similar circumstances and hence, *ex hypothesi*, we have good reason to believe, would give false predictions. Whereas if we leave the formula L unmodified, it will, we have good reason to believe, give correct predictions in all other conceivable circumstances. Hence if we are to say that any law of nature is operative in the field in question we must say that it is L. The only alternative is to say that no law of nature operates in the field. Yet saying this does not seem to do justice to the (in general) enormous success of L in predicting occurrences in the field.

For these latter reasons it seems not unnatural to describe E as a non-repeatable counter-instance to a law of nature L. If we do say this we have to understand the operation of a universal law of the form "so-and-so's always do such-and-such" as logically compatible with "this is a so-and-so and does not do such-and-such." To say that a certain such formula is a law is to say that virtually invariably its predictions are true and that any exceptions to its operation cannot be accounted for by another formula which could be taken as a law (by the criteria discussed earlier), including any statistical substitute for the universal law. One must thus distinguish between a formula being a law *and* a formula being (universally) true or being a law which holds without exception.

I believe this second account of the way to describe the relation between a formula which otherwise we have good reason to believe to be a law of nature, and an isolated exception to it, to be more natural than the first, that is, to do more justice to the way in which most of us ordinarily talk about these matters. However that may be, it is clearly a coherent way of talking, and it is the way adopted by those who talk of violations of natural laws. For if any exception to its operation was incompatible with a law being a true law, there appears to be no ready sense which could be given to "a violation of a law of nature." Hence I shall in future presuppose the second account. Since the second account is a possible account, the concept of a violation of a law of nature is coherent, and we must reject the views of McKinnon and others who claim that it is not logically possible that a law of nature be violated.

If, as seems natural, we understand by the physically impossible what is ruled out by a law of nature, then our account of laws of nature suggests that it makes sense to suppose that on occasion the physically impossible occurs. (If this seems too paradoxical a thing to say we shall have to give a different sense to the "physically impossible.") Substantially the same conclusion is reached by Holland [6]. For Holland a violation of a law of nature is a "conceptual impossibility." He terms it this because the supposition that there is an object behaving in a way other than that laid down by laws of nature is the supposition that there is an object behaving in ways other than the ways embodied in our normal understanding of it, and so, in wide senses of "involved" and "concept," involved in our ordinary concept of it. Therefore, having shown that it makes sense to suppose a law of nature violated, Holland argues that in such a case the conceptually impossible would occur. That being so, he concludes, one cannot deduce from a thing having happened that it is a possible occurrence—*ab esse ad posse non valet consequentia.* (When assessing Holland's conclusion, we should remember what he means by "conceptual impossibility." He does not mean what most philosophers mean by that expression—viz. something the description of which involves a self-contradiction—but merely something the occurrence of which is ruled out by our ordinary (and with this exception basically correct) understanding of the way objects behave.)

Evidence as to Which Events, if They Occurred, Would Be Violations of Laws of Nature

The crucial question however is what would be good reason for believing that an event E, if it occurred, was a non-repeatable as opposed to a repeatable counter-instance to a formula L which we have on all other evidence good reason to believe to be a law of nature. The evidence that E is a repeatable counter-instance would be that a new formula L^1 better confirmed than L as a law of nature can be set up, which, unlike L, predicted E. A formula is confirmed by data, it will be recalled, in so far as the data obtained so far are predicted by the formula, new predictions are successful, and the formula is a simple one relative to the collection of data (viz. a natural extrapolation from the data). Now L^1 will be better confirmed than L if it, like L, predicts the data so far obtained, other than E; unlike L, predicts E; and is no more complex than L. If it is considerably more complex than L, that counts against it and might perhaps balance the fact that it, unlike L, predicts E. And if it is so much more complicated than L that it is not of sufficient simplicity relative to the data (see our earlier discussion) to be a law of nature, it will clearly have to be rejected. In so far as there is a doubt whether any proposed law L^1 is more satisfactory than L, clearly the scientist will, if he can, test between the further predictions of the two laws. If, for matters where they make conflicting predictions, L^1 predicts successfully and L unsuccessfully, L^1 will be preferred, and vice versa. It follows from all this that L will have to be retained as a law of nature and E regarded as a non-repeatable counter-instance to it, if any proposed rival formula L^1 were too much more complicated than L without giving better new predictions, or predicted new phenomena unsuccessfully where L predicted successfully. L^1 would certainly be too much more complicated if it were not of sufficient simplicity relative to the data to be a law of nature at all (see our earlier discussion). L would have to be abandoned if some proposed rival formula L^1 which predicted E were not much more complicated than L, or predicted new phenomena successfully where L predicted unsuccessfully.

Here is an example. Suppose E to be the levitation (i.e., rising into the air and remaining floating on it, in circumstances where no known forces other than gravity (e.g., magnetism) are acting) of a certain holy person. E is thus a counter-instance to otherwise well-substituted laws of nature L (viz. the laws of mechanics, electro-magnetism, etc.) which together purport to give an account of all the forces operating in nature. We could show E to be a repeatable counter-instance if we could construct a formula L^1 which predicted E and also successfully predicted other divergences from L, as well as all other tested predictions of L; or if we could construct L^1 which was comparatively simple relative to the data and predicted E and all the other tested predictions of L, but predicted divergences from L which had not yet been tested. L^1 might differ from L in postulating the operation of an entirely new kind of force, e.g., that under certain circumstances bodies exercise a gravitational repulsion on each other, and those circumstances would include the circumstances in which E occurred. If L^1 satisfied either of the above two conditions, we would adopt it, and we would then say that under certain circumstances people do levitate and so E was not a counter-instance to a law of nature. However it might be that any modification which we made to the laws of nature to allow them to predict E might not yield any more successful predictions than L and they might be so clumsy that there was no reason to believe that their predictions not yet tested would be successful. Under these circumstances we would have good reason to believe that the levitation of the holy person violated the laws of nature.

If the laws of nature are statistical and not universal, as the quantum theory suggests, it is not in all cases so clear what counts as a counter-instance to them. A universal law is a law of the form "all so-and-sos do such-and-such," and a counter-instance is therefore a so-and-so which does not do such-and-such. The occurrence of such a counter-instance is the occurrence of an exception to the law. A statistical law is a law of the form "n % of so-and-sos do such-and-such." But here however many so-and-sos are observed which do not do such-and-such, their occurrence is not completely ruled out by the theory. The theory tells us the proportion of so-and-sos which do such-and-such in an infinite class, and however many so-and-sos are found not to do such-and-such in a finite class, this finite class may be just an unrepresentative selection from the infinite class. It *may* be. But if something occurs which, given the truth of the law, is highly unlikely, that counts against the law, is counter-evidence to it, even if not formally ruled out by it. If the proportion of so-and-sos which do such-and-such in one of the very few, albeit large, finite classes studied is vastly different from that stated to hold in the law, that is counter-evidence to the law. Such an event is therefore not unnaturally described as an exception to a statistical law and the question can therefore be discussed whether it is a repeatable or a non-repeatable exception. It is formally compatible with the currently accepted statistical version of the second law of thermodynamics that a kettle of water put on a fire freeze instead of boiling. But it is vastly improbable that such an event will ever happen within human experience. Hence if it does happen, it is not unnaturally described as an exception to the law. If the evidence does not lead to our adopting a rival law, the event can then be described as a violation of the second law of thermodynamics. Any who speak of a violation of statistical laws would presumably mean the occurrence of a non-repeatable counter-instance to such laws, in the above sense of counter-instance.

All claims about what are the laws of nature are corrigible. However much support any purported law has at the moment, one day it may prove to be no true law. So likewise will be all claims about what does or does not violate the laws of nature. When an event apparently violates such laws, the appearance may arise simply because no one has thought of the true law which could explain the event, or, while they have thought of it, it is so complex relative to the data as rightly to be dismissed before even being tested, or too complex to be adopted without further testing and the tests too difficult in practice to carry out. New scientific knowledge may later turn up which forces us to revise any such claims about what violates laws of nature. But then all claims to knowledge about the physical world are corrigible, and we must reach provisional conclusions about them on the evidence available to us. We have to some extent good evidence about what are the laws of nature, and some of them are so well established and account for so many data that any modifications to them which we could suggest to account for the odd counter-instance would be so clumsy and *ad hoc* as to upset the whole structure of science. In such cases the evidence is strong that if the purported counter-instance occurred it was a violation of the law of nature. There is good reason to believe that the following events, if they occurred, would be violations of the laws of nature: levitation; resurrection from the dead in full health of a man whose heart has not been beating for twenty-four hours and who was dead also by other currently used criteria; water turning into wine without the assistance of chemical apparatus or catalysts; a man getting better from polio in a minute. We know quite enough about how things behave to be reasonably certain that, in the sense earlier (p. 80) delineated, these events are physically impossible.

9

J. L. MACKIE*

Miracles and Testimony

Hume's Argument

WHAT HUME HAS been expounding in [3] are the principles for the rational acceptance of testimony, the rules that ought to govern our believing or not believing what we are told. But the rules that govern people's actual acceptance of testimony are very different. We are fairly good at detecting dishonesty, insincerity, and lack of conviction, and we readily reject what we are told by someone who betrays these defects. But we are strongly inclined simply to accept, without question, statements that are obviously assured and sincere. As Hume would say, a firm association of ideas links someone else's saying, with honest conviction, that *p*, and its being the case that *p*, and we pass automatically from the perception of the one to belief in the other. Or, as he might also have said, there is an intellectual sympathy by which we tend automatically to share what we find to be someone else's belief, analogous to sympathy in the original sense, the tendency to share what we see to be someone else's feelings. And in general this is a useful tendency. People's beliefs about ordinary matters are right, or nearly right, more often than they are wildly wrong, so that

*J.L. Mackie died in 1981. He was Reader in Philosophy, University of Oxford, and had taught previously in other universities in England, Australia, and New Zealand. He made important contributions to many branches of philosphy. This extract is from *The Miracle of Theism* (Oxford: Clarendon Press, 1982), pp. 18–29.

intellectual sympathy enables fairly correct information to be passed on more smoothly than it could be if we were habitually cautious and constantly checked testimony against the principles for its rational acceptance. But what is thus generally useful can sometimes be misleading, and miracle reports are a special case where we need to restrain our instinctive acceptance of honest statements, and go back to the basic rational principles which determine whether a statement is really reliable or not. Even where we are cautious, and hesitate to accept what we are told—for example by a witness in a legal case—we often do not go beyond the question "How intrinsically reliable is this witness?" or, in detail, "Does he seem to be honest? Does he have a motive for misleading us? Is he the sort of person who might tell plausible lies? Or is he the sort of person who, in the circumstances, might have made a mistake?" If we are satisfied on all these scores, we are inclined to believe what the witness says, without weighing very seriously the question "How intrinsically improbable is what he has told us?" But, as Hume insists, this further question is highly relevant. His general approach to the problem of when to accept testimony is certainly sound.

Hume's case against miracles is an epistemological argument: it does not try to show that miracles never do happen or never could happen, but only that we never have good reasons for believing that they have happened. It must be clearly distinguished from the suggestion that the very concept of a miracle is incoherent. That suggestion might be spelled out as follows. A miracle is, by definition, a violation of a law of nature, and a law of nature is, by definition, a regularity—or the statement of a regularity—about what happens, about the way the world works; consequently, if some event actually occurs, no regularity which its occurrence infringes (or, no regularity-statement which it falsifies) can really be a law of nature; so this event, however unusual or surprising, cannot after all be a miracle. The two definitions together entail that whatever happens is not a miracle, that is, that miracles never happen. This, be it noted, is not Hume's argument. If it were correct, it would make Hume's argument unnecessary. Before we discuss Hume's case, then, we should consider whether there is a coherent concept of a miracle which would not thus rule out the occurrence of miracles *a priori*.

If miracles are to serve their traditional function of giving spectacular support to religious claims—whether general theistic claims, or the authority of some specific religion or some particular sect or individual teacher—the concept must not be so weakened that anything at all unusual or remarkable counts as a miracle. We must keep in the definition the notion of a violation of natural law. But then, if it is to be even possible that a miracle should occur, we must modify the definition given above of a law of nature. What we want to do is to contrast the order of nature with a possible divine or super-natural intervention. The laws of nature, we must say, describe the ways in which the world—including, of course, human beings—works when left to itself, when not interfered with. A miracle occurs when the world is not left to itself, when something distinct from the natural order as a whole intrudes into it.

This notion of ways in which the world works is coherent and by no means obscure. We know how to discover causal laws, relying on a principle of the uniformity of the course of nature—essentially the assumption that there are some laws to be found—in conjunction with suitable observations and experiments, typically varieties of con-trolled experiment whose underlying logic is that of Mill's "method of difference". Within the laws so established, we can further mark off basic laws of working from derived laws which hold only in a particular context or contingently upon the way in which something is put together. It will be a derived law that a particular clock, or clocks of a particular sort, run at such a speed, and this will hold only in certain conditions of temperature, and so on; but this law will be derived from more basic ones which describe the regular behavior of certain kinds of material, in view of the way in which the clock is put together, and these more basic laws of materials may in turn be derived from yet more basic laws about sub-atomic par-ticles, in view of the ways in which those materials are made up of such particles. In so far as we advance towards a knowledge of such a system of basic and derived laws, we are acquiring an understand-ing of ways in which the world works. As well as what we should ordinarily call causal laws, which typically concern interactions, there are similar laws with regard to the ways in which certain kinds of things simply persist through time, and certain sorts of continuous process just go on. These too, and in particular the more basic laws of these sorts, help to constitute the ways in which the world works. Thus there are several kinds of basic "laws of working".[1] For our

1. The notion of basic laws of working is fully discussed in Chapters 8 and 9 of my *The Cement of the Universe: A Study of Causation* (Oxford University Press, 1974 and 1980).

present purpose, however, it is not essential that we should even be approaching an understanding of how the world works; it is enough that we have the concept of such basic laws of working, that we know in principle what it would be to discover them. Once we have this concept, we have moved beyond the definition of laws of nature merely as (statements of) what always happens. We can see how, using this concept and using the assumption that there are some such basic laws of working to be found, we can hope to determine what the actual laws of working are by reference to a restricted range of experiments and observations. This opens up the possibility that we might determine that something *is* a basic law of working of natural objects, and yet also, independently, find that it was occasionally violated. An occasional violation does not in itself necessarily overthrow the independently established conclusion that this *is* a law of working.

Equally, there is no obscurity in the notion of intervention. Even in the natural world we have a clear understanding of how there can be for a time a closed system, in which everything that happens results from factors within that system in accordance with its laws of working, but how then something may intrude from outside it, bringing about changes that the system would not have produced of its own accord, so that things go on after this intrusion differently from how they would have gone on if the system had remained closed. All we need do, then, is to regard the whole natural world as being, for most of the time, such a closed system; we can then think of a supernatural intervention as something that intrudes into that system from outside the natural world as a whole.

If the laws by which the natural world works are deterministic, then the notion of a violation of them is quite clear-cut: such a violation would be an event which, given that the world was a closed system working in accordance with these laws, and given some actual earlier complete state of the world, simply could not have happened at all. Its occurrence would then be clear proof that either the supposed laws were not the real laws of working, or the earlier state was not as it was supposed to have been, or else the system was not closed after all. But if the basic laws of working are statistical or probabilistic, the notion of a violation of them is less precise. If something happens which, given those statistical laws and some earlier complete state of the world, is extremely improbable—in the sense of physical probability: that is, something such that there is a strong propensity or tendency for it *not* to happen—we still cannot say firmly that the laws have been violated: laws of this sort explicitly allow that what is extremely improbable may occasionally come about. Indeed it is highly probable (both physically and epistemically) that some events, each of which is very improbable, will occur at rare intervals.[2] If tosses of a coin were governed by a statistical law that gave a 50 per cent propensity to heads at each toss, a continuous run of ten heads would be a highly improbable occurrence; but it would be highly probable that there would be some such runs in a sequence of a million tosses. Nevertheless, we can still use the contrast between the way of working of the natural world as a whole, considered as a normally closed system, and an intervention or intrusion into it. This contrast does not disappear or become unintelligible merely because we lack decisive tests for its application. We can still define a miracle as an event which would not have happened in the course of nature, and which came about only through a supernatural intrusion. The difficulty is merely that we cannot now say with certainty, simply by reference to the relevant laws and some antecedent situation, that a certain event would not have happened in the course of nature, and therefore must be such an intrusion. But we may still be able to say that it is very probable—and this is now an epistemic probability—that it would not have happened naturally, and so is likely to be such an intrusion. For if the laws made it physically improbable that it would come about, this tends to make it epistemically improbable that it did come about through those laws, if there is any other way in which it could have come about and which is not equally improbable or more improbable. In practice the difficulty mentioned is not much of an extra difficulty. For even where we believe there to be deterministic laws and an earlier situation which together would have made an occurrence actually impossible in the course of nature, it is from our point of view at best epistemically very probable, not certain, that those are the laws and that that was the relevant antecedent situation.

Consequently, whether the laws of nature are deterministic or statistical, we can give a coherent definition of a miracle as a super-

2. The distinction between physical and epistemic probability has been drawn in [Mackie's] Introduction; the exact form of statistical laws is discussed in Chapter 9 of *The Cement of the Universe*.

natural intrusion into the normally closed system that works in accordance with those laws, and in either case we can identify conceivable occurrences, and alleged occurrences, which if they were to occur, or have occurred, could be believed with high probability, though not known with certainty, to satisfy that definition.

However, the full concept of a miracle requires that the intrusion should be purposive, that it should fulfil the intention of a god or other supernatural being. This connection cannot be sustained by any ordinary causal theory; it presupposes a power to fulfil intentions directly, without physical means, which [as is argued at length in Chapters 5 and 7 of *The Miracle of Theism* —ed.] is highly dubious; so this requirement for a miracle will be particularly hard to confirm. On the other hand it is worth noting that successful prophecy could be regarded as a form of miracle for which there could in principle be good evidence. If someone is reliably recorded as having prophesied at t_1 an event at t_2 which could not be predicted at t_1 on any natural grounds, and the event occurs at t_2, then at any later time t_3 we can assess the evidence for the claims both that the prophecy was made at t_1 and that its accuracy cannot be explained either causally (for example, on the ground that it brought about its own fulfilment) or as accidental, and hence that it was probably miraculous.

There is, then, a coherent concept of miracles. Their possibility is not ruled out *a priori*, by definition. So we must consider whether Hume's argument shows that we never have good reason for believing that any have occurred.

Hume's general principle for the evaluation of testimony, that we have to weigh the unlikelihood of the event reported against the unlikelihood that the witness is mistaken or dishonest, is substantially correct. It is a corollary of the still more general principle of accepting whatever hypothesis gives the best overall explanation of all the available and relevant evidence. But some riders are necessary. First, the likelihood or unlikelihood, the epistemic probability or improbability, is always relative to some body of information, and may change if additional information comes in. Consequently, any specific decision in accordance with Hume's principle must be provisional. Secondly, it is one thing to decide which of the rival hypotheses in the field at any time should be provisionally accepted in the light of the evidence then available; but it is quite another to estimate the weight of this evidence, to say how well supported this favored hypothesis is, and whether it is likely that its claims will be undermined either by additional information or by the suggesting of further alternative hypotheses. What is clearly the best-supported view of some matter at the moment may still be very insecure, and quite likely to be overthrown by some further considerations. For example, if a public opinion poll is the only evidence we have about the result of a coming election, this evidence may point, perhaps decisively, to one result rather than another; yet if the poll has reached only a small sample of the electorate, or if it was taken some time before the voting day, it will not be very reliable. There is a dimension of reliability over and above that of epistemic probability relative to the available evidence. Thirdly, Hume's description of what gives support to a prediction, or in general to a judgment about an unobserved case that would fall under some generalization, is very unsatisfactory. He seems to say that if *all* so far observed *As* have been *Bs*, then this amounts to a "proof" that some unobserved *A* will be (or is, or was) a *B*, whereas if some observed *As* have been *Bs*, but some have not, there is only a "probability" that an unobserved *A* will be a *B* ([3] pp. 24–26). This mises up the reasoning *to* a generalization with the reasoning *from* a generalization to a particular case. It is true that the premises "All *As* are *Bs*" and "This is an *A*" constitute a proof of the conclusion "This is a *B*", whereas the premises "*x* percent of *As* are *Bs*" and "This is an *A*" yield—if there is no other relevant information—a probability of *x* percent that this is a *B*: they *probabilify* the conclusion to this degree, or, as we can say, the probability of the conclusion "This is a *B*" relative to that evidence is *x* percent. But the inductive argument from the observation "All so far observed *As* have been *Bs*" to the generalization "All *As* are *Bs*" is far from secure, and it would be most misleading to call this a proof, and therefore misleading also to describe as a proof the whole line of inference from "All so far observed *As* have been *Bs*" to the conclusion "This as yet unobserved *A* is a *B*". Similarly, the inductive argument from "*x* percent of observed *As* have been *Bs*" to the statistical generalization "*x* percent of *As* are *Bs*" is far from secure, so that we cannot say that "*x* percent of observed *As* have been *Bs*" even probabilifies to the degree *x* percent the conclusion "This as yet unobserved *A* is a *B*". A good deal of other information and background knowledge is needed, in either case, before the generalization, whether universal or statistical, is at all well supported, and hence before the stage is properly set for either proof or probabilification about an as yet unobserved A. It is harder than Hume allows here to arrive at well-supported generalizations of either sort about how the world works.

These various qualifications together entail that what has been widely and reasonably thought to be a law of nature may not be one, perhaps in ways that are highly relevant to some supposed miracles. Our present understanding of psychosomatic illness, for example, shows that it is not contrary to the laws of nature that someone who for years has seemed, to himself as well as to others, to be paralyzed should rapidly regain the use of his limbs. On the other hand, we can still be pretty confident that it is contrary to the laws of nature that a human being whose heart has stopped beating for forty-eight hours in ordinary circumstances—that is, without any special life-support systems—should come back to life, or that what is literally water should without addition or replacement turn into what is literally good-quality wine.

However, any problems there may be about establishing laws of nature are neutral between the parties to the present debate, Hume's followers and those who believe in miracles; for both these parties need the notion of a well-established law of nature. The miracle advocate needs it in order to be able to say that the alleged occurrence is a miracle, a violation of natural law by supernatural intervention, no less than Hume needs it for his argument against believing that this event has actually taken place.

It is therefore not enough for the defender of a miracle to cast doubt (as he well might) on the certainty of our knowledge of the law of nature that seems to have been violated. For he must himself say that this *is* a law of nature: otherwise the reported event will not be miraculous. That is, he must in effect *concede* to Hume that the antecedent improbability of this event is as high as it could be, hence that, apart from the testimony, we have the strongest possible grounds for believing that the alleged event did not occur. This event must, by the miracle advocate's own admission, be contrary to a genuine, not merely a supposed, law of nature, and therefore maximally improbable. It is this maximal improbability that the weight of the testimony would have to overcome.

One further improvement is needed in Hume's theory of testimony.

It is well known that the agreement of two (or more) *independent* witnesses constitutes very powerful evidence. Two independent witnesses are more than twice as good as each of them on his own. The reason for this is plain. If just one witness says that p, one explanation of this would be that it was the case that p and that he has observed this, remembered it, and is now making an honest report; but there are many alternative explanations, for example that he observed something else which he mistook for its being that p, or is misremembering what he observed, or is telling a lie. But if two witnesses who can be shown to be quite independent of one another both say that p, while again one explanation is that each of them has observed this and remembered it and is reporting honestly, the alternative explanations are not now so easy. They face the question "How has there come about this *agreement* in their reports, if it was not the case that p? How have the witnesses managed to misobserve to the same effect, or to misremember in the same way, or to hit upon the same lie?" It is difficult for even a single liar to keep on telling a *consistent* false story; it is much harder for two or more liars to do so. Of course if there is any collusion between the witnesses, or if either has been influenced, directly or indirectly, by the other, or if both stories have a common source, this question is easily answered. That is why the independence of the witnesses is so important. This principle of the improbability of coincident error has two vital bearings upon the problem of miracles. On the one hand, it means that a certain sort of testimony can be more powerful evidence than Hume's discussion would suggest. On the other, it means that where we seem to have a plurality of reports, it is essential to check carefully whether they really are independent of one another; the difficulty of meeting this requirement would be an important supplement to the points made in Part II of Hume's essay. Not only in remote and barbarous times, but also in recent ones, we are usually justified in suspecting that what look like distinct reports of a remarkable occurrence arise from different strands of a single tradition between which there has already been communication.

We can now put together the various parts of our argument. Where there is some plausible testimony about the occurrence of what would appear to be a miracle, those who accept this as a miracle have the double burden of showing both that the event took place and that it violated the laws of nature. But it will be very hard to sustain this double burden. For whatever tends to show that it would have been a violation of natural law tends for that very reason to make it most unlikely that it actually happened. Correspondingly, those who deny the occurrence of a miracle have two alternative lines of defense. One is to say that the event may have occurred, but in accordance with the laws of nature. Perhaps there were unknown circumstances that made it possible; or perhaps what were thought to be the relevant laws of nature are not strictly laws; there may be as yet unknown kinds of natural causation through which this event might have come about. The other is to say that this event would indeed have violated natural law, but that for this very reason there is a very strong presumption against its having happened, which it is most unlikely that any testimony will be able to outweigh. Usually one of these defenses will be stronger than the other. For many supposedly miraculous cures, the former will be quite a likely sort of explanation, but for such feats as the bringing back to life of those who are really dead the latter will be more likely. But the *fork*, the disjunction of these two sorts of explanation, is as a whole a very powerful reply to any claim that a miracle has been performed.

However, we should distinguish two different contexts in which an alleged miracle might be discussed. One possible context would be where the parties in debate already both accept some general theistic doctrines, and the point at issue is whether a miracle has occurred which would enhance the authority of a specific sect or teacher. In this context supernatural intervention, though *prima facie* unlikely on any particular occasion, is, generally speaking, on the cards: it is not altogether outside the range of reasonable expectation for these parties. Since they agree that there is an omnipotent deity, or at any rate one or more powerful supernatural beings, they cannot find it absurd to suppose that such a being will occasionally interfere with the course of nature, and this *may* be one of these occasions. For example, if one were already a theist and a Christian, it would not be unreasonable to weigh seriously the evidence of alleged miracles as some indication whether the Jansenists or the Jesuits enjoyed more of the favor of the Almighty. But it is a very different matter if the context is that of fundamental debate about the truth of theism itself. Here one party to the debate is initially at least agnostic, and does not yet concede that there is a supernatural power at all. From this point of view the intrinsic improbability of a genuine miracle, as defined above, is very great, and one or other of the alternative explanations in our fork will always be much more likely—that is, either that the alleged event is not miraculous, or that it did not occur, that the testimony is faulty in some way.

This entails that it is pretty well impossible that reported miracles should provide a worthwhile argument for theism addressed to those who are initially inclined to atheism or even to agnosticism. Such reports can form no significant part of what, following Aquinas, we might call a *Summa contra Gentiles*, or what, following Descartes, we could describe as being addressed to infidels. Not only are such reports unable to carry any rational conviction on their own, but also they are unable even to contribute independently to the kind of accumulation or battery of arguments referred to in the Introduction. To this extent Hume is right, despite the inaccuracies we have found in his statement of the case.

One further point may be worth making. Occurrences are sometimes claimed to be literally, and not merely metaphorically, miracles, that is, to be genuine supernatural interventions into the natural order, which are not even *prima facie* violations of natural law, but at most rather unusual and unexpected, but very welcome. Thus the combination of weather conditions which facilitated the escape of the British Army from Dunkirk in 1940, making the Luftwaffe less than usually effective but making it easy for ships of all sizes to cross the Channel, is sometimes called a miracle. However, even if we accepted theism, and could plausibly assume that a benevolent deity would have favored the British rather than the Germans in 1940, this explanation would still be far less probable than that which treats it as a mere meteorological coincidence: such weather conditions can occur in the ordinary course of events. Here, even in the context of a debate among those who already accept theistic doctrines, the interpretation of the event as a miracle is much weaker than the rival natural explanation. *A fortiori*, instances of this sort are utterly without force in the context of fundamental debate about theism itself.

There is, however, a possibility which Hume's argument seems to ignore—though, as we shall see, he did not completely ignore it. The argument has been directed against the acceptance of miracles on testimony; but what, it may be objected, if one is not reduced to reliance on testimony, but has observed a miracle for oneself? Surprisingly, perhaps, this possibility does not make very much difference. The first of the above-mentioned lines of defense is still available: maybe the unexpected event that one has oneself observed did indeed occur, but in accordance with the laws of nature. Either the relevant circumstances or the operative laws were not what one had supposed them to be. But at least a part of the other line of defense is also available. Though one is not now relying literally on another witness or other witnesses, we speak not inappropriately of the evidence of our senses, and what one takes to be an observation of one's own is open to questions of the same sort as is the report of some other person. I may have misobserved what took place, as anyone knows who has ever been fooled by a conjurer or "magician", and, though this is somewhat less likely, I may be misremembering or deceiving myself after an interval of time. And of course the corroboration of one or more independent witnesses would bring in again the testimony of others which it was the point of this objection to do without. Nevertheless, anyone who is fortunate enough to have carefully observed and carefully recorded, for himself, an apparently miraculous occurrence is no doubt rationally justified in taking it very seriously; but even here it will be in order to entertain the possibility of an alternative natural explanation.

As I said, Hume does not completely ignore this possibility. The Christian religion, he says, cannot at this day be believed by any reasonable person without a miracle. "Mere reason is insufficient to convince us of its veracity: And whoever is moved by *Faith* to assent to it, is conscious of a continued miracle in his own person, which subverts all the principles of his understanding". ([3] p. 40). But of course this is only a joke. What the believer is conscious of in his own person, though it may be a mode of thinking that goes against "custom and experience", and so is contrary to the ordinary rational principles of the understanding, is not, as an occurrence, a violation of natural law. Rather it is all too easy to explain immediately by the automatic communication of beliefs between persons and the familiar psychological processes of wish fulfilment, and ultimately by what Hume himself was later to call "the natural history of religion".

10

ANTONY FLEW *

Scientific Versus Historical Evidence

THE TIME HAS NOW come to consider how the inadequacy of Hume's analysis of causality must equally infect any account which he could give of a law of nature. We shall argue that the lack of an adequate conception of a law of nature would make it impossible for Hume himself to justify a distinction between the marvelous or the unusual and the truly miraculous, and that it prevented him from exploiting to the full his own distinctive conception of the opposition of proofs.

Since to say that A is the cause of B is in his view to say that all A's are followed by B's, and that we habitually associate A's with B's, he would presumably have to say that a law of nature holds wherever A's are constantly conjoined with B's, and a similar habitual association obtains. Since to the logical analysis of the conceptions of either cause or law such habitual psychological associations are clearly quite irrelevant, this must reduce statements of lawful connection to statements of a merely numerical universal conjunction. But if that were indeed all that a law of nature asserted then it would give no ground at all for saying that the occurrence of an exception to such a law is physically impossible. Any attempt to use our knowledge, or presumed knowledge, of such a merely numerical universal proposition as an evidential canon by which to justify the outright re-

*Hume's Theory of Belief (London: Routledge and Kegan Paul, 1961), pp. 204–8.

jection of any testimony to the occurrence of a falsifying exception would be a preposterous piece of question begging.

In one deservedly notorious passage Hume seems to be doing just that: "It is no miracle that a man, seemingly in good health, should die on a sudden, because such a kind of death, though more unusual than any other, has yet been frequently observed to happen. But it is a miracle that a dead man should come to life, because that has never been observed in any age or country." Hume can provide no conception of law of nature sufficiently strong to allow for any real distinction between the miraculous and the extremely unusual. For if a law of nature really was no more than an epitome and an extrapolation of a long and uninterruptedly uniform series of observations, then an exception to the law—a breach in the uniformity of the series—could be only an unusual, and no doubt unexpected, event. While if in laws of nature we had only what we have called merely numerical universal propositions, then to dismiss out of hand all testimony to the occurrence beyond the range of our observations of a counter example, on the sole ground that such an occurrence would falsify the universal generalization based upon our observations to date, would indeed be arbitrary and bigotted. This particular remark of Hume's, if nothing else, provides some justification for the harsh interpretation: "He first answers, 'Yes', to the question whether Nature is absolutely uniform: and then uses this 'Yes' as a ground for answering, 'No,' to the question, 'Do miracles occur?'" (C. S. Lewis [31] p. 107).

Once the essential nomological element in the meaning of statements of laws of nature is recognized, then it becomes clear that knowledge—or presumed knowledge—of a law of nature could be a ground for dismissing as in fact impossible the occurrence of anything inconsistent with that law. Of course by itself this does not improve matters greatly. It would be as irrational to deny the occurrence of an event simply on the ground that this would show some nomological proposition to be false as it would be to deny it just on the ground that it would falsify a merely extensional universal proposition. But once we have achieved a better understanding of what a law of nature is the way is open to a more adequate view of the sort of evidence needed to justify us in believing that some given candidate law actually does hold. Then this in turn can be used to bring out more clearly why it is rational to employ among our canons for the assessment of historical testimony whatever well grounded nomological propositions may from time to time be available to us.

Hume himself, as might be expected, can give us very little help here. His account in this Section of the evidence on which we ground our knowledge of laws of nature is almost as paralytic as those which he gives elsewhere of how we come to believe causal propositions. There is throughout the same concentration on observations and what is observed. Where—as in his curiously literal interpretation of the weighing of probabilities—he does talk of "a hundred uniform experiments" and of "an opposition of experiments and observations," he is still employing *experiment* in his usual sense as a synonym for the merely passive *experience*. In only three places does he use phrases which suggest the need for more active tests of reliability. Twice in considering those cases where we are justified in entertaining only probable conclusions he contrasts them with others where sound judgments "are founded on an infallible experience." Later, after defining *a miracle* as "a violation of the laws of nature," he argues from the premise that "a firm and unalterable experience has established these laws." But there is, unfortunately, no reason to think that he himself appreciated these hints.

Nevertheless they do hint at the crucial difference between the merely extensional and the truly nomological kinds of universal proposition. A law of nature, or what is taken to be a law of nature, is always a proposition of the latter sort. [At the end of Chapter VI of *Hume's Theory of Belief* ed.] we urged that the criterion of a nomological is at the same time a criterion of reliability; and that the appropriate way to test for reliability is to subject to strains. If this is correct then to be justified in asserting that some law of nature in fact obtains you must know that the appropriate nomological has been thoroughly tested for reliability, whether directly on its own account separately, or indirectly via the testing of some wider structure of theory from which it follows as a consequence. To be in this position is to be both warranted and required to employ this nomological as one of your critical canons.

Consider now Hume's conception of the opposition of proofs. "There must be a uniform experience against every miraculous event, otherwise the event would not merit that appellation." So here we have "a direct and full *proof*, from the nature of the fact, against the existence of any miracle; nor can such a proof be destroyed, or the

miracle rendered credible, but by an opposite proof which is superior."
(Italics in original.) Since Hume has himself earlier defined *proofs*
as "such arguments from experience as leave no room for doubt or
opposition" his account of the situation is certainly paradoxical. (*Enquiry Concerning Human Understanding*, Section 6). But then the
paradoxical dilemma of anyone trying to establish the occurrence
of a miracle is just what he wants to show.

However, at least in its purely secular aspect, the paradox can now
be resolved. The nomologicals which we know, or think we know,
must serve as fundamental canons of our historical criticism. Finding what appears to be historical evidence for an occurrence inconsistent with such a nomological, we must always insist on interpreting
that evidence in some other way: for if the nomological is true then
it is physically impossible that any event incompatible with it could
have occurred. Nevertheless it is always possible, since we are none
of us infallible, that an accepted nomological may in fact be false.
It must therefore remain at least theoretically possible that an occasion might arise in which in the light of historical evidence it would
be rational to take another look at the credentials of what had
previously been thought to be a law of nature.

It might have happened—to adapt Hume's own example—in the
early days of the science of astronomy. Historical evidence might have
been found suggesting that an eclipse had been observed at some time
and place at which on the prevailing theory it would have been impossible for this to have happened. And this might have been in the
circumstances a sufficient reason for demanding that the theory be
more thoroughly tested. Again, the medical investigations to which
Middleton refers might have been—even if in fact they were not—
partly prompted by curiosity about the impressive testimony in the
Case of the African Witnesses. If such a supposition were to be realized
we should indeed be confronted by an opposition of "proofs," involving
"a mutual destruction of arguments." Since we could not consistently insist that both constituted proofs we should of course have to choose
either to reject one or to suspend judgment.

This might present itself as a conflict between Science and History.
For on the one side we have what purports to be an historical proof:
while on the other the nomological is supposed to have been established by methods which might in a very broad sense be classed as

scientific. But the antagonists in this contest are unevenly matched. Certainly the historical evidence could constitute a sufficient reason for re-examining the nomological; and under this re-examination it might fail to sustain its claim to be believed. But if, on the contrary, it survived such testing then it would be rational—though of course it could always be mistaken—to reject the historical "proof": on the single and sufficient ground that we now have the best of reasons for insisting that what it purports to prove is in fact impossible.

The justification for giving the "scientific" this ultimate precedence here over the "historical" lies in the nature of the propositions concerned and in the evidence which can be deployed to sustain them. It derives—to borrow the expression of Hume's material mode of thought—"from the very nature of the fact." The candidate historical proposition will be particular, often singular, and in the past tense. (It is this which is—or should be—all that is meant by the assertion that the subject matter of historical enquiry is always and essentially individual and unique.) But just by reason of this very pastness and particularity it is no longer possible for anyone to examine the subject directly for himself. All that there is left to examine is the present detritus of the past, which includes the physical records of testimony. This detritus can be interpreted as evidence only in the light of our present knowledge, or presumed knowledge, of men and things; a category which embraces, although it is certainly not exhausted by, our stock of general nomologicals. This surely is and must always be the fundamental principle of historical interpretation. Nor can it be upset by an appeal to the undeniable importance in actual historical enquiry of a knowledge of and a feel for the particular period. For any claims to posses such a particular knowledge and feeling can in the end be rationally justified only by reference to precisely this general knowledge, or presumed knowledge. It alone can provide the warrant for any evidential interpretation of the present historical relics. (Here consider again *Enquiry Concerning Human Understanding*, Section 8(i), and compare *Treatise of Human Nature* II (iii) 1.)

The "law of nature" will, unlike the candidate historical proposition, be a general nomological. It can thus in theory—though obviously not always in practice—be tested at any time by any person. Whatever falls within its scope is physically necessary, and whatever it precludes is physically impossible. So just as it possesses, and is designed to posses, the logical strength required, when combined with appropriate particular premises, both to license and to demand inferences to substantial conclusions transcending those premises: it is also constitutionally adapted to serve as a criterion of exclusion, which must rule out a range of logical possibilities as impossible in fact.

11

RICHARD TAYLOR*

Two Kinds of Explanation

I NOTED EARLIER the great difference in kind between two such statements as

(1) This match started the forest fire,

and

(2) This man started the forest fire.

These two statements are identical except for their subjects, but they are utterly different in meaning. The first cannot be literally true, though the second might be.

The first statement expresses the idea that the ignition of the match in question was significantly involved in the beginnings of the fire mentioned; more precisely, that its igniting was, under only those other conditions that are assumed to have existed, necessary for the beginning of that fire, and also sufficient. It does not suggest that the match actually did anything, or that it performed any act. It, or its igniting, was simply a necessary link in a whole series of causes and effects. The statement does not suggest that the match ignited its own head, and in that sense literally *started* something that spread to the magnitude of a forest fire.

*Action and Purpose (Englewood Cliffs, NJ: Prentice-Hall, 1966), pp. 210–20.

The second statement, however, might be literally true, conveying the idea that the man in question did perform an act, that he literally did *start* the fire, presumably by means of a match or something of that sort. He, or some event in which he was significantly involved, was not merely a link in a whole series of causes and effects; that series itself was presumably started by him. And unlike the match, which did not ignite its own head, the man did, presumably, move his own arm, or perform some other simple act, thus starting what the statement alleges he started.

Both statements, it is clear, are incomplete as explanations of the fire, but they are incomplete in totally different ways. An explanation involving the first statement would be completed by stating how the match came to be where it was in the first place, what conditions raised the temperature of its head to its igniting point, and so on. Disregarding the fact that matches themselves are the products of human agency, this explanation might be completely given, as a "natural catastrophe," without implying any agency anywhere—by noting, for example, that the match was ignited by the heat of the sun, or by being blown by the wind against a stone, or whatnot.

An explanation involving the second statement would not ordinarily be completed in the same way. It might be the case, for example, that nothing other than the man himself made him be where he was, that nothing put him there, nothing carried him there, but that, unlike the match, he went there himself—for a *reason*, perhaps, but from no ordinary *cause*. It might be the case that, unlike the match, nothing other than the man himself caused his body to move as it did, thus igniting a match or whatever and, by its means, starting a fire. The explanation involving this second statement would, however, be completed by discovering the man's motive or purpose, by finding out *why*, in that sense, he did what the statement affirms that he did. This, however, would be an explanation in terms of his purpose or goal, a kind of explanation that is so radically different from the other that it would be senseless if the explanation involving the first statement were expanded in such terms. There is, or normally would be, an answer to the question why the man started the fire, but there can be no *similar* answer to the question why the match started the fire.

It was also remarked earlier that the second statement, but normally not the first, might constitute an ultimate causal explanation, even though neither statement is a complete explanation. It is now fairly easy to see how this is so.

If we begin with the first statement it is perfectly reasonable to wonder what caused the match to ignite. This is a question concerning those conditions, whatever they were, that occurred and were causally necessary and sufficient for that igniting. Having found such conditions, it would be perfectly reasonable to inquire what caused these, that is, what further conditions occurred and were causally necessary and sufficient for them, and so on. Sooner or later such a quest for causes might become hopeless, due simply to the limits of our possible knowledge, but it need not otherwise be the least unreasonable.

If we begin with the second statement, however, it might, and normally would, be unreasonable to seek further causes lying behind the one mentioned, namely, a certain agent himself. There is here no question about what caused the man's body to move as it did, grasping a match, presumably, and striking it against something. The supposition is that he caused these motions himself, that they were his own actions. Something *may* literally have caused him to act in this fashion, but it is by no means necessary to think so. If we ask *why* he behaved in that way, the explanation sought would ordinarily be a teleological rather than a causal one. If we were given true statements about his aims or goals, about what he was trying to accomplish, and if his actions could be properly viewed as his means of attaining those aims, then we would have an explanation of that behavior. It would not, however, be an explanation in terms of what had caused his behavior, for that, it is already assumed, or might reasonably be assumed, was the man himself.

This suggests that the explanation of human behavior, or rather of some human actions, should be sought in terms of purposes or goals rather than causes. Indeed, it is purposeful explanations that are usually sought and accepted in all areas except, curiously, certain of the anthropological sciences, where explanations of a more "scientific" character are vainly desired. In these areas of science, however, the term "scientific" has become a commendatory adjective, and at the same time has somewhat uncritically come to suggest those types of explanation which the physical sciences have yielded in such abundance. In these such notions as purposes, ends, or goals have, quite rightly, no place whatsoever. We can admit at once that considerations of purpose have no place in the understanding of inanimate things. It hardly follows that, in order to be scientific, we must pretend that they have no place in the understanding of human behavior. Indeed, it is naîve even to entertain such an idea, for the actions of men can often be understood in no other way. To explain human actions in the manner in which the behavior of inanimate things is explained is, as I have tried to show, not merely difficult, but logically impossible. No such explanation can be true unless what is explained is in fact *not* the act of an agent.

A purposeful explanation of an event or series of events is some statement that represents the events in question as the *means* to some *end* or goal. A natural way of expressing such a statement is by use of the locution "in order that" or "in order to." Indeed, this can probably serve as a criterion of a purposeful explanation; namely, whether it can naturally and easily be expressed in those terms.

For example, such statements as "He is running in order to catch the train," "He raised his hand to get the speaker's attention," "He burned the woods in order to destroy the evidence," are all clearly purposeful. They would, moreover, ordinarily be considered explanatory—they explain why the agents referred to did the things they are said to have done. They describe actions which are performed with some near or remote goal or end in mind, things that are done in order that certain results may be achieved. Different thinkers interpret such statements variously; some even seem to have wanted to maintain that no such statements can be really true. It is nevertheless clear that, whatever they might mean, such statements as these *are* sometimes true. Raising one's hand, for example, is a way of gaining someone's attention, and it is a way that is frequently employed. On learning, moreover, that a given man has performed such an act in order to get that result, one does not doubt that his action has been at least partially explained; one knows, in the most straightforward sense, why he did it.

Some statements—indeed, probably most of those referring to the actions of men—are implicitly purposeful, in the sense that it is natural to construe them as referring indirectly to the purpose of some agent or agents. Thus, "She has gone shopping" would ordinarily convey the idea that the person in question has gone somewhere in order to make purchases, and this expresses a purpose or goal, for the accomplishment of which something is done. Such similar statements as "He has gone to his grave" or "He has gone to prison" would not ordinarily be so construed, however, and in fact these do not, at least on the most natural interpretation of them, lend themselves to being re-expressed in terms of the locution, "in order that." There are *some* circumstances in which they might—for example, in case a man has gone to prison in order to visit an inmate there, or gone to his previously prepared grave to see whether it is ready to receive him at the appropriate time, and so on. But that is not how one would ordinarily understand those statements. A man is carried to his grave, is sent and transported to a prison—for a purpose, no doubt, but for no purpose of his. A housewife, however, can go shopping without being sent or transported thither. If one said she was sent by her avarice and transported by her legs he would only speak whimsically.

Any statement embodying the purposeful locution "in order that," in the way that it is ordinarily used, is of course a purposeful statement, but not all such statements, it seems needless to say, are true. Like any other statements they can be false. Thus, to say that rain is falling in order to make the corn grow, that the river is rushing to join the sea, that the plant is opening its leaves in order to capture the sunlight, and so on, is to make statements expressive of purposes, but false ones. They are at best only poetic.

This suggests, which I believe to be true, that only the actions of agents can be purposeful, although, of course, the converse does not follow. A man might do something quite purposelessly, for no reason, without any aim or goal. It is not necessary to say whether this ever happens or not. In any case, any true assertion that something *does* occur *in order that* some result may be achieved does seem to entail that the event in question is not merely an event, but the act of some agent. This suggests why the odd statements considered in the previous paragraph are poetic; in ascribing purposes to inanimate things one is enabled to view them in a false but charming light. To say, for example, that the river is rushing to join the sea suggests that the waters are not merely carried along, passively, by the force of gravity, but that they are active, that they are moving themselves, perhaps in the face of obstacles, toward some goal. . . .

This suggests further, I think, one reason why purposeful statements are viewed with such abhorrence in the sciences, including, quite marvelously, even the sciences of human behavior; namely, that they

carry with them the suggestion of agency, even in those cases where
no agent is apparent. If one proposes, for example, that the heart
beats in order to circulate the blood, or that the pupil of the eye dilates
in order to admit more light, and so on, then he seems to suggest that
these occurrences are the acts of an agent. Since, however, neither
the heart nor the eye is an agent—neither acts with a view to attaining any ends or goals of its own—such descriptions or "explanations"
suggest agency on the part of some other being—some god, for instance. That is, a purposeful explanation of such behavior intimates
that the things in question, not themselves agents, were designed or
constructed by some agent for the purpose of achieving some end
or goal of that agent. And such a hypothesis is, needless to say, quite
useless for scientific understanding of events.

It is nevertheless wonderful that this abhorrence of purposeful explanations, which is so appropriate an attitude in the study of things
that are *not* agents, should be carried over into the study of men,
who *are* agents. It may indeed be true that the behavior of inanimate
things cannot be understood teleologically or purposefully, it may be
true that to view inanimate things from a perspective of purposes
or ends would be to presuppose, or at least to suggest, all sorts of
anthropomorphic and even theological notions, and it may also be
true that no understanding of the organs of living things can be gained
by the postulation of goals and purposes. It nevertheless remains that
men, at least, are sometimes agents, that they do sometimes act purposefully, that their behavior can sometimes be understood through
an understanding of their purposes, aims, and goals. Indeed, this
seems to be the only way it can be understood, in case it is purposeful.
To rule out purposeful explanations in human psychology, accordingly,
where such explanations can have no possible theological implica-
tions is to rule out the only kind of explanation that renders certain
kinds of human behavior intelligible.

A purposeful explanation of someone's behavior does not interpret
it in the same way that, for example, a causal explanation would.
Nevertheless it is sometimes perfectly adequate in that it renders intelligible what no other explanation possibly could.

Suppose, for example, I see a friend hurrying along the walk, and
I ask for an explanation of his behavior. He replies, we can suppose,
that he needs some cigarettes, and the store closes in two minutes.

Now here is a bit of perfectly typical human behavior, and the answer given to my question, it must be obvious, *explains* that behavior. Having heard that answer I then know, assuming the answer to be true, exactly why he is doing what he is doing—his behavior is intelligible to me. And the explanation is clearly purposeful; it has, or at least appears to have, nothing whatever to do with causes and effects, but only with a goal and the means thereto. Whether it can be reduced to an explanation in terms of causes and effects is another question, and an important one, which I shall turn to shortly.

There are two obvious remarks to make on this simple illustration before contrasting it with another. The first is that the explanation, and its truth, are not affected in the slightest in case the goal referred to is never attained, or did not even exist in the first place. If the store had closed before my friend reached it, such that he failed to achieve his end, it would still be true, if it was true in the first place, that his behavior was goal-directed or purposeful. A true statement to the effect that an agent is behaving in a certain way in order to realize a certain result does not entail that he realizes it. Purposeful behavior that is frustrated is no less purposeful for that. Indeed, even if there had been no cigarettes in that store to begin with, and even if there had been no such store, and hence no actual goal to attain, his behavior would have been no less purposeful, no less goal-directed. It would only have been misdirected.

The second observation, already implied in what was just said, is that there is nothing in such an explanation to imply that goals or ends are causes that come after their effects, which is a fairly standard misunderstanding of purposeful explanations. It is, accordingly, no criticism whatever of a purposeful explanation to say that it represents causes as "working backward," of following their effects in time, and so on, for no such notion is implied in the least. If a man explains his behavior by saying that he is doing something in order that a certain end may be achieved, he does not at all imply that this end, which does not yet and may never exist, is causing him to behave that way. Such a criticism, in short, is simply irrelevant. Sometimes (but not always) the *cause* of an effect is the *means* to that effect, but an end or goal of an action is never in any kindred sense the *cause* of that action. It is for this reason that the expression "final cause" is misleading, though it need not mislead anyone who understands it.

Next contrast the situation just described with this one. We suppose that I am watching the turbulent flow of a stream, and I somewhat naively ask someone for an explanation of this behavior. Now if this were explained to me by saying that the water is hurrying to join the sea, the author of such an explanation would be speaking absurdly. The absurdity does not arise, however, from an inherent meaningless or uselessness in the purposeful explanation but only from the absurdity of the application. A purposeful explanation is not useless or meaningless as applied to the behavior of a man, as we have just seen. On the contrary, it is sometimes the best explanation that can be given, and a perfectly adequate one. This suggests what should be fairly obvious; namely, that streams and similar inanimate things are not agents, whereas men sometimes are. If such things as streams really acted, there is no reason why they might not do so purposefully. But the behavior they exhibit is in fact never purposeful just because it is always the passive effect of something else. A purposeful explanation applied to an inanimate, inactive thing is for this reason never more than a poetic, metaphorical utterance which may charm with its allusion to activity and purpose, but which is nevertheless never a true explanation. Here is why purposeful explanations are so utterly out of place in any physical science, and rightly scorned in those areas. It is not because they never explain anything, but rather because they never explain certain things, namely, the behavior of inanimate and inactive things. The fault, then, lies not with purposeful explanations as such, but in the misapplication of them.

Now there are some apparent exceptions, for sometimes it does appear meaningful and informative, up to a point, to explain the behavior of certain inanimate things in teleological terms. Thus one might say of a telephone that it is ringing in order to summon its owner; that a whistle is blowing in order to release the workmen from their labors for the day; or that water is flowing into a lock in order to lift a ship therein to the level of another lock, and so on. In every such case, however, the implied purposefulness of the behavior in question has only a borrowed meaning, which is derived from the activity of some agent or agents, who have arranged that the inanimate things should behave as they do. Thus the telephone does not literally ring in order to summon its owner; but another person literally makes it ring, or arranges for it to ring, for that purpose. Similarly, the water does not literally flow into a lock in order to raise a vessel, but some agent makes it behave thus, with the view to attaining some purpose of his. Remove the element of agency that is presupposed as part of the context or background of all such examples and the element of purpose simultaneously disappears.

It seems hardly doubtful, then, that purposeful explanations are often useful, true, and adequate in the realm of human behavior. Indeed, it is precisely the kind of explanation that is usually sought in almost every aspect of life. If one asks why a given man has, for example, ignited some leaves, he wants to know what he was trying to accomplish by that behavior, what his goal or purpose was. This is not what he would want to know if he asked why a given match or bolt of lightning has ignited some leaves. Normally, whenever we ask for the why's of human behavior—why this man did that, why this group of men are doing whatever they are doing, and so forth—we are asking for some indication of purposes or goals, some intended result. We are asking for an explanation that will represent the behavior in question as the means to some end. When such explanations are given, they are sometimes *adequate*; they set curiosity at rest, they render the behavior inquired about intelligible. They may, in fact they certainly do, differ radically from other types of explanation—from those sought in the physical sciences, for instance—but they do not differ by explaining nothing. The answers they provide are sometimes the only possible answers to the questions that are asked.

Now there is, to be sure, a sense of "explanation" much in vogue according to which teleological explanations, even in the realm of human behavior, are not real explanations, or are at least dubious as such. According to this interpretation, something is alleged to be "explained" only if it was *predictable*; that is, only if there is some general *law* from which, together with certain data consisting of the observable occurrences of other things, the thing in question could have been predicted. Now it is doubtful whether the purposeful behavior of men, or at least of individuals, is always explicable in that sense. Apart from the behavior of fairly large groups of men in certain situations having a common pattern, there seem to be no such laws. If there are, they certainly are not known. There are, for example, no laws in terms of which the purposeful behavior of an individual man from one moment to the next can in fact be predicted. It is doubtful, moreover, whether there could be such laws, because typically a man is able to pursue his various ends or goals in a variety of ways, and there seems to be no way anyone could predict which of these ways, to the exclusion of every other, a given man might choose on a given occasion.

Suppose, however, that this should all be true; suppose, that is, that at least some instances of purposeful behavior are in principle unpredictable, that there are no laws, known or unknown, under which a given purposeful act could be subsumed. We need not affirm that this *is* so, but let us for the moment suppose it is. What follows? Does it follow that such a purposeful act would be inexplicable? Hardly. All that follows is that it would not be predictable. If it could nevertheless be explained, it would follow that explanation does not consist simply of predictability.

And that is, in any case, obvious from what has already been said. Predictability is *one* sense of explanation, very useful in the study and understanding of inanimate things, but utterly out of place in the understanding of *some* cases of human behavior. I am not here saying that human behavior is in principle unpredictable, for to some extent, of course, it is. I am saying instead that in some cases the question whether it is predictable is irrelevant to the question whether it is explained. The behavior of the man hurrying down the walk to get some cigarettes, for example, is explained as soon as we know what his purpose is, what he is trying to accomplish, and are able to view that behavior as an appropriate *means* to that *end*. This has absolutely nothing to do with the predictability of his or any other man's behavior. If his actions were quite unprecedented, they would nevertheless be understood, intelligible, and in that sense explained, if they satisfied these conditions—that is, if they could be truly represented as an appropriate means to some end. It is in courts of law often of the highest importance to understand why a given crime was committed. Now this kind of understanding *never* takes the form of subsuming the crime in question under some general law of behavior which would have enabled anyone to predict it. This would simply be irrelevant. It is understood, instead, in terms of the *motive* of him who committed it—in terms of what the criminal was trying to accomplish. It is thus, and thus only, that it becomes intelligible. The question whether any similar man in similar circumstances and with similar purposes or motives would have done the same thing is an interesting philosophical question, the answer to which is not known by anyone, but it has absolutely no relevance whatever to understanding in this way, and in that sense explaining, why this man performed the acts he did perform. If this were not so, then we would be forced to conclude that hardly any crime, if indeed any crime at all, has ever really been explained by any detective or prosecuting attorney; for *in fact* no general laws are known to such people in terms of which the specific crimes coming to their attention could have been predicted. If such laws exist, they are in any case not known, and hence are not invoked for explanations. It is nevertheless true that ever so many individual crimes, which no one was in fact able to predict, and which have accordingly never been "explained" in the sense of having been shown to have been predictable, *have* been explained, in the sense that they have been quite thoroughly understood. Courts have been satisfied, and rightly satisfied, that they knew exactly why those crimes were committed by those who committed them. The explanations of them that were produced were explanations in terms of motives, purposes, ends, or goals of certain individual agents. For one to insist that they were not *genuine* explanations, since they were not in fact explanations in terms of any laws of human behavior, would only show that one was trying to cram the whole concept of explanation into the specialized meaning it has in areas far removed from human behavior, a sense that is often wholly irrelevant to the explanation of certain individual instances of human behavior.

12

DAVID OWEN*

Hume *Versus* Price on Miracles and Prior Probabilities

I

HUME'S ESSAY ON miracles[1] is one of his most celebrated arguments. It is also, perhaps, the second most discussed and argued-over of his skeptical positions. Reading it in the light of a recent controversy over Bayesianism and the appropriateness of taking prior probabilities into account when judging the likelihood of an event's occurrence on the basis of reliable testimony[2], I have been struck by the thought that Hume can best be seen as applying a proto-Bayesian argument to a celebrated eighteenth-century controversy. There is some evidence[3] that it struck Hume's critics that way as well, yet none of the recent major commentators (e.g., Broad, Flew, Gaskin)

Philosophical Quarterly, 1987, 37: 187–202.

1. David Hume, *An Inquiry Concerning Human Understanding*, Section X, ed. C.W. Hendel (1955). All page references to this section are to [3] in this volume.

2. See L.J. Cohen, "Can Human Irrationality Be Experimentally Demonstrated?" and replies, *The Behavioral and Brain Sciences* (1981) 4.

3. Richard Price, *Four Dissertations* (3rd ed. 1772); Bernard Peach, "Miracles, Methodology and Metaphysical Rationalization," *International Journal for Philosophy of Religion*, 9 (1978) 69–74; David Raynor, "Hume's Mistake—Another Guess," *Hume Studies* 8 (1981). Raynor rightly pleads for an examination of Hume and Price on miracles. This paper can be seen, I hope, as a start.

mention Bayes[4] or Hume's contemporary critic Richard Price, who most clearly discussed Hume's argument in this light. This is doubly unfortunate; not only does it make difficult a clear appreciation of what Hume was up to in the argument about miracles, but it also insulates the modern debate about prior probabilities from its history.[5] In this paper I should like to do a little to rectify this and, in passing, to make some independent observations about Hume's argument as well.

II

In Part I of Section X of the *Inquiry*, Hume formulates a position about judging probabilities according to the available evidence. He distinguishes, perhaps misleadingly, between proofs and probabilities in just the way he has already done in the footnote to section VI, "Of Probability." "Proofs" are those arguments from "infallible experience" that provide "the last degree of assurance" (p. 24) concerning an event. Such arguments from experience "leave no room for doubt or opposition." Events supported by such arguments, such as the sun's rising tomorrow, are expected with the highest degree of probability for Hume. What Hume calls "probabilities" as opposed to "proofs" are those arguments where past experience concerning whether or not a particular sort of event has occurred is mixed. We expect the event in proportion as to how many times it has occurred in these circumstances and how many times it has not.

> In all cases we must balance the opposite experiments where they are opposite, and deduct the smaller number from the greater in order to know the exact force of the superior evidence (p. 25).

In such cases, the probability that such an event will occur, accor-

4. Although Hume's *Dialogues Concerning Natural Religion* have been discussed in the light of Bayes (see e.g., W. C. Salmon, "Religion and Science: A New Look at Hume's Dialogues," *Philosophical Studies* 33 (1978) and Raynor's reply, same journal, 38 (1980)) Hume's arguments about miracles are not mentioned. Raynor suggests that Hume may have come to know Bayes' theorem through Price.

5. Although both Blackburn and Mackie in their replies to Cohen, *op. cit.*, mention Hume on miracles as relevant to the modern debate, neither of them mention Price or his criticisms of Hume, which can to some extent be seen as precursors of Cohen's position on when to take prior probabilities into account.

ding to the evidence, will be less than the full assurance given by proofs.

Hume then argues that our assurance concerning testimony is to be calculated in the same way. Our assurance concerning testimony should vary as past experience dictates.

> And as the evidence derived from witnesses and human testimony is founded on past experience, so it varies with the experience and is regarded either as a *proof* or a *probability*, according as the conjunction between any particular kind of report and any kind of object has been found to be constant or variable (p. 25).

What is interesting is that Hume insists that *more than a person's general propensity to tell the truth* (or speak falsely) needs to be taken into account. It is true that "A man delirious or noted for falsehood and villainy has no manner of authority with us," (p. 25), but such considerations are not exhaustive. Hume claims that the contrariety of evidence "may be derived from several different causes," (p. 26), and he mentions "opposition of contrary testimony," "the character or number of the witnesses," "the manner of their delivering their testimony" as well as "many other particulars of the same kind" (p. 26). Of course the particular Hume is most interested in is the case when

> the fact which testimony endeavours to establish partakes of the extraordinary and the marvellous—in that case the evidence resulting from the testimony admits of a diminution, greater or less in proportion as the fact is more or less unusual (p. 26).

So here is his central case. Although many factors are relevant when judging the likelihood of the occurrence of a reported event (and Hume discusses some of these factors in great detail in Part II) Hume is mainly concerned about weighing the conformity we are accustomed to find "between testimony and reality" as against the likelihood of an event "as has seldom fallen under our observation." (p. 26).

How are we to weigh up these two competing considerations? Hume, typically, first gives us a quasi-mechanical account:

here is a contest of two experiences, of which one destroys the other
as far as its force goes, and the superior can only operate in the mind
by the force which remains (p. 26).

After he has characterized a miracle as a violation of a law of nature,
Hume considers the case of testimony which "considered apart and
in itself, amounts to an entire proof" (p. 27) that affirms the occurrence of a miracle. Now since a miracle is a violation of a law of nature,
and the evidence in favor of a law of nature is exceptionless, i.e., constitutes a "proof," we have a standoff. One proof destroys the other,
and we are left indifferent as to whether the event testified to occurred or whether the testimony is false. Given the nature of miracles,
no testimony can be good enough to command our assent.

Hume, at this stage, is a little careless. He talks as if the proof in
favor of the law of nature and against its violation, i.e., the occurrence of a miracle, could be overcome "by an opposite proof which
is suprior" (p. 28). But since a proof, by his own account, provides
full assurance based on exceptionless experience, the notion of a
superior proof seems incoherent.[6] But the general point remains.
Hume is simply talking about greater and lesser probabilities in a

___

6. See J.H. Sobel, "On the Evidence of Testimony for Miracles: A Bayesian reconstruc-
tion of David Hume's Analysis" ([29] of the bibliography) for an interesting but technical
way of retaining the notion of a "superior proof" and a literal reading of "testimony . . .
of such a kind that its falsehood would be more miraculous than the fact which it endeavours
to establish" (p. 28). Sobel treats our assurance in a law of nature as having probability
infinitely close to one, and the corresponding violation as infinitely close to zero. I prefer
to think of Hume's notion of proof as being simply an argument with very high probability
indeed. This allows there to be such a thing as a superior proof without resort to the un-
Humean notion of "infinitely close to," and thus allows one to treat seriously Hume's important example of the real possibility of being rationally convinced that the earth was
covered in darkness for eight days (p. 37). It is entirely in line with Hume's motivation
for introducing "proof" as well as "probability," which is simply to avoid the oddness of
saying "that it is only probable all men must die, or that the sun will rise tomorrow". (Hume,
Enquiry Concerning Human Understanding, sec. 6.) One bit of evidence that this reading
concurs with Hume's intentions is mentioned by I. Hacking in another context. ("Hume's
Species of Probability," *Philosophical Studies* 33 (1978) pp. 21–37). Hacking points out (pp.
27–28) that while Hume allows, in theory, a species of probability connected with exceptionless uniformities, he further claims that in fact "no one who is arrived at the age of
maturity can any longer be acquainted with it" (*Treatise of Human Nature*, Book I Part
III Section XII). So unless in maturity we also lose our acquaintance with proofs, proofs
cannot be based on exceptionless experience and have probability infinitely close to one.
We must be content with proofs yielding simply very high probabilities indeed. Nothing
in the subsequent argument hinges on the exact interpretation of "proof" as long as it is
understood that it does not mean "demonstrative proof."

graphic way. No matter how reliable the testimony, it cannot in general overcome the intrinsic improbability of a violation of a law of nature. Suppose that the testimony is as reliable as possible; the case is still a standoff. The two proofs destroy each other, and we have no more reason to believe that the miracle occurred than that the testimony is false. And furthermore suppose, *per impossible*, that the reliability of the testimony that a miracle occurred is slightly greater than our assurance of the relevant law of nature. We should not then believe that the miracle occurred with the same degree of assurance that we have in the reliability of the testimony. Rather, Hume says,

> even in that case there is a mutual destruction of arguments, and the superior only gives an assurance suitable to that degree of force which remains after deducting the inferior (p. 28).

(Again, notice the mechanical metaphor.) The general rule is clear. We should only believe that the miraculous or unlikely event occurred, on the basis of testimony, if the likelihood of the testimony's being false is less than the likelihood of the law of nature's being violated. In Hume's words,

> The plain consequence is (and it is a general maxim worthy of our attention) that no testimony is sufficient to establish a miracle unless the testimony be of such a kind that its falsehood would be more miraculous than the fact which it endeavours to establish (p. 28).

Given the nature of miracles, this situation can never occur. And even if, *per impossible*, it did occur, the strength of our belief that the miracle occurred would be substantially less than the strength of our belief in the reliability of the testimony.

It is this last point that may appear puzzling. If we believe in the reliability of the testimony with a certain degree of assurance, surely we believe that the event reported by the testimony occurred with exactly the same degree of assurance. How could the likelihood of the event lessen that already held belief? As long as there is *some* probability that the event occurred, surely our belief in the reliability of the testimony is exactly the same as our belief that the event occurred. This is the point that puzzled Price and, apparently, Cohen.

It is easy enough to make the point in terms of the mechanical metaphor. If the argument in favor of the belief is of a certain force, and the argument against the event's occurring is of an opposite force, even if one ends up believing that the event occurred, the degree of assurance will be lessened proportionately to the amount of the countervailing force. But in order to pursue this, let us recast Hume's argument in the light of Bayes' theorem.

III

The relevant application of Bayes' theorem which I shall use,[7] states that if p is the prior probability of a certain event, and if t is the probability that a certain witness tells the truth, i.e., the probability that the witness asserts that the event took place, given that it did take place, then the probability that the event took place, given that the witness asserts that it has taken place, is

$$\frac{pt}{pt + (1 - p)(1 - t)}$$

It is easily seen that this formula gives just the results that Hume asserts. For instance, consider the claim that we should be indifferent (or judge with probability of .5) when the probability that the witness speaks falsely is the same as the probability that the unlikely event occurred. Suppose that both these probabilities are .1. In this case, since p, the prior probability that the event did take place, is .1, and

---

7. The formula is given by Niiniluoto in his reply to Cohen, *op. cit.*, p. 349. He claims that it was known as early as 1785 to Condorcet. For doubts, see Sobel, *op. cit.*. It is important to remember that the formula gives the conditional probability that an event took place, given that a witness said it took place. Let us symbolize this as $(Pr(e/says\ e)$. Bayes' theorem then gives us this formula:

$$Pr(e/says\ e) = \frac{Pr(e) \times Pr(says\ e/e)}{[Pr(e) \times Pr(says\ e/e)] + [Pr(\sim e) \times Pr(says\ e/\sim e)]}$$

If $p = Pr(e)$ and $t = Pr(says\ e/e)$, then our formula is derivable from the long formula as long as $Pr(says\ e/e) = Pr(says \sim e/\sim e)$. Where that assumption does not hold, the long formula can be used instead of our short one.

t, the probability that the witness tells the truth, is $1 - .1 = .9$, then the probability that the event did take place, given that the witness asserts that it did take place, is, according to our formula,

$$\frac{(.1)(.9)}{(.1)(.9) + (1 - .1)(1 - .9)} = .5,$$

In fact, it is easily seen that for any $p = 1 - t$,

$$\frac{pt}{pt + (1 - p)(1 - t)} = .5,$$

Similarly, if it is more probable that the witness speaks falsely than that the unlikely event occurred, i.e. if $(1 - t) > p$, the relevant probability is less than .5, and if it is more probable that the event occurred than that the witness spoke falsely, i.e., if $p > (1 - t)$, then the relevant probability is greater than .5. Furthermore, it is interesting to see how much less the probability that the event occurred, given that the witness said it occurred, is than the reliability of the witness, even when it is less likely that the witness spoke falsely than that the event occurred. Suppose the witness is 99% reliable, so that there is only a 1% chance that he spoke falsely, and that the likelihood of the event is 2%. Then with $p = .02$ and $t = .99$, our formula yields:

$$\frac{(.02)(.99)}{(.02)(.99) + (1 - .02)(1 - .99)} = .67$$

This is a surprising result, but in accordance with Hume's view that when

> the fact which testimony endeavours to establish partakes of the extraordinary and the marvellous—in that case the evidence resulting from the testimony admits of a diminution, greater or less in proportion as the fact is more or less unusual. (p. 26)[8]

8. The surprising result is that $Pr(e/says\ e)$, the probability that the event took place, given that the witness said it took place, is only .67, while $Pr(says\ e/e)$, the probability that the witness said it took place, given that it took place, is 99%. The figure of .67, however, should also be contrasted with the prior probability of the event's occurring, i.e. 2%. Hume certainly didn't intend to argue that testimony should have *no* effect on our belief, but rather that in certain circumstances it might have less effect than we might at first think.

IV

Price finds Hume's results on testimony and prior probabilities "contrary to all reason".[9] He argues, partially by example and partially by appeal to general principles, that Hume is wrong to allow prior probabilities any impact at all in our judgments concerning whether the event reported by the witness actually occurred.[10] Part of his point is that our assent to testimony is not based on induction, because

> One conversation with a man may convince us of his integrity and induce us to believe his testimony, though we never, in a single instance, experienced his veracity (p. 399).

As a result Price thinks, testimony for miracles is *not* a matter of using a feebler experience to overthrow another of the same kind which is stronger. Rather, it is proof of an event which at best, prior to its happening, would have appeared to have a presumption against its happening (p. 401). This is a weak point, and does not show that likelihood of testimony being correct is not calculated in the same manner as induction. Hume himself admits that a single instance can serve as an inductive basis for a causal belief.[11] Price further argues that we *never* have an absolute proof that a very probable sort of event will happen again, nor the *least reason* to believe that it will *always* happen (pp. 394–95). But there is nothing in this to bother Hume, and at most it shows only that Price has not noticed that Hume is using a reasonably well-defined technical sense of "proof" in the section on miracles.

After this unpromising start, Price has some most interesting things to say about prior probabilities. Concerning a case where the probability of the truth of testimony is ten to one, and the event attested to is the success of a person engaged in a pursuit against the success of which there was a probability of a hundred to one, Price says,

9. Richard Price, *op. cit.*, fourth dissertation entitled "On the Importance of Christianity, the Nature of Historical Evidence, and Miracles," p. 407. Subsequent page references to Price will be given in the body of the paper.

10. Not allowing prior probabilities to have any effect at all is the same as using our formulae, but stipulating that p always equals .5. Then the formula results in $Pr(e/says\ e)$ being simply equal to t, i.e. to $Pr(says\ e/e)$. According to Diaconis and Freedman in their reply to Cohen, *op. cit.* (note 4, p. 334) this is an application of Laplace's principle of insufficient reason, first published around 1780.

11. *Treatise*, Book I, Part III, Section 8.

> The truth is, that the testimony would give the probability of ten
> to one to the event, unabated by the supposed probability against
> it . . . (because) the very experience which teaches us to give credit
> to testimony, is an experience by which we have found, that it has
> informed us rightly concerning facts, in which there would have
> appeared to us, previously, a great improbability (pp. 407–8).

The argument here is that in making judgments about the likelihood
of an event's occurring, on the basis of testimony, we should ignore
the prior probability of the likelihood of the event, because our judgment about the reliability of the testimony (in this case ten to one)
is a judgment about testimony *concerning unlikely events.* In other
words, the likelihood of the event's occurring has *already been taken
into account* when we make the judgment about the reliability of
testimony. It would be double counting if we then proceeded to further calculate probabilities in the way Hume, and our application
of Bayes' theorem, suggests.

Price then proceeds to give a series of apparently persuasive examples.[12] Suppose a newspaper is generally accurate two out of
three times, and suppose it reports, separately and individually, the
occurrence of nine quite improbable events. Hume, Price claims,
would reject all nine reports, i.e., he would say,

> that what, by supposition, reports truth six times in nine, does not
> report truth once in nine times (p. 409).

Or suppose that the same newspaper reported the loss of a ferry boat
during a crossing it had previously made safely two thousand times.
In this case, Price asserts, testimony that is accurate only two out of
three times would overcome odds of thousands to one against.

Later (p. 418) Price admits that prior probabilities should *sometimes*

---

12. Including the lottery example, a favorite in the nineteenth century and also mentioned by Cohen. Here is Cohen's formulation: (p. 329)

> A witness of 99% reliability asserts that the number of the single ticket drawn in
> a lottery of 10,000 tickets was, say, 297; ought we really to reject that proposition
> just because of the size of the lottery?

The lottery problem is different from the other problems discussed here as there is not just
one way of being wrong about 297, but 9,999 ways. Proper application of Bayes' theorem
does not result in rejecting the witness's testimony because of the size of the lottery. See
Diaconis and Freedman, *op. cit.*, and Sobel, *op. cit.*.

be taken into account. We should not, for example, believe reports, however reliable the bearers of such reports are in general, of impossibilities. It remains unclear at this stage when prior probabilities are relevant, and when they are not. Price could say consistently with his argument so far, that our previous experience concerning the accuracy of testimony has presented us with cases of accurate testimony concerning improbable events, but never of accurate testimony concerning impossible events. This, however, might well just simply give the game away to Hume concerning miracles. But in a footnote at the end of his dissertation, Price gives a better reason, and strengthens his argument about the usual irrelevance of prior probabilities (p. 444). Price says that two events are independent when the happening of one of them has no influence on the happening of the other, and with this account of independence he goes on to enunciate the principle that the improbabilities of independent events are the same whether they are considered jointly or separately. As it stands, this point does not seem to amount to much of an argument against Hume. Testimony that an event occurred is, when accurate, related both causally and logically to the occurrence of the event. However, it is easy enough to reformulate the point in an apparently telling way against Hume. One could argue that the *likelihood* of the event reported, or the distribution of past occurrences or non-occurrences, is independent of the accuracy of the testimony, so that when we are to consider whether or not to believe testimony, only its accuracy should be taken into account. Alternatively, if we want to retain the generality of Bayes' theorem, we should treat the prior probability of the event as .5 when we judge the known prior probability of that event to be irrelevant to the accuracy of the testimony we are considering (see note 10). If sound, this point entirely undermines Hume's use of prior probabilities in his discussion of the rationality of belief in miracles based on testimony.

V

In the article already cited, L.J. Cohen, during the discussion of empirical tests of rationality, comes to conclusions remarkably similar to Price's, and for apparently similar reasons.

First of all, let me outline two examples Cohen mentions (pp. 328–29). In one case, subjects were told that, in a certain town where blue and green cabs operated in a ratio of 85 to 15, respectively, a witness identified a cab in a crash as green. The court is told that in the relevant light conditions such a witness can distinguish blue from green cabs 80% of the time. The subjects were then asked, what is the probability that the cab involved in the accident was blue? The usual answer was .2, indicating that the subjects were ignoring the prior probability based on the distribution of cabs in the town. But if that probability were taken into account, the right answer, according to our formula, would be

$$\frac{(.85)(.2)}{(.85)(.2) + (1 - .85)(1 - .2)} = .59$$

An 80% reliable witness, sincerely claiming that the cab was green, would be judged to have .59 chance of misidentifying the color of the cab.[13]

Cohen's second example, concerning diagnosis, is this. Suppose you are suffering from symptoms which indicate that you have either disease A or disease B, which require different treatments. Disease A is nineteen times as common as B, but you take a test, which always distinguishes A and B, and in the past has been right 80% of the time. The test results indicate that you have disease B. Should you opt for treatment for B, on the grounds that the probability that you have B is, as Price would apparently calculate it, 4/5, or should you opt for treatment for A, on the grounds that the probability that you have A is, as Hume would apparently calculate it, 19/23? If you decide with Hume, of course, you need not have taken the test at all.

Cohen admits, as Price probably would not, that if one were concerned only with long term frequencies or instances thereof, one should calculate as we have claimed Hume would. But, Cohen argues, if we are concerned with the likelihood of a particular witness correctly identifying a particular cab, or if a patient is concerned with successful diagnosis in his own particular case, then we should ig-

---

13. Again, note that while the prior probability that the cab was green is only 15%, the probability that the cab was green, given that the witness said it was green, is .41.

nore prior probabilities, i.e., treat them as .5 in the Bayesian calculation. And his reason for this seems to be precisely Price's: since the distribution of past instances has no causal efficacy on, i.e., is independent of, the individual event (the witnessing, the taking of the test) then the prior probability based on such chance distribution is irrelevant.[14]

VI

How are we to decide between Hume and standard statistical methods, on the one hand, and Cohen and the eighteenth century theologians on the other? To what extent does the modern debate deepen our understanding of what is at issue between Hume and Price, or *vice versa*? These are large questions, and only a partial unravelling of the issues will be attempted here. My main purpose has been to show that Hume's argument has a larger significance than is generally realized, that Price saw this and has been unjustly neglected, and that their debate is extremely similar to an important modern issue. The parallel between the two debates is significant, I think, and not merely of historical interest. It indicates that the issue is a long-standing one, and that there are unresolved divisions (some would say "persistent cognitive illusions"[15]) over what constitutes a rational decision concerning prior probabilities. Which side one comes down on could be of profound importance. The patient has to decide whether to believe the result of the test; the doctor has to decide whether even to administer it: both might be risking the patient's life. Or suppose that the likelihood of a nuclear attack is one in a thousand, but that the accuracy of one's radar or other early warning devices is only 99.8%. Would it be rational to act on the information given by one's equipment, or more rational not to set up such warning devices at all? If one in a hundred new food stuffs is carcinogenic, but one's tests are only 90% accurate, should one bother to carry out the tests or not? There are no easy answers to

14. See also Cohen's interesting discussion of this point in terms of detaching unconditional probabilities from conditional probabilities only when the conditions include, not just the knowledge we have (i.e., in the examples mentioned, chance distribution) but "a substantial amount of the causally relevant factors" (p. 365).
15. See Diaconis and Freedman, *op. cit.*.

these questions, and apparently good arguments can be provided on both sides.[16]

On first pass, one's intuitions seem to side with Price and Cohen, and for the reasons they give. If the prior probabilities are not causally relevant to the actual case of visual perception that grounds the witness's testimony, why should we take them into account when deciding whether or not to believe him? As Cohen says,

> if the green cab company suddenly increased the size of its fleet relative to that of the blue company, the accuracy of the witness's vision would not be affected, and the credibility of his testimony would therefore remain precisely the same in any particular case of the relevant kind (p. 329)[17]

Similarly, it is hard not to side, at least initially, with Price concerning the particular examples that he gives.

On the other hand, consider this way of formulating the diagnosis case. One *could* argue that, given the 19 to 1 distribution of the disease, and the 80% accuracy of the test, the test will indicate that an individual has disease B 4.75 times more often when he has A than when he has B. Consider a population of 20,000 who take the test. 19,000 will have A and 1,000 will have B. Out of the 19,000 who have A, the test will indicate that 3,800 of them have B. Out of the 1,000 who have B, the test will indicate that 800 of them have B. So out of 4,600 instances of the test indicating B, 3,800 of them will actually have A. The 80% accurate test will be right in only 800 cases out of 4,600 indications of B, or only 17.39% of the time.[18] But how could a test of 80% accuracy be right in only 17.39% of B—indicating cases? We need to make a distinction between two claims:[19]

(1) Concerning people who have disease B, the test is right 80% of the time.

16. It is of interest that most of those who replied to Cohen seemed to think that he was clearly right (and that his point had been obvious since the early days of probability theory) or clearly, perhaps even dangerously, wrong.

17. It is significant, surely, that the median answer given by the people to whom the cab problem was posed chose to answer with Cohen.

18. See Krantz's reply to Cohen, p. 341, for this line of reasoning. Note that the same figures can be arrived at by using our formula and that the 17.39% figure contrasts also with the one in twenty prior probability.

19. See Mackie's reply to Cohen, p. 346.

(2) Concerning people whom the test indicates as having B, it is right 80% of the time.

It is clear that the above line of reasoning, which is simply another way of advocating taking prior probabilities into account in the way our formula recommends, requires that we treat 80% accuracy claim as equivalent to claim (1) above. And if that is what the claim did mean, we would be wise not to trust the results of the test. But given the way we have outlined the example, there is no reason whatsoever to treat the claim as meaning (1) rather than (2), or for that matter as (2) rather than (1). But any company that marketed such a test, and claimed that it was 80% accurate, had better mean, by 80% accuracy, claim (2), or they would, I suspect, be deluged by lawsuits.

Throughout this paper, I have talked of "accuracy of testimony," "probability that the witness tells the truth," "reliability of testimony," "probability of the truth of testimony," "general accuracy of a newspaper" and the like, and used the value of t to reflect what such expressions meant when using the formula

$$pt + (1 - p)(1 - t)$$

to calculate the probability that an event did take place, given that the witness said that it took place. Strictly speaking, for this formula to operate at all, t must be the probability that the witness said that the event took place, given that the event did take place. Let us symbolize the former probability as $Pr(e/says\ e)$ and the latter probability as $Pr(says\ e/e)$.[20] Our discussion of the diagnosis case, and the distinction between claim (1) and claim (2), shows that the terms "accuracy," "reliability" etc. are ambiguous. Though we have treated them throughout as giving $Pr(says\ e/e)$, and hence giving a value for t, it may be the case, as our discussion of claim (2) shows, that sometimes they are meant instead to indicate $Pr(e/says\ e)$. But $Pr(e/says\ e)$ is just what our formula was meant to calculate. If a degree of accuracy or reliability is given, and is meant to give $Pr(e/says\ e)$, then it would be a gross mistake to treat it as $Pr(says\ e/e)$ and use it as a value for t in our formula. On the other hand, if the reliability figure gives $Pr(says\ e/e)$, it would be an equally bad mistake not

20. See note 7.

to use our formula in deciding on a value for $Pr(e/says\ e)$ when a value for the prior probability $Pr(e)$ (i.e., p in our formula) is available. Although no ordinary language expression unequivocally expresses the distinction between $Pr(e/says\ e)$ and $Pr(says\ e/e)$, for the remaining discussion let us mean by "credibility of testimony" the former and by "reliability of the witness" the latter. Then our formula is a means of calculating credibility of testimony in terms of the reliability of the witness and the prior probability of the event reported.

It is my contention that Hume argued, rightly, that the credibility of testimony in favor of miracles would never be high enough to command our assent, even if the reliability of the witnesses was high. Price thought otherwise, and argued so both by means of general principles and by example. It is obvious, I think, that neither was absolutely clear about the distinction between credibility and reliability that has just been drawn and in terms of which the dispute between them can be adjudicated. But in the end, I think, Hume's insistence on the distinction between our degree of belief in the occurrence of an event on the sole grounds that a witness reported its happening, and our degree of belief in the reliability of the witness[21], shows him to have a better grip on the matter, and to be the better proto-Bayesian.

What of Price's arguments, and the other examples mentioned? As has already been said, the diagnosis case is underdescribed; but it would be grossly irresponsible of those marketing the test not to mean "credibility" rather than "reliability" by their 80% accuracy figure. The cab example is also underdescribed. The crucial datum was given as, "a witness can distinguish blue from green cabs 80% of the time." Does this mean credibility or reliability? It is charitable to assume that the subjects of the experiment took it to mean credibility, as that interpretation shows their answer to be correct, though one would have to look at details of the original experiment to see whether their taking it that way was correct. In any event, a close look at the original data on which the 80% figure in the cab case (or, for that matter, the diagnosis case) was reached would reveal how to disambiguate that figure. It should not be a difficult matter to determine whether the data support an 80% probability that the

---

21. Most graphically expressed by his quoting, "I should not believe such a story were it told me by Cato" (p. 26).

cab was blue, given that the witness said it was blue (credibility) or an 80% probability that the witness said that the cab was blue, given that it was blue (reliability).

What of Price's persuasive newspaper example? Again, everything hinges on what is meant by the claim that a newspaper is accurate two out of three times. Does it mean that, given that the newspaper said the event happened, it has a two out of three chance of being right, or rather that, given that it happened, the newspaper has a two out of three chance of being right? To the extent that we are persuaded by Price's example, we are taking him to be making the former claim. On intuitive grounds the two-thirds figure for newspaper accuracy does seem more likely to mean credibility ($Pr(e/says\ e)$) rather than reliability ($Pr(says\ e/e)$) as we would normally come up with that figure by starting with the newspaper reports, and then checking to see whether what it reported actually occurred.

Although Price at some points seems near to grasping the distinction between what we have called credibility and reliability[22], in the end it seems to elude him. Most of his examples and his argument concerning "double counting" make sense only if he is thinking of credibility. If the figure we are given is a value for $Pr(e/says\ e)$ then of course we cannot use that as a value for t (i.e., $Pr(says\ e/e)$) in our formula. On the other hand, his argument from independence is only plausible if he is talking about reliability. The argument was that, unless the prior probability was causally operative on the accuracy of the witness's testimony, it had no effect on that accuracy. If accuracy here means reliability, the point may stand. But if accuracy here means credibility, i.e., $Pr(e/says\ e)$, the prior probability $Pr(e)$ is crucial, as we have seen.[23]

Price's arguments and examples do not add up to a coherent position as a result of his confusion concerning crucial terms such as "accuracy." Hume's admirable insistence on the distinction between the degree of belief we should have concerning the occurrence of a

22. See, for instance, pp. 417—8, where he claims that though prior probabilities as *such* should not be considered as invalidating counter-evidence to testimony (or, as he puts it on p. 413, do not "lessen the capacity of testimony to report truth") they nonetheless may affect the *credit* of testimony.

23. The passage already quoted from Cohen about the irrelevance of the green cab company's increasing the size of its fleet merits similar treatment. It is irrelevant if we are concerned about the witness's reliability, but not at all irrelevant if it is the credibility of witnesses' testimony that is at issue.

reported event and the degree of belief we should have in the veracity of the reporter, stands in marked contrast. However, there is a very simple point that might be made, on grounds adduced by Price, against Hume on miracles. Why, it might be asked, should we not treat the evidence based on testimony in favor of miracles as a matter of credibility, rather than reliability, just as we should in the newspaper example? Hume's answer is, I think, clear. Given the incredibly high odds against the occurrence of a miracle (it is, after all, a violation of a law of nature), what possible grounds could there be for treating the evidence based on testimony as a matter of credibility rather than reliability? One who argues in such a way should be challenged to defend his attribution of credibility to the witness's testimony. If it is to be a matter of *credibility*, then the reliability of the witness must be greater than the probability that the law of nature holds. And what witness is so reliable?

At this point Hume's argument leaves the realm of abstract probability theory. As is little noted, Hume does admit that it is conceivable that the reliability of testimony may exceed the evidence in favor of a law of nature, and hence that the credibility of testimony may exceed .5. This is shown by his example of the earth being covered in darkness for eight days (p. 37). What he dennies is that such a possibility should ever be "proved so as to be the foundation of a system of religion" (p. 37). A miracle is not simply a violation of a law of nature, but must also be "by a particular violation of the Deity, or by the interposition of some invisible agent" (p. 28). It is conceivable that reliability of witnesses may be enough to render credible the violation of a law of nature:

> The decay, corruption and dissolution of nature is an event rendered probable by so many analogies that any phenomenon which seems to have a tendency towards catastrophe comes within the reach of human testimony if that testimony be very extensive and uniform (p. 37f).

Hume thinks that no such instance is to be found "in all the records of history" (p. 37). But even if it were found, and the violation were credible, what possible grounds could be adduced so that it became plausible to treat the phenomenon as owing to a particular violation of the Deity rather than as an instance of the already experienced dissolution of nature? If one *already* believed in the God of the Christian religion, then if the sort of evidence envisaged became available, it might be rational to treat the violation as a result of God's volition. But if one was not already a believer, then even if such evidence obtained, one would still have no good reason to change one's mind.

Hume argued that the evidence of testimony in favor of miracles could never be good enough to provide a rational basis for the foundation of a religion. His argument was designed not, as Price thought (p. 379), as an objection to Christianity, but as an argument against a certain way of trying to rationally ground belief in Christianity. Given the difficulties we have discussed, it surely must be admitted that he succeeded in this limited task.[24]

24. An ancestor of this paper was read at the University of Calgary, where I received many helpful comments, especially from T. Hurka and J. Heintz. Correspondence with P. Maher and L.J. Cohen was also most useful. A shorter version was read at the 28th Annual Congress of the Canadian Philosophical Association, Guelph, Ontario, June 11th, 1984. J.H. Sobel replied. His paper, *op. cit.*, and his subsequent discussion with me greatly contributed to the revision of my paper. Ian Hacking was also of great help.

13

RICHARD SWINBURNE*

Historical Evidence

THE CLAIM OF the chapter published as [8] in this volume was that we could have good reason to suppose that an event E, if it occurred, was a violation of a law of nature L. But could one have good evidence that such an event E occurred? At this point we must face the force of Hume's own argument. This, it will be remembered, runs as follows. The evidence, which *ex hypothesi* is good evidence, that L is a law of nature is evidence that E did not occur. We have certain other evidence that E did occur. In such circumstances, writes Hume, the wise man "weighs the opposite experiments. He considers which side is supported by the greater number of experiments" ([3] p. 24. Since he supposes that the evidence that E occurred would be that of testimony, Hume concludes "that no testimony is sufficient to establish a miracle, unless the testimony be of such a kind, that its falsehood would be more miraculous, than the fact which it endeavors to establish" ([3] p.28).

Four Kinds of Historical Evidence

We have four kinds of evidence about what happened at some past instant—our own apparent memories of our past experiences, the testimony of others about their past experiences, physical traces and our contemporary understanding of what things are physically im-

*This is a shortened version of Chapter 4 of my book *The Concept of Miracle* London: Macmillan and Co., 1970.

possible or improbable. (The fourth is only a corrective to the other three, not an independent source of detailed information.) A piece of evidence gives grounds for believing that some past event occurred, except in so far as it conflicts with other pieces of evidence. In so far as pieces of evidence conflict, they have to be weighed against each other.

Let us consider more fully the kinds of evidence. Firstly we have our own apparent memories. I remember, in my opinion, to some extent what I was doing yesterday or last year, what happened to me, and what was going on in the neighborhood. True, though I may think that I remember these things I may be mistaken, and evidence of other types about what happened may convince me that I am mistaken. However in the usual use of "remember," if I remember that p, then of logical necessity it was the case that p. Hence the memory evidence for what happened to be weighed against other evidence is best described as evidence of apparent memory. While I may be mistaken about what happened (my claims to memory may be wrong), I can be certain about my apparent memories. Secondly we have the testimony of others—what they say that they did and saw and what happened to them. This may be testimony spoken to us personally or written down long ago. Thirdly we have physical traces of what happened—footprints, fingerprints, ashes, bomb craters. Such physical states are evidence for us that certain past events probably happened, of which events they may be termed traces. A particular present state or event, that is change of state, A_1 is a trace for us of a particular past state or event B_1 if the two events are members of classes of events A's and B's, when the occurrence of A's is highly correlated in our experience with prior occurrence of B's.[1]

---

1. The classes must be classes described by what philosophers of science call projectible predicates. That is to say A's and B's must be events of the kind which if we know that they have been correlated in the past, we thereby have reason to believe that they will be correlated in the future. Thus "fall of barometer" and "rainy day" are projectible. If a number of falls of barometers have all been followed by rainy days in the past, that is reason to suppose that falls of barometers will be so followed in the future. But if a jule day is defined as 3 June or 18 June or 1 July or 3 July or 4 July, then "jule day" is not projectible. If the jule days 3 June, 18 June, 1 July, 3 July and 4 July, have all been rainy days this year, that is in itself no reason for supposing that all the jule days next year will be rainy days. The problem of distinguishing between projectible and non-projectible predicates is the problem of which extrapolation is a natural or simple one, discussed in [8] in this volume. Philosophers of science have not yet solved the problem of providing a general rule for when a predicate is projectible, but there are obvious clear cases of when predicates are and when they are not projectible.

This correlation (unless—which is highly unlikely—it is coinciden-
tal) will arise either because B's cause A's (and A's are seldom caused
by anything else) or because C's cause both B's and A's, first B's and
then later A's (and A's are seldom caused by anything else). Thus a
particular human footprint (in the sense of a mark in the shape of
a human foot) in the sand is for us a trace that someone with a foot
of that size has walked there recently, because we have observed that
men walking on sand produce footprints, and that these are seldom
produced by any other cause. Fourthly we have our contemporary
understanding of what things are physically impossible or improbable,
that is, ruled out or rendered improbable by the laws of nature or
generalizations of what usually happens. This scientific knowledge
serves as a check on the evidence of apparent memory, testimony and
traces. Evidence as to what is physically impossible is, as Humeans
have emphasized, a very strong check on other evidence. If a witness
says that he saw a man recover within a minute from polio, or a man
walk on air, we, with our contemporary scientific knowledge, have
reason to believe that such things are not physically possible, and so
have strong evidence against that testimony. Evidence about what
is physically improbable is a check, but a less strong one, on other
evidence. It counts against evidence that Smith was dealt all thirteen cards of a suit one Friday night at bridge that only extremely
rarely are all thirteen cards of a suit dealt at bridge to one player's
hand, i.e., that such an event is highly improbable.

My classification of kinds of evidence is, I believe, exhaustive (viz.
there are no other kinds), but the classes do to some extent overlap.
Thus testimony to the occurrence of X may also be a trace of an event
Y. If Jones tells the police that Smith did the robbery, then this event
is testimony to Smith having done the robbery. But if we know that
on past occasions Jones has only betrayed men to the police when
Mrs. Jones has persuaded him to do so, then on this occasion his telling the police is also a trace of Mrs. Jones having persuaded him to
do so.

Now Hume says a great deal about evidence of the second and
fourth kinds, but nothing at all about evidence of the first and third
kinds. Hume supposes that the conflict about what happens is a conflict between testimony and scientific knowledge. And so no doubt
were most conflicts known to Hume—e.g., conflicts about whether
the biblical miracles took place. But sometimes the evidence available
to an inquirer consists not merely of the testimony of others but of

one's own apparently remembered observations. Some men have the evidence of their own eyes, not merely the testimony of others. What, one wonders, would Hume say, if he himself apparently saw a man walk on water? And Hume says nothing at all about traces, finger-prints, footprints and cigarette ash, the impersonal kind of evidence on which detectives like to rely a great deal. But then Hume lived before the era of scientific criminology, and so would hardly be like-ly to be aware of what could be established by such methods.

However, the evidence of traces could be of considerable impor-tance in assessing whether some event E occurred which if it occurred would have violated a law of nature. Thus if E consists in a state X being followed by a state Y, and we have a trace of the state X and an observed later state Y, or a trace thereof, then we have evidence of traces that E occurred. Thus we might have evidence of footprints in soft mud that Jones was on one side of a broad river one minute ago, and evidence of Jones on the other side now not in the least wet, with not the slightest indication of water having touched his body or clothes (viz. no traces of his having swum across the river), and no bridge, boats, airplanes or rope by which he could have crossed. Hence the evidence indicates that he must have walked or flown across. Traces alone, unsupported by testimony, could thus provide evidence that such an event occurred.

It must, however, be admitted that traces are of more use in in-quiring into alleged recent miracles than into alleged miracles of long ago. For it is a sad fact which detectives bemoan that many traces become obliterated in the course of time. Footprints in the sand and cigarette ash still warm are useful indications of what happened a minute or two ago—but footprints get smudged out, and ash gets cold and scattered, and they do not serve as indications of what hap-pened centuries ago. Yet there are many traces which do not become obliterated and which historians are now learning to use—C_{14} dating to determine the age of artifacts, errors of transcription to determine the history of documents, peculiarities of style to deter-mine authorship, etc. Science is continually discovering new kinds of traces which reveal facets of ancient history. Who knows how much detail about the past the science of the future will be able to infer from then current remains?

So much for the kinds of evidence which we have about the past and their sources. Clearly one piece of evidence will often conflict with another. The testimony of Jones may conflict with what I appear to remember, or with the testimony of Smith. Jones says that he stayed with Robinson at home all day yesterday, while I "distinctly remember" having seen him at the Pig and Whistle, and Smith claims to have seen him at the Horse and Hounds. Testimony may conflict with traces. Jones has a scar of a certain type normally caused by a knife wound, but denies having been slashed. Or traces may conflict with each other. A bomb crater may indicate a recent explosion, but the healthy state of the surrounding vegetation count against this. And our contemporary understanding of the physically possible may count against the evidence of particular traces, testimony or apparent memory. I appear to remember having seen the conjurer take the rabbit out of the hat, but he cannot have done so, because the laws of light are such that, had the rabbit been in the hat, I would have seen it.

Principles for Weighing Conflicting Evidence

Conflicting evidence has to be weighed, and the fundamental idea involved in such weighing seems to be to obtain as coherent a picture as possible of the past as consistent as possible with the evidence. We can express this idea in the form of one basic principle for assessing evidence and several subsidiary principles limiting its operation. The most basic principle is to accept as many pieces of evidence as possible. If one witness says one thing, and five witnesses say a different thing, then, in the absence of further evidence (e.g., about their unreliability) take the testimony of the latter. If one method of dating an artifact gives one result, and five methods give a different result, then, in the absence of further information accept the latter result.

The first subsidiary principle is—apart from any empirical evidence about their relative reliability—that evidence of different kinds ought to be given different weights. How this is to be done can only be illustrated by examples. Thus one's own apparent memory ought as such to count for more than the testimony of another witness (unless and until evidence of its relative unreliability is forthcoming). If I appear to remember having seen Jones yesterday in Hull, but Brown says that he had Jones under observation all day yesterday and that he went nowhere near to Hull, then—ceteris paribus—I ought to stand by my apparent memory. This is because when someone else gives testimony it always makes sense to suppose that he is lying; whereas, when I report to myself what I appear to remember, I cannot be lying. For the liar is someone who says what he believes to be false. But if I report what I appear to remember (and I can *know* for certain what I appear to remember), I cannot be lying. Secondly, if I feel highly confident that I remember some event, my apparent memory ought to count for more than if I am only moderately confident. My apparent memory has a built-in weight, apart from empirical evidence which may be forthcoming about its reliability in different circumstances (e.g., that it is not reliable when I am drunk). In these and other ways for non-empirical reasons different pieces of evidence ought to be given different weights in assessing the balance of evidence.

The second subsidiary principle is that different pieces of evidence ought to be given different weights in accordance with any empirical evidence which may be available about their different reliability, obtained by a procedure which I may term narrowing the evidence class. In general we necessarily assume or have reason to believe that apparent memory, testimony and states of particular types are reliable evidence about past states and events. But clash of evidence casts doubt on this. So we test the reliability of a piece of evidence by classifying it as a member of a narrow class, and investigating the reliability of other members of that class which—see note 1—would have to be classes whose members were described by projectible predicates. If the testimony of Jones conflicts with the testimony of Smith, then we must investigate not the worth of testimony in general, but the worth of Jones' testimony and of Smith's testimony. We do this by seeing if on all other occasions when we can ascertain what happened Jones or Smith correctly described what happened. In so far as each did, his testimony is reliable. Now this procedure will only work in so far as we can at some stage ascertain with sufficient certainty what happened without bringing in empirical evidence about the reliability of the evidence about what happened. Unless we could establish with sufficient certainty by mere balance of evidence what happened on a certain past occasion, without testing the worth of each piece of evidence by considering the worth of evidence of a narrow class to which it belongs, we could never establish anything at all. For the testing of evidence of one class can only be performed if we presuppose the reliability in general of other evidence. Thus, to test Jones' testimony we have to find out—by the testimony of others and traces—what happened on a number of occasions and then see whether Jones correctly reported this. But to do this we have to be able to ascertain what did happen on those occasions, and we will have various pieces of evidence as well as that of Jones about this. Unless the agreement of evidence apart from the testimony of Jones suffices to do this, we could never show Jones to be a reliable or unreliable witness. We may have empirical evidence about the reliability of such other evidence, but as such evidence will consist of more empirical evidence, we have to stop somewhere, with evidence which we can take to be reliable without empirical evidence thereof.

Similar tests to these tests of the reliability of testimony can be made of the reliability of traces, e.g., of methods of dating ancient documents.

For a given number of pieces of evidence in the class, the narrower the evidence class chosen for the assessment of the worth of a particular piece of evidence, the more reliable the assessment yielded by it. If we examine the worth of a particular piece of testimony given by a certain Soviet diplomat, Stamkovsky, to an official of M.I.5 by examining the worth of n pieces of testimony given by Soviet diplomats, then we have some knowledge of its worth, better than our knowledge of the worth of testimony in general. But we have a better assessment of its worth if we examine the worth of n pieces of testimony given by Stamkovsky and an even better estimate if we consider the worth of n pieces of testimony given by Stamkovsky to British counter-intelligence officers. But this raises a well-known difficulty about evidence classes—that the narrower the evidence class we choose, the fewer pieces of evidence we will have on which to base our assessment. We will have plenty of pieces of evidence by Soviet diplomats the reliability of which we can check, but few pieces of evidence given by Stamkovsky to British counter-intelligence agents the reliability of which we can check. The narrower the evidence class the better, but so long only as we have sufficient evidence to put in it to reach a well-substantiated conclusion.

The third subsidiary principle is not to reject coincident evidence (unless the evidence of its falsity is extremely strong) unless an explanation can be given of the coincidence; and the better substantiated is that explanation, the more justified the rejection of the coincident evidence. If five witnesses all say the same thing and we wish to reject their evidence, we are in general not justified in doing so unless we can explain why they all said the same thing. Such explanations could be that they were subject to common illusions, or all plotted together to give false testimony. The better substantiated is such an explanation the better justified is our rejection of the evidence. Substantiation of the theory of a common plot would be provided by evidence that the witnesses were all seen together before the event, that they stood to gain from giving false testimony etc. But ultimately the evidence rests on evidence about particular past events and would itself need to be substantiated in ways earlier described.

These subsidiary principles, and perhaps others which I have not described, then qualify the basic principle of accepting the majority of the evidence. They are the standards of investigation adopted, I would claim, by and large by all historical investigators.

However, those whose standards of historical evidence are by and large very similar may have *slightly* different standards, and with their slightly different standards may reach different conclusions about which way the balance of evidence tends. Such disputes will arise between people who in general accept the principles of evidence which I set forward, but who differ about the details or the interpretation of these principles, or the different weight to be given to each principle.

I stated the principles in a fairly general way which all would accept, but when we come down to details and interpretation differences are likely to arise. Thus I described the basic principle as that of accepting as many pieces of evidence as possible. But what constitutes one piece of evidence? Does each footprint constitute separate evidence of a man's presence, or is a set of footprints just one piece of evidence? Are fingerprints separate evidence from footprints? The subsidiary principles are also open to an enormous variety of interpretations—if I am absolutely convinced that I remember some event, how many pieces of confidently given testimony ought to make me abandon my claim? And how ought one to narrow the evidence class? Given that the class of all pieces of testimony made by Soviet diplomats the truth or falsity of which we can ascertain independently is too wide a class for ascertaining the value of Stamkovsky's testimony to an M.I.5 official, how shall we narrow it? Shall we choose the class of all pieces of testimony given to British counter-intelligence agents by Soviet diplomats the truth or falsity of which we can ascertain independently? Or the class of all pieces of testimony given by

Stamkovsky to anyone the truth of falsity of which we can ascertain independently? And so on.

In answer to these questions a number of standard examples can sometimes be provided which illustrate the correct application of the basic or subsidiary principles. We can give examples in detail of witnesses whose combined testimony ought to outweigh a firm claim to memory, of good and bad explanations of the occurrence of coincident but false evidence. Or further principles, which I shall term minor principles, can sometimes be provided which show how different kinds of evidence ought to be taken into account. Thus if in general we can show that the behavior of individuals in different circumstances is more of a pattern than is the behavior of members of a group in similar circumstances, that would show that the reliability of Stamkovsky's testimony to an M.I.5 official is better estimated by the reliability of Stamkovsky's testimony to anyone than by the reliability of the testimony of Soviet diplomats to British counter-intelligence agents. But how we apply this principle depends on what counts as "a group" and "similar circumstances." Further principles and examples could perhaps elucidate this. But there will be people who will dispute more generally accepted standards in some of these matters, disagreeing with our standard examples or minor principles. With regard to some minor principles or standard examples people may indeed be evenly divided—there may be no generally accepted standards. In such a case when the area of disagreement is fairly small argument can take place. Argument will consist in a man trying to show his opponent that the opponent's disputed principle coheres less well with commonly accepted principles of evidence than does a rival principle of his own; or that a standard example proffered by the opponent is importantly unlike the other standard examples on which both would agree. These points about the nature of argument in such cases will be confirmed by considering how people do and can argue about the principles in dispute crucial for our topic of miracles.

Principles for Assessing Conflicts between Evidence of the First Three Kinds and Evidence of the Fourth Kind

Bearing in mind these considerations about conflicting evidence and these principles for assessing different ways of weighing evidence, what are we to say when there is a conflict between evidence of the first three kinds that an event E occurred and evidence of the fourth kind that an event of the type of E is physically impossible? Hume's official answer, it will be recalled, was that exceedingly strong evidence of other kinds, in particular testimony, would be needed for evidence about physical impossibility to be outweighed. A more extreme answer is given by Antony Flew in a passage in his *Hume's Philosophy of Belief*.[2]

> The justification for giving the "scientific" this ultimate precedence here over the "historical" lies in the nature of the propositions concerned and in the evidence which can be displayed to sustain them . . . the candidate historical proposition will be particular, often singular, and in the past tense. . . . But just by reason of this very pastness and particularity it is no longer possible for anyone to examine the subject directly for himself . . . the law of nature will, unlike the candidate historical proposition, be a general nomological. It can thus in theory, though obviously not always in practice, be tested at any time by any person ([10] p.101).

Flew seems here to be taking the view that evidence of the fourth kind ("scientific" evidence) could never be outweighed by evidence of the first three kinds ("historical" evidence), an answer suggested also by Hume's detailed discussions of three purported miracles. Flew's justification for this view is that while a historical proposition concern a past event of which we have only the present remains (viz. evidence of the first three kinds), the scientific proposition, being a general statement (viz. about all entities of some kind at all times and places), can go on and on being tested by any person who wishes to test it. Flew's suggestion seems to be that the historical proposition cannot go on and on being tested by any person at any time.

If this is Flew's contrast, it is mistaken. Particular experiments on particular occasions only give a certain and far from conclusive support to claims that a purported scientific law is true. Any person can test for the truth of a purported scientific law, but a positive result to one test will give only limited support to the claim. Exactly the same holds for purported historical truths. Anyone can examine the evidence, but a particular piece of evidence gives only limited support to the claim that the historical proposition is true. But in the historical as in the scientific case, there is no limit to the testing which we can do. We can go on and on testing for the truth of historical as of scientific propositions. True, the actual traces, apparent memories and testimony, which I may term the direct evidence, available to an inquirer are unlikely to increase in number, at any rate after a certain time. Only so many witnesses will have seen the event in question and once their testimony has been obtained no more will be available. Further, it is an unfortunate physical fact, as we have noted, that many traces dissipate. But although the number of pieces of direct evidence about what happened may not increase, more and more evidence can be obtained about the reliability of the evidence which we have. One could show the evidence yielded by traces of certain types, or testimony given by witnesses of such-and-such character in such-and-such circumstances was always correct. This indirect evidence could mount up in just the way in which the evidence of the physical impossibility of an event could mount up. Hence by his examining the reliability of the direct evidence, the truth of the "historical" proposition like the "scientific" can also "be tested at any time by any person".

But if Flew's justification of his principle is mistaken, what can we say positively for or against the principle itself? Now I would urge that it is an unreasonable principle since claims that some formula L is a law of nature, and claims that apparent memory, testimony or traces of certain types are to be relied on are claims established ultimately in a similar kind of way (not exactly the same kind of way—a difference is discussed in note 2) and will be strong or weak for the same reasons, and so neither ought to take automatic preference over the other. To make the supposition that they are to be treated differently is to introduce a complicating *ad hoc* procedure for assessing evidence. As we have seen, formulae about how events succeed each other are shown to be laws of nature by the fact that they provide the most simple and coherent account of a large number of observed data. Likewise testimony given by certain kinds of people or traces of certain kinds are established as reliable by well-established correlations between present and past phenomena. (The reliability of apparent memory could also be assessed in the same way but we will ignore this for the moment, as important only for the few who claim to have observed miracles.) The reliability of C_{14} dating is established by showing that the postulated correlation between the proportion of C_{14} in artifacts and their age since manufacture clearly established by other methods holds of the large number of cases studied without exception and is the simplest correlation that does. That testimony given by Jones on oath is to be relied on is to be established by showing that whatever Jones said on oath is often by other methods shown to be true and never shown to be false, and there is no other simple account of the matter coherent with the data than that Jones tells the truth on oath (e.g., the account that in each of these cases he told the truth because he knew that a lie could be detected).

So then a claim that a formula L is a law of nature and a claim that testimony or trace of a certain type is reliable are established in basically the same way—by showing that certain formulae connect observed data in a simple coherent way. This being so, whether we take the evidence of an established law of nature that E did not occur or the evidence of trace or testimony that it did would seem to be a matter of the firmness with which the law, if reliable, forbids and the firmness with which the trace or testimony, if reliable, establishes the occurrence of E, and of the reliability of each. If the law is universal, it will firmly rule out an exception; if it is statistical, it will merely show an exception to be highly improbable. (On our understanding—see [8]—whatever, given a statistical law, is highly improbable is considered an exception to it.) Likewise traces or testimony may, in virtue of the correlation used, either show to be certain or show to be highly probable the event in question.

If the correlation between (e.g.) testimony of a certain kind of witness and the past event testified to is statistical (e.g. "witnesses of such and such a type are reliable in 99% cases") then it shows that the event in question (what the witness reported) having happened is highly probable. If the correlation is universal ("witnesses of such and such a type are invariably reliable") then it makes certain the occurrence of the event in question (viz. given the truth of the correlation, it is then certain that the event happened). So whether the evidence on balance supports or opposes the occurrence of E is firstly a matter of whether the law or correlation in question is universal or statistical in form. It is secondly a matter of how well established the law or correlation is: a statistical law may have very strong evidence in its favor. The basic laws of quantum theory are statistical in form but the evidence in their favor is enormously strong. On the other hand, some universal laws are, though established, not very strongly established. Such are, for example, many of the generalizations of biology or anthropology. If L is a law, universal or statistical, to which the occurrence of E would be an exception, and T is a trace or piece of testimony of the occurrence of E, shown to be such by an established correlation C, whether the evidence on balance supports or opposes the occurrence of E is a matter of whether L and C are universal or statistical, and how well established respectively are L and C.[2]

If C is universal and better established than L, then, surely, whether L is universal or statistical, the evidence on balance supports the occurrence of E; whereas if L is universal and is better established than C, then, whether C is universal or merely statistical, the evidence is against the occurrence of E. If C and L are both statistical, and C is no less well established than L, and C renders the occurrence of E more probable than L renders it improbable, then the evidence on balance supports the occurrence of E. If C and L are both statistical, and L is no less well established than C, and L renders the occurrence of E more improbable than C renders it probable, then the evidence on balance is against the occurrence of E. What we are to say in other cases depends on whether we can measure quantitatively how well established are C and L and compare these figures with the probability and the improbability which they respectively ascribe to E. How well established or confirmed are L or C is a matter of how well they (or the scientific theory of which they are part) integrate a large number of data into a simple and coherent pattern. Whether one can measure and how to measure quantitatively this

2. C correlates present events of some type with past events of some type and therefore cannot be a scientific law or part of a scientific theory, because the laws of science are necessarily forward-moving—they show the necessary consequents, not necessary antecedents of some present state. (For argument on this point, see my *Space and Time* (Macmillan, London, 2nd ed., 1981,) pp. 139, 148.) It is a consequence of this point that while we can test laws experimentally (viz. by producing an event and seeing whether the predicted event occurs subsequently), we cannot test correlations of the above type in this way. For they correlate a present event with a past event, and we cannot produce an event now in order to make a past event have happened. Yet although scientific laws can be tested experimentally, and correlations of the type in which we are interested can only be tested observationally (viz. by collecting observations), it does not follow that such correlations cannot be established with as great a degree of probability as scientific laws. For the only value of experiments (producing the relevant events ourselves instead of waiting for them to happen) is to secure particularly crucial observations, and there is no reason to suppose that we cannot secure equally crucial observations simply by waiting for them to happen. There may be practical difficulties in securing as good confirmation of correlations of present with past phenomena as of scientific laws, but there seems no reason to suppose that there are logical difficulties.

degree of confirmation of scientific laws and of generalizations are disputed issues. They are the subject of a branch of philosophy of science known as confirmation theory which has not yet yielded any results of the kind which we could apply to our concern.

In so far as we have several traces or pieces of testimony that E occurred, to that extent the evidence provided by traces and testimony will be very much the weightier. Suppose for example that we have traces or pieces of testimony T_1 and T_2 that E occurred, and that E if it occurred would be an exception to a universal law of nature L. T_1 is evidence that E occurred in virtue of a universal correlation C_1, and T_2 is evidence that E occurred in virgue of a universal correlation C_2. If L is true with no exceptions at all then E did not occur, but (given the existence of T_1 and T_2) if *either* C_1 or C_2 is true, then E did occur. It will be more likely that one of C_1 and C_2 is true than that C_1 is true or that C_2 is true. Hence T_1 and T_2 together produce more evidence in favor of E having occurred than does just one of them. It is clearly in virtue of such considerations that the principle of coincident evidence, which I cited earlier, holds. This is the principle that we should not reject coincident evidence that an event E occurred unless the evidence that E did not occur is extremely strong or an explanation can be given of the coincidence. Evidence that E did not occur would be extremely strong if L was very well supported and far better supported than any of the very few correlations $C_1 \ldots C_n$ adduced as evidence of the reliability of traces or testimony $T_1 \ldots T_n$ to the occurrence of E. Evidence that the coincident evidence is susceptible of another explanation is evidence of further traces and testimony backed by other correlations $C_{n+1} \ldots C_p$ that exceptional circumstances hold under which $T_1 \ldots T_n$ are not evidence that E occurred. But in general we assume (because $T_1 \ldots T_n$ being traces, it is highly likely) or have evidence that those circumstances do not hold.

It is not always easy even to compare the strength of support for various proposed laws or correlations, let alone measure such strength quantitatively. But, as we have seen, laws and correlations are supported in a similar kind of way by instances. Hence it seems reasonable to suppose that in principle the degree of support for any correlation C or disjunction of correlations could exceed the degree of support for any law and hence render it more probable than not that the cited event E occurred. Flew's principle can only be saved if we suppose that support for the C's and support for L are to be treated differently just because of the different role which the C's and L play in supporting or opposing the occurrence of E. But this seems to be to make a complicating, *ad hoc* supposition. Flew's principle advocates treating evidence for generalizations in a different way from the way in which we ordinarily treat it, and is therefore for this reason to be rejected.

It must however be admitted that in general any one correlation C will be less well established than L, and since L will usually be a universal law, its evidence will in general be preferred to that of C. However, the more pieces of evidence there are that E occurred (e.g., the testimony of many independent witnesses), the more such evidence by its cumulative effect will tend to outweigh the counter-evidence of L. This accounts for our previous third subsidiary principle.

Although we do not yet have any exact laws about the reliability of testimony of different kinds, we have considerable empirical information which is not yet precisely formulated. We know that witnesses with axes to grind are less to be relied on than witnesses with no stake in that to which they testify; that primitive people whose upbringing conditions them to expect unusual events are more likely to report the occurrence of unusual events which do not occur than are modern atheists (perhaps too that modern atheists are more likely to deny the occurrence of unusual events which in fact occur in their environment than are primitive people); and so on.

I venture to suggest that generalizations of this kind about the reliability of testimony, although statistical in character, are extremely well established, perhaps better established than many laws of nature. However it must be added that while we can construct wide and narrow generalizations about the reliability of contemporary witnesses which are well confirmed, generalizations about the reliability of past witnesses will be more shaky, for we have less information about them and it is in practice often difficult to obtain more.

Now, although we are in no position yet (if ever we will be) to work out numerically the degree or balance of support for a violation E of a law of nature L having taken place, since *a priori* objections have been overruled, we can surely cite examples where the combined testimony of many witnesses to such an event is in the light of the above considerations to be accepted.

One interesting such example is given by Hume himself:

> Thus, suppose, all authors in all languages agree, that, from the first of January 1600, there was a total darkness over the whole earth for eight days: suppose that the tradition of this extraordinary event is still strong and lively among the people: that all travellers, who return from foreign countries, bring us accounts of the same tradition, without the least variation or contradiction: it is evident, that our present philosophers, instead of doubting the fact, ought to receive it as certain, and ought to search for the causes whence it might be derived ([3] p. 37).

Hume unfortunately spoils this example by going on to suggest that such an event, although extraordinary, is not physically impossible, since

> The decay, corruption, and dissolution of nature, is an event rendered probable by so many analogies, that any phenomenon, which seems to have a tendency towards that catastrophe, comes within the reach of human testimony, if that testimony be very extensive and uniform. ([3] p. 37).

We with our knowledge of natural laws, in particular the laws of meteorology and the Earth's motion, would not judge the matter in this way, but would surely judge the event to be physically impossible. Indeed Hume originally introduced it as an example of "violations of the usual course of nature, of such a kind as to admit proof from human testimony" ([3] p. 37). (He allowed in theory, it will be remembered, that there could be such, "though, perhaps, it will be impossible to find any such in all the records of history.") The example is similar to many which might be artifically constructed in which the amount, diversity and detail of testimony to the occurrence of E surely suffices to overwhelm any information provided by science that E is physically impossible.

The Weight of Apparent Memory

The argument of the preceding pages is that we can assess any testimony or trace of the past on evidence of the reliability of testimony or traces of similar kind. It suggests that we can assess our own apparent memory, or claims to knowledge of our own past experience, by similar tests. It suggests also that any apparent memory of having observed some event E has to be weighed against any other evidence that E did not occur, and that sufficient of the latter could always outweigh the former.

There is an argument against all this by Holland [6] who proposes another principle for assessing evidence, the adoption of which would mean that evidence could on balance easily be favorable to the occurrence of a violation of a law of nature. This is the principle that sometimes evidence of apparent memory is strong enough (quite apart from evidence of its reliability) to outweigh any rival evidence, for sometimes, according to Holland, we can know incorrigibly (viz. in such a way that nothing could count against our claim to knowledge) what we observed on a particular occasion. Holland does not give any rules for distinguishing occasions where we know incorrigibly what happens (whatever science etc. may tell us about what can or cannot happen)—e.g., how long ago our incorrigible knowledge can extend, how familiar we have to be with the subject matter etc. He would probably say that sometimes we just do know and realize that we know incorrigibly and that is all there is to it. Holland claims that unless we do say this, "a distinction gets blurred which is at least as important as the distinction between a law and a hypothesis—namely the distinction between a hypothesis and a fact. The distinction between my saying when I come across an infant who is screaming and writhing and holding his ear 'he's got an abscess' and my making this statement after looking into the ear, whether by means of an instrument or without, and actually seeing, coming across the abscess" ([6] p. 61).

The only argument that I know of to support the claim that we know some truths about the physical world incorrigibly, that some judgments of observations which we report cannot possibly be mistaken, is that given by Holland ([6] p. 61) that "if there were not things of this kind of which we can be certain we wouldn't be able to be uncertain of anything either." This argument is given more fully by Norman Malcolm in his *Knowledge and Certainty* (Englewood Cliffs, N.J.: Prentice-Hall, 1963), pp. 66–72. Malcolm claims (p. 69) that "in order for it to be possible that any statements about physical things should *turn out to be false* it is necessary that some statements about physical things *cannot* turn out to be false." By "statements about physical things" Malcolm means empirical statements, statements about the world (as opposed to, e.g., statements of mathematics) other than statements about mental states (e.g., the statement that I am now experiencing a pain). I can only consider, he claims, e.g., who did a murder, if there are some physical things about which I cannot be mistaken, e.g., that Jones had blood on his hands. The latter is a fact, the former an hypothesis. Only if there are facts, the argument goes, can I consider hypotheses.

This argument seems mistaken. Certainly for argument, discussion, inference to take place about physical things, there must be some statements about physical things of which we are at present with reason highly confident, and other statements about physical things of which we are more doubtful. Then using the former as premises, we can discuss the truth of the latter. In this context we treat the former statements as statements of facts and the latter as hypotheses. But all this is quite compatible with the claim that anything taken for granted in one discussion could be seriously questioned in another discussion. In a new discussion what was previously not open to question could be treated as an hypothesis and evidence could be adduced for and against it. A historian may take it for granted in general in discussing ancient history that Trajan became emperor in A.D. 98 but if another historian presents arguments against this assertion, then it in its turn could be discussed. The argument that argument can only take place about physical things and hypotheses about them be rejected if we know some physical things incorrigibly is mistaken.

Given that this particular argument fails, the question remains whether I can ever rightly treat something as a fact if I alone claim to have observed it, its occurrence is apparently physically impossible, and there is no evidence to show the reliability of my memory. My own view is that our standards of evidence are unclear here, that some people would certainly stand by some of their apparent memories despite any amount of counter-evidence and that other people would not and that there are no relevant commonly accepted standards to which members of the two groups can appeal to decide who is right. Thus consider an example of Holland's:

Suppose that a horse, which has been normally born and reared, and is now deprived of all nourishment (we could be completely certain of this)—suppose that, instead of dying this horse goes on thriving (which is again something we could be completely certain about). A series of thorough examinations reveals no abnormality in the horse's condition: its digestive system is always found to be working and to be at every moment in more or less the state it would have if the horse had eaten a meal an hour or two before. ([6] p. 64)

Now if only one observer is involved can he really be certain (even without evidence on the reliability of his own memory) that the horse is not being surreptitiously fed? It is not clear, nor is it clear how we can settle whether he can be certain. But if the testimony of others comes in as well as apparent memory (many others claim to have watched the horse in turn day and night), then surely a man can be sure that the horse has not been fed, and so that a law of nature has been violated. (This latter may be Holland's claim in the particular example. Whether he is considering only one observer or many observers who give testimony to each other is unclear from his paper.)

So I conclude that although standards for weighing evidence are not always clear, apparent memory, testimony and traces could sometimes outweigh the evidence of physical impossibility. It is just a question of how much evidence of the former kind we have and how reliable we can show it to have been. Hume's general point must be admitted, that we should accept the historical evidence, viz. a man's apparent memory, the testimony of others and traces, only if the falsity of the latter would be 'more miraculous,' i.e., more improbable 'than the event *which* he relates". However, my whole discussion in this chapter has ignored "background evidence." In so far as there is substantial other evidence in favor of the existence of God, less would be required in the way of historical evidence in favor of the occurrence of a miracle than this chapter has supposed hitherto. If we have already good grounds for believing that there is a gorilla loose in snowy mountains, we require less by way of evidence of footprints to show that he has visited a particular place. Conversely, if there is substantial evidence against the existence of God, more is required in the way of historical evidence in favor of the occurrence of a miracle than this chapter has supposed—for we have then substantial evidence for supposing that nothing apart from laws of nature determines what happens.

14

TERENCE PENELHUM*

∽୧୬∽

Petitionary Prayer

∽୧୬∽

THE STAGE IS now set for a discussion of the very complex question of the relation between belief in the reign of natural law and belief in the efficacy of prayer. Christians are enjoined to pray, and at least some of the prayers they offer are prayers for things to happen. Unless such procedures are thought to be efficacious, it is hypocritical to engage in them. But surely if they are efficacious, it must be possible that God intervenes in nature from time to time in such a way that something happens that would not have happened unless the prayer had been addressed to him. And does this not mean that the processes of natural law that would normally be operative over phenomena of the sort prayed for are set aside?

Prayer and Miracle

This is very close to the issue of the possibility of miracle in a law-abiding world, but it is not quite identical, because sometimes Christians would want to say that a prayer has been efficacious even though the event prayed for happened in accordance with natural law. In fact it is probable that the majority of cases of alleged answers to prayer fall into this category. And this category is not that of miracle. Yet clearly sometimes what is prayed for is prayed for because it seems

*Chapter 20 of his *Religion and Rationality* (New York: Random House, 1971).

153

otherwise unlikely to happen (for example, the recovery of a desperately ill patient); and this makes it very probable indeed that the suppliant is asking that something should happen even if its happening would involve a violation of natural law. Prayers, then, often seem to involve, if not direct requests for miracles, at least direct requests for happenings which might, for all the suppliant knows, be miraculous if they were to occur. The request is made subject to the will of God; but it would be very specious to suggest that this is intended to coincide with some such notion as "subject to the laws of nature." So it is hard to see how someone who does not believe that there are any miracles can believe in the efficacy of prayer, unless "efficacy" is tendentiously defined.

There are two other, less serious, differences between miracles and answered prayers. First, I suggested above that it is conceptually necessary that miracles be relatively rare occurrences. It certainly seems that believers would suppose answered prayers to be far more frequent occurrences than miracles are. This is a minor difference, however, since all that matters for our present purposes is the fact that only some alleged instances of answers to prayer are also alleged instances of miracles. But this would be a major difference if it were held that answers to prayer that are violations of natural law are frequent. The delicate differences I have tried to sketch between miraculous events (if any) and apparent natural anomalies would no doubt vanish if believers were committed to the expectation of frequent miracles—hence the absurdity of the notion. Similarly, if believers were committed to the expectation of frequent violations of natural law as answers to prayer, the world they thought they lived in and the world the skeptic believed himself to inhabit would be very different indeed. So even if the suggestion that there might be frequent violations of natural law is not the absurdity it appears to be, I shall assume in what follows that believers would regard divine intervention in nature in response to prayer as rare. Second, I have written as though the purpose of a miracle must be more or less pedagogical; yet men may think their prayers are answered without feeling that God's beneficence to them has been confined to this purpose or that it has even perhaps included it. I think in this case the best recourse is to suggest that the point of a miracle may not be pedagogical; or to say that all acts of divine beneficence are also acts of teaching. Consequently I shall speak in what follows as though someone who says that a prayer is answered by the occurrence of some event that involves the violation of natural law is saying that his prayer has been answered by a miracle.

When the point is put this way, any difficulty there may be about those answers to prayer that are thought to be miraculous is the same difficulty we face about combining a belief in miracles with a belief in natural law. I shall say no more about this, except to repeat that a belief in the efficacy of prayer does seem to entail a belief in the (occasional) occurrence of miracles. Perhaps the belief that something someone has prayed for would violate natural law is a reason for thinking that God might not grant his request. Perhaps also if that person believes that an answer to his prayer would violate natural law, this is a reason for not praying for this event to happen. But in neither case need it be a conclusive reason. For the fact is that men are enjoined to pray for things that at least sometimes seem very unlikely to happen, and this fact logically suggests that God might grant the request even when the things prayed for would not happen at all in the normal course of events that God has laid down.

The problem of petitionary prayer now has to take a different turn. Instead of concentrating our attention on miraculous answers to prayer, we should consider the case of alleged answers to prayer that are not also alleged to be miracles. Surely if they were the outcome of natural causes there is no point in anyone's having prayed for them. Would they not have happened anyway? (We can leave aside the special case of those events that occur as a result of natural causes which include the performance of praying itself. They are only of interest as possible instances where prayer might have been causally effective without being efficacious in the theological sense, that is, without having been *answered*.) Is there not some absurdity in saying that the events had natural causes and yet were answers to prayer?

The Purpose of Prayer

Before dealing with this question it is necessary to deal with sophisticated attempts to evade it. Such suggestions take the form of arguing that, properly understood, prayer is not petitionary. It may appear petitionary, but this is a mere surface relic from a prescientific age. This view is espoused by T. R. Miles.[1] It need not be extended, although Miles does extend it, to include a denial that prayer is a form of actual or intended communication with God. Whether or not one wants to extend the thesis this far will depend on whether or not one wishes to desupernaturalize one's theism to the extent that one rejects the very notion of a divine individual who could hear the prayers addressed to him. Even if one did not extend the thesis this far, one might hold, for example, that prayers are not really petitions but some other form of address. Many prayers are, for example, prayers of thanksgiving.

Miles, who does reject the belief in a divine individual, takes as the paradigm of prayer the sentence "Thy will be done," interpreting it as some sort of self-directed performative utterance. He regards it as an attempt by means of a linguistic device to induce an attitude or resignation in oneself, perhaps after the manner of ancient Stoicism. It is hard to see how such a device could be effective unless it carried with it the associations that accrue to it from a less sophisticated tradition—presumably some belief in the power of this utterance to do something toward bringing about some action of the deity if the deity so chooses. It is also hard to see how anyone who took this view of the practice of prayer would wish to recommend its continuance when so many who practice it seem to do so for what would seem to be confused or mistaken reasons. This difficulty is merely one more instance of the emptiness of the claim that such desupernaturalized versions of Christianity are defenses of it rather than thinly disguised recommendations to replace it by something else. While the spiritual stance required for prayer is undoubtedly regarded as of primary value within the Christian tradition, the reasons that tradition offers for this evaluation of it could not be sincerely countenanced by a desupernaturalized world view. The traditional reasons for valuing spiritual prayer are the need for man to recognize his dependence upon God and his need to submit to the divine will. A willingness to submit without prideful complaint to *what happens*, rather than to what *God wills*, is not a Christian state of mind at all, even if what happens is in fact the will of God. And if one does not believe that there is a God who wills anything, to recommend that men should behave

1. See T. R. Miles, *Religion and the Scientific Outlook* (London: Allen & Unwin, 1959).

toward the world as if they did believe this because it is somehow good for them to do so and should reinforce this behavior by engaging in rituals that used to be followed because men did believe this is to infer from one's theory of religion a rule of conduct which is, at best, a form of deliberate self-deception which would be rendered unsuccessful by the acceptance of the very theory it is based upon.

But Miles' suggestion is worth examining because it might be made by someone who did believe that God is a supernatural individual, either because of alleged difficulties about natural law or for theological reasons. Such a person might hold that Miles' paradigmatic "Thy will be done" is indeed the proper paradigm of prayer, rather than the self-seeking or childlike request for things to happen. It is easy enough to find theologically respectable grounds for emphasizing the submissive aspects of prayer or for stressing that prayer is a form of thanksgiving as well as a form of request, and these forms of prayer do not run into snags about natural law. One also finds occasional arguments to the effect that it is prideful or impertinent, if not even logically absurd, to think that a man could change God's mind about the future course of events in the world by asking that they take place in one way rather than another, since God's plans must already be better than any that his creatures could have the temerity to recommend to him.

A few brief comments must be added before we return to the compatibility of a belief in the efficacy of prayer and a belief in the reign of natural law. I propose to take it as a datum that the tradition whose logical character we are examining throughout is one in which petitionary prayer is not merely tolerated, but required. In this tradition men are enjoined to take their wishes and needs to God. All the normative documents of the tradition contain clear injunctions to its adherents to engage in petitionary prayer and contain, moreover, many such prayers. The obvious and basic case is the Lord's Prayer itself, which is, apart from the often omitted "For thine is the Kingdom, the power and the glory, for ever and ever," a series of such petitions. This includes, as Peter Geach has correctly pointed out, "Thy will be done."[2] This is not just a verbal gesture of submission, though it can function in this way from time to time. It is a request

---

2. Peter Geach, "Praying for Things to Happen," in *God and the Soul* (London: Routledge & Kegan Paul, 1969), p. 86.

that the petitioner himself be enabled to submit to God's will when it does not coincide with his own inclinations and a request that men in general, including the petitioner, should follow the injunctions to conduct that the Christian tradition lays upon them. This is not to say that the only purpose of prayer is to ask for changes in the course of nature. Nor is it to deny that there is bound to be some tension in the petitioner between asking for what he wishes to happen and submitting to the will of God when it does not in fact coincide with his wishes. Nor is it, consequently, to say that the concept of an answer to prayer is adequately analyzable in terms of God arranging the course of the world so that what the petitioner asks for comes about. It is merely to say that men are enjoined, in the Christian tradition, to place their wishes before God in the form of requests which God may (because of his grace, not their right) grant; and to say that God answers the prayers that they place before him must include the claim that on some occasions he does so arrange the course of events that it turns out in the way the petitioners request, in part *because* they so request it.[3]

This last point seems to some to smack of presumption or even absurdity. If it does, then so does the tradition of which the procedure of offering prayers is at the heart. We can say a little more than this, however. We must recall from our discussions of the problem of evil (earlier in *Religion and Rationality*) that the scheme of values that the Christian tradition ascribes to God is one in which human free choice has a uniquely high place or at the very least is a logically necessary condition of states of mind and forms of conduct that are highly valued. I have already suggested that some form of libertarian view of human choice seems to be required by this, if only to maintain the "freewill defense" and that it is a more natural framework in which to understand certain key elements in our moral discourse.

---

3. There seems no obvious reason for holding that such an interpretation of petitionary prayer is a form of superstitition or belief in magic. Such notions apply rather to cases where the suppliant considers he can influence God or place him under an obligation, or where he regards the mouthing of prayers as in themselves efficacious after the manner of spells or incantations. It at least needs to be shown that a request that is not analyzable as something else must, if addressed to God, be on a level with such performances. Emphasis on the special context of religiously genuine prayers need not efface the distinction between the one and the other. Although I may misunderstand, it seems to me to do this in the case of the discussion of petitionary prayer in D. Z. Phillips, *The Concept of Prayer* (London: Routledge & Kegan Paul, 1965), Chapter 6.

This implies that we cannot properly think of the created order as one in which a divine plan is worked out inexorably, detail by detail, without free human participation or free human opposition. Although human freedom may not prevent the fulfillment of broad divine purposes, if men are free they can do other than God wishes them to do and thus frustrate the divine will over details. This freedom, and in consequence this power, is accorded to them by God's choice to make them free agents. One form of free action in which they can engage or refuse to engage, as they choose, is prayer. If prayer is enjoined in the tradition, then praying is something that God wishes them to do, although they may not do it. And like all the acts God enjoins men to do, they can not only do it or not do it, they can do it as he wishes them to do it or in some selfish and perverted way.

Insofar as prayer includes requests for things to happen, three consequences follow. First, men may or may not pray for something to happen, or may pray for good or bad things to happen, or may pray for things to happen for good or bad reasons. For God to create free agents with the power to pray or not is for him to create agents who may act in any of these ways. Second, if something comes to pass because someone has prayed for it, then it comes to pass because of an action that they might very well not have done or might have done differently. Third, just as free actions in the world have natural consequences that would not have come about unless those actions had been done, so events that are answers to prayer might not have come about unless the prayers had been offered.[4] In giving men the freedom to pray, God would not have given them a pointless freedom. And in giving them freedom to pray, God has created a world in which he takes their freely expressed wishes into account in directing nature's course, just as they can take one another's requests into account in their actions. Whatever analyses we may offer of the intractable notion of possibility here, it is idle to suggest that prayers would be answered in a world in which it is not possible for things to happen differently if a man does pray from the way they would happen if he did not. So the fact that God creates free beings who share with him the power to direct the course of events by their free choices frees from absurdity (though it does not entail) the statement that he ex-

---

4. I do not refer here, of course, to cases where one can plausibly connect the act of praying itself with subsequent events as natural cause and effect.

tends their freedom to include the possibility of his being influenced in the way he directs the world by the requests that they can direct to him if they choose. His omnipotence and wisdom is not put into question by such a statement, since it merely entails that he gives them some of the freedom, and puts at their service some of the power, which otherwise would belong exclusively to him.[5]

Natural Events as Answers to Prayer

We can now return to our earlier question. Is there any absurdity in saying that some event is both the answer to a prayer and is due to natural causes? On the assumption that the last phrase implies that the event took place in accordance with some natural law, does not the fact that it had natural causes mean that it would have taken place even if the prayer had not been offered?

I have argued that belief in the efficacy of prayer entails that the suppliant must be able, without absurdity or presumption, to request something that might turn out to be a miracle, for all he knows. Many prayers (again one thinks naturally of prayers for the recovery of the sick) are offered in circumstances where the situation seems hopeless except for the possibility of a special answer to prayer, and it is unfortunately easy enough to find circumstances in which the prayer for daily bread or freedom from temptation is one that seems similarly hopeless. But in spite of this it would certainly be objectionable to say to someone who has prayed for something that has later happened, apparently in accordance with natural law and not in violation of it, that there was no need for him to have prayed. He may insist that his prayers have been answered by the event. Must he be committed to holding that natural causes were not sufficient to have produced it? The temptation to say so comes from the fact that the acceptance of a natural explanation entails the acceptance that the event would have taken place even if the prayers had not been offered at all. This is clear, except in the special and uninteresting cases where some natural connection can be found between the offering of the prayer itself and the occurrence of the event. What needs to be scrutinized is the further assumption that if the event would have happened anyway it is for this reason not an answer to prayer.

5. It would seem to require independent argument, therefore, to show that a positive answer to a prayer must always be in the best interest of the suppliant. Such independent argument is no doubt easy to supply, but not relevant here.

Professor Geach, in his interesting essay on this theme, points out that "To say that God brought something about because of a man's prayers is not at all to say that, once the prayers had been said, God could not but grant them; for this is not at all what we mean when we use similar language about petitions men address to other men."[6] This seems unexceptionable and entails that if God answers prayers, the offering of them is only a logically necessary condition of their being answered. He goes on, however, to suggest that if a prayer is answered or if, as he puts it, God brings something about because he is asked, then it cannot be the case that he would have brought it about even if he had not been asked. He bases this conclusion on the argument that if one person does something because another asks him, this entails that he would not have done it unless that other person had asked him. He continues: "The upshot is that if we are to be justified in saying that a state of affairs S came about from somebody's impetratory prayer, then at the time of the prayer S must have had two-way contingency: it could come about, it could also not come about."[7] I will return to his development of the notion of two-way contingency shortly. For the moment, however, let us look at the argument that has led to Geach's use of it. I must begin by echoing his unease over the necessity to use notions like "might not have happened" and "could have happened," which, as our brief discussion of free will is enough to make clear, are notoriously difficult to analyze. But here one has to use them.

If the event would have taken place even if the petitioner had not prayed for it to take place, then, let us say, God would have brought it about even if he had not been asked to, since the operation of natural law is the normal operation of God's creation. It follows from this that God did not bring the event about *only* because he was asked. Does it also follow that he did not bring about the event because he was asked? If someone asks me to give him a lift home, and I do, and I had planned to do so whether he had asked me or not, is it the case that I gave him a lift because he asked me, or is it the case that I did not give him a lift because he asked me? Surely neither is quite right as it stands. What we would say would depend on whether or not I would have given him a lift, once asked, even if I had *not* intended to do so otherwise. Though it is often hard to decide whether or not this is so, the suggestion that it is so makes sense and may be true

6. Geach, *op. cit.* p. 87.
7. Ibid., p. 89.

sometimes and not at other times. When it is not true, it is also not true that I gave him a lift because he asked me. For the latter to have been true, I would have had to consider his request a sufficient reason in itself for doing the action, and it was not. But the fact that I would have had to regard his request as a sufficient reason for the action does not mean that I would have had to regard it as the only sufficient reason that such an action could have or that there was no other sufficient reason actually present. Human choices are sometimes made with a superabundance of reasons. At such a time it is artificial and misleading to single out one of them and say that it was *the* reason. But if the agent would have regarded it as sufficient even if there had not been the others, then it is not mistaken to say that the action was done because of it. It is merely misleading to interpret this last phrase to mean "only because of it." If his asking me for the ride would have been enough by itself, then although it is false that his asking me was the only reason I had, it is not false that I granted his request because he asked me. If I only gave him the lift because of the other reasons that prompted me, and would not have done so if they had been absent and he had asked me, then although I did what he asked, I did not do it because he asked, and he would be deceiving himself if he said without qualification that I had granted his request. I might make this clear by telling him that I am only doing it for those other reasons.

I would suggest that it is proper for the theist to say that prayers are answered in one of two cases: either when the event in question would not have taken place at all unless the prayer had been offered—the case of a miraculous answer to prayer—or when the event would have taken place even if the prayer had not been offered, but where the offering of the prayer would have been enough for the deity to have brought the event about had natural causes not already been sufficient. (I make no comment on how the theist could ever be sure which situation obtained. He does not need to be sure.) In the latter case God will necessarily have a superabundance of reasons for bringing that event about, whereas in the former he may not have more than one reason. Another way of expressing the same point is to say that God's act is a manifold one. Just as a human action can be at one and the same time the composition of a letter, the replying to a friend, the fulfillment of an obligation, the enriching of the postmaster, and the unburdening of one's heart; so God's bringing about an event can be the unfolding of the progress of nature, the watering of the crops, and the answer to a prayer. Although if it is several things at once, it is false that it is *only* one of them, it is also false that if it is several at once it is *not at all* one of them.

I have one further suggestion that I would offer only tentatively. One instinctively feels that cases of answered prayer that are in accordance with natural law must be more frequent than cases that are violations of it—if, that is, any prayers are answered at all. This is partly because of the necessary rarity of miracles. It is also because there seems no absurdity in the belief that if prayers are ever answered many are. Now if the above argument is sound, to say that a prayer is answered in the natural course of things is to say that the supplication would have been sufficient for God to bring it about even if this would have involved a miracle. What theological reason could there be, in this situation, for any greater frequency of law-abiding answers over law-violating ones? One possible answer is that God anticipates our free requests in the very structure of creation, that is, in natural law itself.

It is difficult, however, to give an acceptable meaning to this. It could mean that human actions, including prayers, are themselves the outcome of natural causes, and that natural causes determine that some of the things asked for in some of the prayers happen to come to pass. This, however, would subsume human actions under natural law, and we have seen both theological and nontheological reasons for refusing to accept that this is compatible with their being designated as free. Another interpretation, however, is that the laws of nature have been so contrived by God that they sometimes provide for the occurrence of the very events that men will in fact (though not by necessity) pray for. Such intricate provision does not seem, in general terms, beyond the scope of omnipotence and omniscience combined. It unfortunately carries the suggestion that men's future actions are in some way fixed and subject to scrutiny from on high before they are done. This suggestion has to be expunged.

There are at least two ways to do this. One is to deny that divine foreknowledge entails any lack of freedom. In other words, even if God knows from all eternity that (for example) Jones will freely pray for X at time T, it is still true that at time T-minus-one Jones *can* refrain from praying for T—it is just that God knows which he will pray for and can so arrange the laws of nature that T will happen. For reasons I shall argue briefly later, I do not think this will do as a general rubric for the discussion of divine foreknowledge and human freedom. For the present I shall merely say that if this were suggested, there would seem no absurdity in the further suggestion that this is how God answers all successful petitionary prayers. Yet this would seem to contradict what I have argued for above, that a petitioner might pray without absurdity for something that he does not believe the operation of natural causes can bring about. On the view now suggested, his being entitled to do this would be necessarily connected with his ignorance of the real operation of natural law. The other way of denying the suggestion that men's actions are predetermined by God is to suggest that in giving men freedom of choice, God makes it genuinely *uncertain* what they will do, and in consequence (since men's actions are uncertain before they happen) even he does not know what their actions will be before they do them. Yet the fact that Jones' doing A rather than B is never *certain* before it happens does not show that his doing A is *no more likely* than his doing B before it happens. If this is true, there is nothing absurd about the suggestion that the laws incorporate answers to *likely* prayers. And since it seems necessarily true that more likely things happen than unlikely ones, we have a good reason for expecting that a majority of likely acceptable prayers will in fact be offered and can thus be provided for.

I do not think, therefore, that we need adopt Professor Geach's view that no petitionary prayer can be answered by the occurrence of an event that would have happened even if the prayer had not been offered. On the other hand, the acceptance of the thesis that the prayer must be sufficient reason for its occurrence even though not a necessary one does mean we must accept his claim that at the time of praying the event prayed for must have a "two-way contingency," that is, it might or might not come about. This, on the view I have offered, has to mean that at the time it is offered, the petitioner and anyone who believes in the efficacy of prayer must think it possible that it be responded to by a miracle if only a miracle would do.

Geach, however, interprets two-way contingency much more strongly. He first of all argues that it must mean that no one can pray for a change in what is past. Since there clearly seems to be a logical absurdity in stating that something that has happened will after all turn out not to have happened, it seems equally absurd to request it, and it is hard to see that such a view needs his ammunition to attack it. He argues further, however, that a future issue "cannot be thus contingent if, miracles apart, it is already determined in its causes." In order to allow for the possibility of petitionary prayer he then is forced to argue that the sphere of real contingency is very wide, and that it is false that in the realm of natural causes events are "in principle' predictable." Many readers would certainly wish to accept the thesis that natural events, if subject to natural law at all, are in principle predictable and do not have the sort of contingency he ascribes to them. They are not necessarily right in this, but to insist that they must be wrong would be to rest the case for the possibility of prayer on the continuance of our present inability to predict as much as we would like. The thesis I have tried to present is that some case for the possibility of petitionary prayer can be made out that is consistent with the conviction of the predictability of natural events, provided the possibility of miracle is not excluded also. If it is not excluded, then no third area of natural contingency is required. This is not to say there *is* none; only that it is not theologically requisite to insist that there is. I will not therefore follow Geach into his defense of it, since if the above arguments are sound petitionary prayer and sufficient natural causation are not incompatible.

15

ELEONORE STUMP*

Petitionary Prayer

ORDINARY CHRISTIAN BELIEVERS of every period have in general taken prayer to be fundamentally a request made of God for something specific believed to be good by the one praying. The technical name for such prayer is "impetration"; I am going to refer to it by the more familiar designation "petitionary prayer." There are, of course, many important kinds of prayer which are not requests; for example, most of what is sometimes called "the higher sort of prayer"—praise, adoration, thanksgiving—does not consist in requests and is not included under petitionary prayer. But basic, common petitionary prayer poses problems that do not arise in connection with the more contemplative varieties of prayer, and it is petitionary prayer with its special problems that I want to examine in this paper.

As much as possible I want to concentrate on just one problem[1]. It is, I think, the problem stemming from petitionary prayer which has most often occurred to ordinary Christian believers from the Patristic period to the present. Discussion of it can be found, for ex-

*American Philosophical Quarterly, 1979, 16: 81–91.

1. Issues I intend to avoid include Peter Geach's worries about prayer for events in the past in God and the Soul (Routledge and Kegan Paul, London, 1969), pp. 89ff., and about "certain tensed propositions about the divine will . . . in connexion with prayer" (op. cit., p. 97).

ample, in Origen's third-century treatise on prayer,[2] in various writings of Aquinas,[3] and, very recently, in a book by Keith Ward.[4]

Put roughly and succinctly, the problem comes to this: is a belief in the efficacy and usefulness of petitionary prayer consistent with a belief in an omniscient, omnipotent, perfectly good God? It is, therefore, a problem only on certain assumptions drawn from an ordinary, orthodox, traditional view of God and of petitionary prayer. If one thinks, for example, as D. Z. Philipps does,[5] that all "real" petitionary prayer is reducible to the petition "Thy will be done," then the problem I want to discuss evaporates. And if one thinks of God as the unknowable, non-denumerable, ultimate reality, which is not an entity at all, as Keith Ward does,[6] the problem I am interested in does not even arise. The cases which concern me in this paper are those in which someone praying a petitionary prayer makes a specific request freely (at least in his own view) of an omniscient, omnipotent, perfectly good God, conceived of in the traditional orthodox way. I am specifying that the prayers are made freely because I want to discuss this problem on the assumption that man has free will and that not everything is predetermined. I am making this assumption, first because I want to examine the problem of petitionary prayer as it arises for ordinary Christian believers, and I think their understanding of the problem typically includes the assumption that man has free will, and secondly because adopting the opposite view enormously complicates the attempt to understand and justify petitionary prayer. If all things are predetermined—and worse, if they are all predetermined by the omnipotent and omniscient God to whom one is praying—it is much harder to conceive of a satisfactory justification for petitionary prayer. One consequence of my making this assumption is that I will not be drawing on important traditional Protestant accounts of prayer such as those given by Calvin and Luther, for instance, since while they may be thoughtful, in-

2. Eric George Jay, *Origen's Treatise on Prayer* (S.P.C.K. London, 1954), vols. V–VI, pp. 92—103.

3. Most notably, *Summa theologiae*, 2a–2ae, 83, 1–17; *Summa contra gentiles*, I.III. 95–96; *In IV. Sent.*, dist. XV, q. 4, a. 1.

4. *The Concept of God* (Blackwell, Oxford, 1974), pp. 221–22. Ward introduces the problem only as an embarrassment for what he calls "Thomistic" theology. *Cf* my review in *The Philosophical Review*, vol. 86 (1977), pp. 398–404.

5. *The Concept of Prayer* (Routledge and Kegan Paul, London, 1965), pp. 112 ff.

6. *Cf. The Concept of God op. cit.*, pp. 62, 101, 111, 185.

teresting accounts, they assume God's complete determination of everything.

I think that I can most effectively and plausibly show the problem which interests me by presenting a sketchy analysis of the Lord's Prayer. It is a prayer attributed to Christ himself, who is supposed to have produced it just for the purpose of teaching his disciples how they ought to pray. So it is an example of prayer which orthodox Christians accept as a paradigm, and it is, furthermore, a clear instance of petitionary prayer. Consequently, it is a particularly good example for my purposes. In what follows, I want to make clear, I am not concerned either to take account of contemporary Biblical exegesis or to contribute to it. I want simply to have a look at the prayer—in fact, at only half the prayer—as it is heard and prayed by ordinary twentieth-century Christians.

As the prayer is given in Luke 11, it contains seven requests. The last four have to do with the personal needs of those praying, but the first three are requests of a broader sort.

The first, "Hallowed be thy name," is commonly taken as a request that God's name be regarded as holy.[7] I am not sure what it means to regard God's name as holy, and I want to avoid worries about the notion of having attitudes towards God's *name*. All the same, I think something of the following sort is a sensible interpretation of the request. The common Biblical notion of holiness has at its root a sense of strong separateness.[8] And it may be that to regard God's name as holy is only to react to it very differently from the way in which one reacts to any other name—and that could happen because it seems specially precious or also (for example) because it seems specially feared. On this understanding of the request, it would be fulfilled if everyone (or almost everyone) took a strongly emotional and respectful attitude towards God's name. But it may be that this is too com-

7. *Cf.*, for example, the similar understanding of this petition in two very different theologians: Augustine, *Homilies on the Gospels*, Serm. 6; and Calvin, *Institutes of the Christian Religion*, III. xx. 41.

8. The most common Old Testament word for "holy" and its correlates is some form of "kādash," the basic, literal meaning of which is separation, withdrawal, or state of being set apart; *cf.* Gesenius, *A Hebrew and English Lexicon of the Old Testament*. In the New Testament, the most frequently used word is "hagiazō" and its correlates, the basic meaning of which also includes the notion of being separate and being set apart; *cf.* Thayer, *A Greek-English Lexicon of the New Testament*, and Arndt and Gringich, *A Greek-English Lexicon of the New Testament and Other Early Christian Literature*.

plicated as an interpretation of the request, and that to regard God's name as holy is simply to love and revere it. In that case, the request is fulfilled if everyone or almost everyone regards God's name very reverentially. And there are New Testament passages which foretell states of affairs fulfilling both these interpretations of the request— prophesying a time at or near the end of the world when all men fear or love God's name, and a time when the inhabitants of earth are all dedicated followers of God.[9]

The second request in the Lord's Prayer is that God's kingdom come. Now according to orthodox Judaeo-Christian beliefs, God is and always has been ruler of the world. What then does it mean to ask for the advent of his kingdom? Plainly, there is at least some sense in which the kingdom of heaven has not yet been established on earth and can be waited and hoped for. And this request seems to be for those millenial times when everything on earth goes as it ought to go, when men beat their swords into plowshares (Is. 2:4) and the wolf dwells at peace with the lamb (Is. 11:6, 65:25). This too, then, is a request for a certain state of affairs involving all or most men, the state of affairs at the end of the world prophesied under one or another description in Old and New Testament passages (cf., e.g., Rev. 21:1–4).

And it seems closely related to the object of the third request, "Thy will be done on earth as it is in heaven." There is, of course, a sense in which, according to Christian doctrine, God's will is always done on earth. But that is the sense in which God allows things to happen as they do (God's so-called permissive will). God permits certain people to have evil intentions, he permits certain people to commit crimes, and so on, so that he wills to let happen what does happen; and in this sense his will is always done. But in heaven, according to Christian doctrine, it is not that God permits what occurs to occur, and so wills in accordance with what happens, but rather that what happens happens in accordance with his will. So only the perfect good willed unconditionally by God is ever done in heaven. For God's will to be done on earth in such a way, everyone on earth would always have to do only good. This request, then, seems to be another way of asking for the establishment of God's kingdom on earth; and it also seems linked with certain New Testament prophecies—there will be a "new earth," and the righteous meek will inherit it (cf., e.g., Mt. 5:5 and Rev. 5:10 and 21:1–4).

9. Cf., e.g., Is. 2: 2–21, 45: 23, and 65: 23; Matt. 24; Mk. 13; Lk. 21; and Rev. 6: 15–17.

What I think is most worth noticing in this context about all three of these first requests of the Lord's Prayer is that it seems absolutely pointless, futile, and absurd to make them. All three seem to be requests for the millenium or for God's full reign on earth. But it appears from New Testament prophecies that God has already determined to bring about such a state of affairs in the future. And if God has predetermined that there will be such a time, then what is asked for in those three requests is already sure to come. But, then, what is the point of making the prayer? Why ask for something that is certain to come whether you beg for it or flee from it? It is no answer to these questions to say, as some theologians have done,[10] that one prays in this way just because Jesus prescribed such a prayer. That attempt at an answer simply transfers responsibility for the futile action from the one praying to the one being prayed to; it says nothing about what sense there is in the prayer itself. On the other hand, if, contrary to theological appearances, the things prayed for are not predetermined and their occurrence or nonoccurrence is still in doubt, *could* the issue possibly be resolved by someone's asking for one or another outcome? If Jimmy Carter, say (or some other Christian), does not ask for God's kingdom to come, will God therefore fail to establish it? Or will he establish it *just because* Jimmy Carter asked for it, though he would not have done so otherwise? Even Carter's staunchest supporters might well find it frightening to think so; and yet if we do not answer these questions in the affirmative, the prayer seems futile and pointless. So either an omniscient, omnipotent, perfectly good God has predetermined this state of affairs or he hasn't; and either way, asking for it seems to make no sense. This conclusion is applicable to other cases of petitionary prayer as well. To take just one example, suppose that Jimmy Carter prays the altruistic and Christian prayer that a particular atheistic friend of his be converted and so saved from everlasting damnation. If it is in God's power to save that man, won't he do so without Jimmy Carter's prayers? Won't a perfectly good God do all the good he can no matter what anyone prays for or does not pray for? Consequently, either God of his goodness will save the man in any case, so that the prayer is pointless,

---

10. See, for example, Martin Luther, *Large Catechism* pt. III. 169. Luther's argument for prayer has more force in the context of the catechism than it does in the context of a philosophical discussion, because Luther's purpose there is the practical one of blocking what he understands as believers' *excuses* for not praying.

or there is some point in the prayer but God's goodness appears impugned.

We can, I think, generalize these arguments to all petitionary prayer by means of a variation on the argument from evil against God's existence.[11] (The argument that follows does not seem to me to be an acceptable one, but it is the sort of argument that underlies the objections to petitionary prayer which I have been presenting. I will say something about what I think are the flaws in this argument later in the paper.)

> (1) A perfectly good being never makes the world worse than it would otherwise be if he can avoid doing so.

The phrase "than it would otherwise be" here should be construed as "than the world would have been had he not brought about or omitted to bring about some state of affairs." In other words, a perfectly good being never makes the world, in virtue of what he himself does or omits to do, worse than it would have been had he not done or omitted to do something or other. *Mutatis mutandis*, the same remarks apply to "than it would otherwise be" in (4) and (7) below.

> (2) An omniscient and omnipotent being can avoid doing anything which it is not logically necessary for him to do.

> ∴(3) An omniscient, omnipotent, perfectly good being never makes the world worse than it would otherwise be unless it is logically necessary for him to do so. (1, 2)

> (4) A perfectly good being always makes the world better than it would otherwise be if he can do so.

> (5) An omniscient and omnipotent being can do anything which it is not logically impossible for him to do.

> ∴(6) An omniscient, omnipotent, perfectly good being always makes the world better than it would otherwise be unless it is logically impossible for him to do so. (4, 5)

11. My approach to the argument from evil, which underlies the following argument, owes a good deal to Carl Ginet and Norman Kretzmann.

(7) It is never logically necessary for an omniscient, omnipotent, perfectly good being to make the world
worse than it would otherwise be; it is never logically impossible for an omniscient, omnipotent, perfectly
good being to make the world better than it would
otherwise be.

∴(8) An omniscient, omnipotent, perfectly good being
never makes the world worse than it would otherwise
be and always makes the world better than it would
otherwise be. (3, 6, 7)

This subconclusion implies that unless the world is infinitely improvable, either the world is or will be absolutely perfect or there
is no omniscient, omnipotent, perfectly good being. In other words,
(8) with the addition of a pair of premisses—

(i) The world is not infinitely improvable and

∴(ii) It is not the case that the world is or will be absolutely
perfect (i.e., there is and always will be evil in the
world)—

implies the conclusion of the argument from evil. That is not a surprising result since this argument is dependent on the argument from
evil.[12]

(9) What is requested in every petitionary prayer is or
results in a state of affairs the realization of which
would make the world either worse or better than it
would otherwise be (that is, than it would have been
had that state of affairs not been realized).

It is not always clear whether a petitionary prayer is requesting just
an earthly state of affairs, or God's bringing about that earthly state
of affairs. So, for example, when a mother prays for the health of
her sick son, it is not always clear whether she is requesting simply

12. There is a noteworthy difference between (ii) and the premiss ordinarily supplied
in its stead in arguments from evil, namely, (ii) "There is evil in the world." The difference
suggests a way to develop an alternative or at least an addition to the standard free will
defense against the argument from evil.

the health of her son or God's restoration of the health of her son. If we can determine the nature of the request on the basis of what the one praying desires and hopes to get by means of prayer, then at least in most cases the request will be just for some earthly state of affairs. What is important to the mother is simply her son's getting well. For a case in which the request is for God's bringing about some earthly state of affairs, we might consider Gideon's prayer concerning the fleece, discussed below. In any event, I intend "state of affairs" in this argument to range broadly enough to cover both sorts of cases.

∴ (10) If what is requested in a petitionary prayer is or results in a state of affairs the realization of which would make the world worse than it would otherwise be, an omniscient, omnipotent, perfectly good being will not fulfill that request. (8)

∴ (11) If what is requested in a petitionary prayer is or results in a state of affairs the realization of which would make the world better than it would otherwise be, an omniscient, omnipotent, perfectly good being will bring about that state of affairs even if no prayer for its realization has been made. (8)

It might occur to someone here that what is requested in at least some petitionary prayers is that God bring about a certain state of affairs *in response to the particular petitionary prayer being made.* In such cases, of course, it is logically impossible that God bring about what is requested in the petitionary prayer in the absence of that petitionary prayer. It is not clear to me that there are such cases. The familiar entreaties such as "Hear the voice of my supplications" (Ps. 28:2) in the Psalms seem to me not to be cases of the relevant sort, because they seem to be an elaborate "Please" rather than anything influencing the nature of what is requested in the prayer. Perhaps one of the best candidates for such a case is Gideon's prayer about the fleece: "If you will save Israel by my hand, as you have said, I will put a fleece of wool on the floor and if the dew is on the fleece only and it is dry on all the earth, then I will know that you will save Israel by my hand, as you have said" (Judges 6:36–37; cf. also 6:39). Gideon here is requesting that God give him a sign by means of the fleece of wool. Does his prayer amount to a request that God produce dew only on the fleece and not on the surrounding ground, or does it come to a request that God do so in response to Gideon's prayer? If there are cases in which the request implicitly or explicitly includes reference to the prayer itself, then in those cases the inference from (8) to (11) is not valid; and such cases ought simply to be excluded from consideration in this argument.

∴ (12) Petitionary prayer effects no change. (9, 10, 11)

There is, of course, a sense in which the offering of a prayer is itself a new state of affairs and accompanies or results in natural, psychological changes in the one praying, but step (12) ought to be understood as saying that no prayer is itself efficacious in causing a change of the sort it was designed to cause. An argument which might be thought to apply here, invalidating the inference to the conclusion (13), is that prayer need not effect any change in order to be considered efficacious, provided the offering of the prayer itself is a sufficient reason in God's view for God's fulfilment of the prayer. [13] In other words, if, for certain reasons apart from consideration of a prayer for a state of affairs S, God has determined to bring about S, a prayer for S may still be considered to be efficacious if and only if God would have brought about S just in response to the prayer for S. But I think that even if this view is correct, it does not in fact invalidate the inference to (13). There is a difference between being efficacious and having a point. This argument about the efficacy of prayer seems to assume that not all answers to prayer will be of the overdetermined type. And as long as a believer is not in a position to know which states of affairs are divinely determined to occur regardless of prayers, there is some point in petitionary prayer—any given case may be one in which God would not have brought about the desired state of affairs without prayer for it. But if it is the case for every fulfilled prayer that God would have brought about the desired state of affairs without the prayer, it does seem that there is no point in petitionary prayer, except for those cases (which I think must at best form a very small minority) in which the real object of the one praying a petitionary prayer is not so much to see the realization of the state of affairs he is requesting as to have some in-

13. See Terence Penelhum, *Religion and Rationality* [14] in this volume, pp. 160–165.

fluence on or contact with the Deity by means of petitionary prayer; and such cases may then simply be excepted from the conclusion of the argument.

∴(13) Petitionary prayer is pointless. (12)

The basic strategy of this argument is an attempt to show that there is an inconsistency between God's goodness and the efficacy of petitionary prayer; but it is possible to begin with other divine attributes and make a case for a similar inconsistency, so that we can have other, very different arguments to the same conclusion, namely, that petitionary prayer is pointless. Perhaps the most formidable of such alternative arguments is the one based on God's immutability, an argument the strategy of which can be roughly summarized in this way. Before a certain petitionary prayer is made, it is the case either that God will bring about the state of affairs requested in the prayer or that he will not bring it about. He cannot have left the matter open since doing so would imply a subsequent change in him and he is immutable. Either way, since he is immutable, the prayer itself can effect no change in the state of affairs and hence is pointless. Even leaving aside problems of foreknowledge and free will to which this argument (or attempted objections to it) may give rise, I think that orthodox theology will find no real threat in the argument because of the doctrine of God's eternality. However problematic that doctrine may be in itself, it undercuts arguments such as this one because it maintains God's atemporality.[14] My thirteen-step argument against petitionary prayer is, then, not the only argument rejecting petitionary prayer on theistic principles, but it (or some argument along the same lines) does, I think, make the strongest case against petitionary prayer, given Christian doctrine.

The premiss that is most likely to appear false in the argument, at first reading, is (9) because one is inclined to think that there are many petitionary prayers which, if they are granted, would not make the world either better or worse than it would otherwise be. Such a view might be accommodated without damaging the argument simply by weakening (9) and the conclusion: many petitionary prayers, and surely the most important ones, are such that if fulfilled

14. Norman Kretzmann and I examine the concept of eternity in ancient and medieval metaphysics and theology in our article "Eternity", *Journal of Philosophy*, 1981, 78, 429–458.

they make the world either a better or a worse place. But I think it is possible to argue plausibly for (9) in the strong form I have given it. Take, for instance, the case of a little boy who prays for a jack-knife. Here, we might think, we have an example of a petitionary prayer the fulfilment of which makes the world neither better nor worse. But, on the one hand, if the little boy has prayed for a jack-knife, surely he will be happier if he gets it, either because he very much wants a jackknife or because God has honored his request. Consequently, one could argue that fulfilling the request makes the world better in virtue of making the one praying happier. Or, on the other hand, if we think of the little boy's prayer for a jackknife from God's point of view, then we see that fulfilment of the prayer involves not just the little boy's acquiring a jackknife but also God's bringing it about in answer to prayer that the little boy acquire a jackknife. Fulfilling the prayer, then, will have an influence on at least the little boy's religious beliefs and perhaps also on those of his parents and even on those of the people in his parents' community. One might argue that the influence in this case would be deleterious (since it is conducive to wrong views of the purpose of prayer and of relationship with God), and consequently that fulfilling this prayer would make the world a worse place than it would otherwise be. So I think it is possible to argue plausibly that the fulfilment of even such a prayer would make the world either a worse or a better place.

Christian literature contains a number of discussions of the problem with petitionary prayer and various attempts to solve it. For the sake of brevity, I want to look just at the proposed solution Aquinas gives. It is the most philosophically sophisticated of the solutions I know; and in the wake of the twentieth-century revival of Thomism, it is the solution adopted by many theologians and theistic philosophers today.[15] Thomas discusses problems of petitionary prayer in his Sentence commentary and in the *Summa contra gentiles*,[16] but the clearest exposition of his views is in the question on prayer in the *Summa theologiae*, where he devotes an entire article to showing that there is sense and usefulness in petitionary prayer.[17] The basic argument he relies on to rebut various objections against the usefulness of prayer is this. Divine Providence determines not only

15. See, for example, the articles on prayer in the *Dictionnaire de Théologie Catholique* and *The New Catholic Encyclopedia*.
16. See *In IV. Sent.*, dist. XV, q.4, a.l, and *Summa contra gentiles*, I. III. 95–96.
17. See 2a–2ae, q. 83, a.2.

what effects there will be in the world, but also what causes will give rise to those effects and in what order they will do so. Now human actions, too, are causes. "For," Thomas says, "we pray not in order to change the divine disposition but for the sake of acquiring by petitionary prayer what God has disposed to be achieved by prayer."[18]

Perhaps the first worry which this argument occasions stems from the appearance of theological determinism in it: God determines not only what effects there will be but also what the causes of those effects will be and in what order the effects will be produced. It is hard to see how such a belief is compatible with freedom of the will. In the preamble to this argument, however, Thomas says he is concerned *not* to deny free will but, on the contrary, to give an account of prayer which preserves free will. So I want simply to assume that he has in mind some distinction or some theory which shows that, despite appearances, his argument is not committed to a thorough-going determinism, and I am going to ignore any troubles in the argument having to do with the compatibility of predestination or foreknowledge and free will.

For present purposes, what is more troublesome about this argument is that it does not provide any real help with the problem it means to solve. According to Thomas, there is nothing absurd or futile about praying to God, given God's nature, because God has by his providence arranged things so that free human actions and human prayers will form part of the chain of cause and effect leading to the state of the world ordained in God's plan. And so, on Thomas's view, prayer should not be thought of as an attempt to get God to do something which he would not otherwise do but rather as an effort to produce an appropriate and preordained cause which will result in certain effects since God in his providence has determined things to be so. Now surely there can be no doubt that, according to Christian doctrine, God wants men to pray and answers prayers; and consequently it is plain that God's plan for the world includes human prayers as causes of certain effects. The difficulty lies in explaining how such a doctrine makes sense. Why should prayers be included in God's plan as causes of certain effects? And what sense is there in the notion that a perfect and unchangeable God, who disposes and plans everything, fulfills men's prayers asking him to do one thing

18. See reply, a.2. "*Non enim propter hoc oramus ut divinam dispositionem immutemus: sed ut id impetremus quod Deus disposuit per orationes sanctorum implendum . . .*"

or another? Thomas's argument, I think, gives no help with these questions and so gives no help with this problem of petitionary prayer.

This argument of Thomas's is roughly similar in basic strategy to other traditional arguments for prayer[19] and is furthermore among the most fully developed and sophisticated arguments for prayer, but it seems to me inadequate to make sense of petitionary prayer. I think, then, that it is worthwhile exploring a sort of argument different from those that stress the connection between God's omniscience or providence and men's prayers. In what follows I want to offer a tentative and preliminary sketch of the way in which such an argument might go.

Judaeo-Christian concepts of God commonly represent God as loving mankind and wanting to be loved by men in return. Such anthropomorphic talk is in sharp contrast to the more sophisticated-sounding language of the Hellenized and scholastic arguments considered so far. But a certain sort of anthropomorphism is as much a part of Christianity as is Thomas's "perfect being theology,"[20] and it, too, builds on intricate philosophical analysis, beginning perhaps with Boethius's attempt in *Contra Eutychen et Nestorium* to explain what it means to say of something that it is a person. So to say that God loves men and wants to be loved in return is to say something that has a place in philosophical theology and is indispensable to Christian doctrine. Throughout the Old and New Testaments, the type of loving relationship wanted between man and God is represented by various images, for example, sometimes as the relationship between husband and wife, sometimes as that between father and child. And sometimes (in the Gospel of John, for instance) it is also represented as the relationship between true friends.[21] But if the relationship between God and human beings is to be one which at least sometimes can be accurately represented as the love of true friendship, then there is a problem for both parties to the relationship, because plainly it will not be easy for there to be friendship between an omniscient, omnipotent, perfectly good person and a fallible, finite, imperfect person. The troubles of generating and maintaining friendship in such a case are

---

19. Cf., e.g., Origen, *op. cit.*, and Augustine, *City of God*, Bk. V, ix.

20. Plainly, a good deal of skilful work is needed to weave such anthropomorphism and scholastic theology into one harmonious whole. The problem is, of course, given lengthy, detailed treatment in various scholastic writings, including Thomas's *Summa theologiae*.

21. See especially Jn. 15: 12–15.

surely the perfect paradigms of which the troubles of friendship between a Rockefeller child and a slum child are just pale copies. Whatever other troubles there are for friendship in these cases, there are at least two dangers for the disadvantaged or inferior member of the pair. First, he can be so overcome by the advantages or superiority of his "friend" that he becomes simply a shadowy reflection of the other's personality, a slavish follower who slowly loses all sense of his own tastes and desires and will. Some people, of course, believe that just this sort of attitude towards God is what Christianity wants and gets from the best of its adherents; but I think that such a belief goes counter to the spirit of the Gospels, for example, and I don't think that it can be found even in such intense mystics as St. Teresa and St. John of the Cross. Secondly, in addition to the danger of becoming completely dominated, there is the danger of becoming spoiled in the way that members of a royal family in a ruling house are subject to. Because of the power at their disposal in virtue of their connections, they often become tyrannical, willful, indolent, self-indulgent, and the like. The greater the discrepancy in status and condition between the two friends, the greater the danger of even inadvertently overwhelming and oppressing or overwhelming and spoiling the lesser member of the pair; and if he is overwhelmed in either of these ways, the result will be replacement of whatever kind of friendship there might have been with one or another sort of using. Either the superior member of the pair will use the lesser as his lackey, or the lesser will use the superior as his personal power source. To put it succinctly, then, if God wants some kind of true friendship with men, he will have to find a way of guarding against both kinds of overwhelming.

It might occur to someone to think that even if we assume the view of God wants friendship between himself and human beings, it does not follow that he will have any of the problems just sketched, because he is omnipotent.[22] If he wants friendship of this sort with men, one might suppose, let him just will it and it will be his. I do not want to stop here to argue against this view in detail, but I do want just to suggest that there is reason for thinking it to be incoherent, at least

22. I want to avoid detailed discussion of the various controversies over omnipotence. For present purposes, I will take this as a rough definition of omnipotence: a being is omnipotent if and only if he can do anything which it is not logically impossible for him to do and if he can avoid doing anything which it is not logically necessary for him to do.

on the assumption of free will adopted at the beginning of this paper, because it is hard to see how God could bring about such a friendship magically, by means of his omnipotence, and yet permit the people involved to have free will. If he could do so, he could make a person freely love him in the right sort of way, and it does not seem reasonable to think he could do so.[23] On the face of it, then, omnipotence alone does not do away with the two dangers for friendship that I sketched above. But the institution of petitionary prayer, I think, can be understood as a safeguard against these dangers.

It is easiest to argue that petitionary prayer serves such a function in the case of a man who prays for himself. In praying for himself, he makes an explicit request for help, and he thereby acknowledges a need or a desire and his dependence on God for satisfying that need or desire. If he gets what he prayed for, he will be in a position to attribute his good fortune to God's doing and to be grateful to God for what God has given him. If we add the undeniable uncertainty of his getting what he prays for, then we will have safeguards against what I will call (for lack of a better phrase) overwhelming spoiling. These conditions make the act of asking a safeguard against tyrannical and self-indulgent pride, even if the one praying thinks of himself grandly as having God on his side.

We can see how the asking guards against the second danger, of oppressive overwhelming, if we look for a moment at the function of roughly similar asking for help when both the one asking and the one asked are human beings. Suppose a teacher sees that one of his students is avoiding writing a paper and is thereby storing up trouble for himself at the end of the term. And suppose that the student *asks* the teacher for extra help in organizing working time and scheduling the various parts of the work. In that case I think the teacher can without any problem give the student what he needs, provided, of course, that the teacher is willing to do as much for any other student, and so on. But suppose, on the other hand, that the student does not ask the teacher for help and that the teacher instead calls

23. Controversy over this point is related to the more general controversy over whether or not it is possible for an omnipotent, omniscient, perfectly good God to create men who would on every occasion freely do what is right. For a discussion of that general controversy and arguments that it is not possible for God to do so, see Alvin Plantinga's *God and Other Minds* (Cornell University Press, Ithaca, 1967), pp. 132–148; I am in agreement with the general tenor of Plantinga's remarks in that section of his book.

the student at home and simply presents him with the help he needs in scheduling and discipline. The teacher's proposals in that case are more than likely to strike the student as meddling interference, and he is likely to respond with more or less polite variations on "Who asked you?" and "Mind your own business." Those responses, I think, are healthy and just. If the student were having ordinary difficulties getting his work done and yet docilely and submissively accepted the teacher's unrequested scheduling of his time, he would have taken the first step in the direction of unhealthy passivity towards his teacher. And if he and his teacher developed that sort of relationship, he could end by becoming a lackey-like reflection of his teacher. Bestowing at least some benefits only in response to requests for them is a safeguard against such an outcome when the members of the relationship are not equally balanced.

It becomes much harder to argue for this defense of prayer as soon as the complexity of the case is increased even just a little. Take, for example, Monica's praying for her son Augustine. There is nothing in Monica's praying for Augustine which shows that *Augustine* recognizes that he has a need for God's help or that *he* will be grateful if God gives him what *Monica* prays for. Nor is it plain that *Monica's* asking shields Augustine from oppressive overwhelming by God. So it seems as if the previous arguments fail in this case. But consider again the case in which a teacher sees that a student of his could use help but does not feel that he can legitimately volunteer his help unasked. Suppose that John, a friend of that student, comes to see the teacher and says, "I don't know if you've noticed, but Jim is having trouble getting to his term paper. And unless he gets help, I think he won't do it at all and will be in danger of flunking the course." If the teacher now goes to help Jim and is rudely or politely asked "What right have you got to interfere?," he'll say, "Well, in fact, your friend came to me and *asked* me to help." And if John is asked the same question, he will probably reply, "But I'm your friend; I had to do *something*." I think, then, that because John asks the teacher, the teacher is in a position to help with less risk of oppressive meddling than before. Obviously, he cannot go very far without incurring that risk as fully as before; and perhaps the most he can do if he wants to avoid oppressive meddling is to try to elicit from *Jim* in genuinely uncoercive ways a request for help. And, of course, I chose Monica and Augustine to introduce this case because, as Augustine tells it in the *Confessions*, God responded to Monica's fervent and continued prayers for Augustine's salvation by arranging the circumstances of Augustine's life in such a way that finally Augustine himself freely asked God for salvation.

One might perhaps think that there is something superfluous and absurd in God's working through the intermediary of prayer in this way. If Jim's friend can justify his interference on the grounds that he is Jim's friend and has to do *something*, God can dispense with this sort of petitionary prayer, too. He can give aid unasked on the grounds that he is the *creator* and has to do something. But suppose that Jim and John are only acquaintances who have discussed nothing more than their schoolwork; and suppose that John, by overhearing Jim's phone conversations, has come to believe that all Jim's academic troubles are just symptoms of problems he is having with his parents. If John asks the teacher to help Jim with his personal problems, and if the teacher begins even a delicate attempt to do so by saying that John asked him to do so, he and John could both properly be told to mind their own business. It is not the *status* of his relationship or even the depth of his care and compassion for Jim which puts John in a position to defend himself by saying "But I'm your friend." What protects John against the charge of oppressive meddling is rather the degree to which Jim has freely, willingly, shared his life and thoughts and feelings with John. So John's line of defense against the charge of oppressive meddling can be attributed to God only if the person God is to aid has willingly shared his thoughts and feelings and the like with God. But it is hard to imagine anyone putting himself in such a relation to a person he believes to be omnipotent and good without his also *asking* for whatever help he needs.

Even if the argument can be made out so far, one might be inclined to think that it will not be sufficient to show the compatibility of God's goodness with the practice of petitionary prayer. If one supposes that God brought Augustine to Christianity in response to Monica's prayers, what is one to say about Augustine's fate if Monica had not prayed for him? And what does this view commit one to maintain about people who neither pray for themselves nor are prayed for? It looks as if an orthodox Christian who accepts the argument about petitionary prayer so far will be committed to a picture of this sort. God is analogous to a human father with two very different children. Both Old and New Testaments depict God as doing many good things for men without being asked to do so, and this human father, too, does unrequested good things for both his children. But one child, who is healthy and normal, with healthy, normal relations to his father, makes frequent requests of the father which the father responds to and in virtue of which he bestows benefits on the child. The other child is selectively blind, deaf, dumb, and suffering from whatever other maladies are necessary to make it plausible that he does not even know he has a father. Now either there are some benefits that the father will never bestow unless and until he is asked; and in that case he will do less for his defective child, who surely has more need of his help than does the healthy child. Or, on the other hand, he will bestow all his benefits unasked on the defective child, and then he seems to make a mockery of his practice with the normal child of bestowing some benefits only in response to requests—he is, after all, willing to bestow the same benefits without being asked. So it seems that we are still left with the problem we started with: either God is not perfectly good or the practice of petitionary prayer is pointless. But suppose the father always meets the defective child's needs and desires even though the child never comes to know of the existence of his father. The child knows only that he is always taken care of, and when he needs something, he gets what he needs. It seems to me intuitively clear that such a practice runs a great risk, at least, of making the defective child willful and tyrannical. But even if the defective child is not in danger of being made worse in some respects in this situation, still it seems plain that he would be better off if the father could manage to put the child in a position to know his father and to frame a request for what he wants. So I think a good father will fulfill the child's needs unasked; but I think that he can do so without making a mockery of his practice of bestowing benefits in response to requests only if putting the child in a position to make requests is among his first concerns.

And as for the question whether God would have saved Augustine without Monica's prayers, I think that there is intermediate ground between the assertion that Monica's prayers are necessary to Augustine's salvation, which seems to impugn God's goodness, and the claim that they are altogether without effect, which undercuts petitionary prayer. It is possible, for example, to argue that God would have saved Augustine without Monica's prayers but not in the same amount of time or not by the same process or not with the same effect. Augustine, for instance, might have been converted to Christianity but not in such a way as to become one of its most powerful authorities for centuries.[24]

With all this, I have still looked only at cases that are easy for my position; when we turn to something like a prayer for Guatemala after the earthquake—which begins to come closer to the sort of petitions in the first half of the Lord's Prayer—it is much harder to know what to say. And perhaps it is simply too hard to come up with a reasonable solution here because we need more work on the problem of evil. Why would a good God permit the occurrence of earthquakes in the first place? Do the reasons for his permitting the earthquake affect his afterwards helping the country involved? Our inclination is surely to say that a good God must *in any case* help the earthquake victims, so that in this instance at any rate it is pointless to pray. But plainly we also have strong inclinations to say that a good God must in any case prevent earthquakes in populated areas. And since orthodox Christianity is committed to distrusting these latter inclinations, it is at least at sea about the former ones. Without more work on the problem of evil, it is hard to know what to say about the difference prayer might make in this sort of case.

I think it is worth noticing, though, that the first three requests of the Lord's prayer do not run into the same difficulties. Those requests seem generally equivalent to a request for the kingdom of God on earth, that state of affairs in which, of their own free will, all men on earth are dedicated, righteous lovers of God. Now suppose it is true that God would bring about his kingdom on earth even if an individual Christian such as Jimmy Carter did not pray for it. It does not follow in this case, however, that the prayer in question is pointless

---

24. I have presented the case of Monica and Augustine in a simplified form in order to have an uncomplicated hard case for the view I am arguing. As far as the historical figures themselves are concerned, it is plain that Monica's overt, explicit, passionate concern for her son's conversion greatly influenced the course of his life and shaped his character from boyhood on. It is not clear whether Augustine would have been anything like the man he was if his mother had not been as zealous on behalf of his soul as she was, if she had not prayed continually and fervently for his salvation and let him know she was doing so. Augustine's character and personality were what they were in large part as a result of her fierce desire for his espousal of Christianity; and just his knowledge that his beloved mother prayed so earnestly for his conversion must have been a powerful natural force helping to effect that conversion. In this context the question whether God could have saved Augustine without Monica's prayers takes on different meaning, and an affirmative answer is much harder to give with reasoned confidence.

and makes no difference. Suppose no one prayed for the advent of God's kingdom on earth or felt a need or desire for those millenial times strongly enough to pray for them. It seems unreasonable to think that God could bring about his earthly kingdom under those conditions, or if he could, that it would be the state of affairs just described, in which earth is populated by people who *freely* love God.[23] And if so, then making the requests in the first half of the Lord's Prayer resembles other, more ordinary activities in which only the effort of a whole group is sufficient to achieve the desired result. One man can't put out a forest fire, but if everyone in the vicinity of a forest fire realized that fact and on that basis decided not to try, the fire would rage out of control. So in the case of the opening petitions of the Lord's Prayer, too, it seems possible to justify petitionary prayer without impugning God's goodness.

Obviously, the account I have given is just a preliminary sketch for the full development of this solution, and a good deal more work needs to be done on the problem. Nonetheless, I think that this account is on the right track and that there is a workable solution to the problem of petitionary prayer which can be summarized in this way. God must work through the intermediary of prayer, rather than doing everything on his own initiative, for man's sake. Prayer acts as a kind of buffer between man and God. By safeguarding the weaker member of the relation from the dangers of overwhelming domination and overwhelming spoiling, it helps to promote and preserve a close relationship between an omniscient, omnipotent, perfectly good person and a fallible, finite, imperfect person. There is, of course, something counter-intuitive in this notion that prayer acts as a buffer; prayer of all sorts is commonly and I think correctly said to have as one of its main functions the production of closeness between man and God. But not just any sort of closeness will result in friendship, and promoting the appropriate sort of closeness will require inhibiting or preventing inappropriate sorts of closeness, so that a relationship of friendship depends on the maintenance of both closeness and distance between the two friends. And while I do not mean to denigrate the importance of prayer in producing and preserving the appropriate sort of closeness, I think the problem of petitionary prayer at issue here is best solved by focusing on the distance necessary for friendship and the function of petitionary prayer in maintaining that distance.

As for the argument against prayer which I laid out at the start of the paper, it seems to me that the flaw lies in step (7), that it is never logically necessary for God to make the world worse than it would otherwise be and never logically impossible for him to make the world better than it would otherwise be. To take a specific example from among those discussed so far, orthodox Christianity is committed to claiming that the advent of God's kingdom on earth, in which all people freely love God, would make the world better than it would otherwise be. But I think that it is not possible for God to *make* the world better in this way, because I think it is not possible for him to *make* men *freely* do anything.[23] And in general, if it is arguable that God's doing good things just in virtue of men's requests protects men from the dangers described and preserves them in the right relationship to God, then it is not the case that it is always logically possible for God to make the world better and never logically necessary for him to make the world worse than it would otherwise be. If men do not always pray for all the good things they might and ought to pray for, then in some cases either God will not bring about some good thing or he will do so but at the expense of the good wrought and preserved by petitionary prayer.

It should be plain that there is nothing in this analysis of prayer which *requires* that God fulfil every prayer; asking God for something is not in itself a sufficient condition for God's doing what he is asked. Christian writings are full of examples of prayers which are not answered, and there are painful cases of unanswered prayer in which the one praying must be tempted more to the belief that God is his implacable enemy than to the sentimental-seeming belief that God is his friend. This paper proposes no answer for these difficulties. They require a long, hard, careful look at the problem of evil, and that falls just outside the scope of this paper.

And, finally, it may occur to someone to wonder whether the picture of God presented in this analysis is at all faithful to the God of the Old or New Testaments. Is this understanding of God and prayer anything that Christianity ought to accept or even find congenial? It seems to me that one could point to many stories in either the Old or New Testament in support of an affirmative answer—for example, Elijah's performance on Mt. Carmel (I Kings 18), or the apostles' prayer for a successor to Judas (Acts 1:24–26). But for a small and particularly nice piece of evidence, we can turn to the story in the

Gospel of Luke which describes Jesus making the Lord's Prayer and giving a lecture on how one is to pray. According to the Gospel, Jesus is praying and in such a way that his disciples see him and know that he is praying. One of them makes a request of him which has just a touch of rebuke in it: teach us to pray, as *John* taught *his* disciples to pray (Lk. 11:1). If there is a note of rebuke there, it seems just. A religious master should teach his disciples to pray, and a good teacher does not wait until he is asked to teach his students important lessons. But Jesus is portrayed as a good teacher of just this sort in the Gospel of Luke.[25] Does the Gospel, then, mean its readers to understand that Jesus would not have taught his disciples how to pray if they had not requested it? And if it does not, why is Jesus portrayed as waiting until he is asked? Perhaps the Gospel means us to understand[26] that Jesus does so just in order to teach by experience as well as by sermon what is implicit throughout the Lord's Prayer: that asking makes a difference.[27]

25. See, for example, the lessons taught in the two incidents described in Lk. 21:1–6.

26. I have used awkward circumlocutions in this paragraph in order to make plain that it is not my intention here to make any claims about the historical Jesus or the intentions of the Gospel writer. I am not concerned in this paper to do or to take account of contemporary theories of Biblical exegesis. My point is only that the story in the Gospel, as it has been part of ordinary Christian tradition, lends itself to the interpretation I suggest.

27. In writing this paper, I have benefited from the comments and criticisms of John Boler, Norman Care, and Bill Rowe. I am particularly indebted to my friend Norman Kretzmann for his thorough reading and very helpful criticism of the paper. And I am grateful to John Crossett, from whom I have learned a great deal and whose understanding of philosophical problems in Christian theology is much better than my own.

16

RICHARD L. PURTILL*

Miracles: What If They Happen?

SOME RELIGIOUS BELIEVERS think that miracles continue to occur; others believe that they have occurred only at specific places and times, where extraordinary needs brought forth extraordinary help from God. But even if events which cannot be explained by science do occur in some religious contexts, what do such events prove?

One traditional way of providing a rational basis for religious belief begins with arguments for the existence of God and goes on to argue that a certain body of religious beliefs can be known to be a revelation from God because miracles have been worked in support of those religious beliefs. For example, a Christian of one traditional sort, when challenged as to the basis of one of his beliefs—say the Second Coming of Christ—would cite certain words said by Christ. When asked why we should believe these words of Christ, he would cite the miracles done by Christ, and especially His Resurrection, as evidence that Christ's words were backed up or authenticated by God. And when asked why he believed that those miracles had indeed occurred, the traditional Christian would argue that if God exists miracles cannot be ruled out, and that miracle is the best or only explanation for certain events recorded by history. If challenged as to the existence

* From his *Thinking About Religion* (Englewood Cliffs, NJ: Prentice-Hall, 1978), pp. 65–79.

of God, he would try to give arguments based on reason and experience for God's existence.

Thus, this kind of traditional Christian, whom we might call a rationalistic believer, nowhere appeals to blind faith or personal experiences not shared by unbelievers, but bases his assent to particular doctrines on authority, his acceptance of authority on the evidence of miracles, and his acceptance of miracles on philosophical arguments for God and historical arguments for the actual occurance of miracles.

Nowadays not only most nonbelievers but many people who would call themselves religious believers would challenge this way of providing a basis for religious belief. They would argue that accounts of miracles are not historically reliable and that a faith based on such accounts is open to historical and scientific objections. The traditional believer understands such objections from nonbelievers in God, but finds them puzzling from people calling themselves believers in God. For if God is the Creator and Ruler of the universe, then surely miracles are possible. Of course, if miracles were impossible, then any historical account which tells of the occurrence of miracles, as the Old and New Testaments plainly do, must be rejected as unhistorical. If miracles are tremendously improbable, then we must reject any account of them unless we get evidence of a kind which, in the nature of the case, history almost never gives us. But if God exists, miracles are not impossible, and unless we have some argument to show that they are improbable, then we cannot assume that they are. This undercuts most of the "historical" objections to miracles, for if we have no metaphysical objections, then we will have to examine the historical evidence on its merits. And if we do this we may find, as many reasonable and hardheaded men have found, that miracle is the best explanation for certain recorded events.

There may, of course, be historical objections to certain accounts of miracles—for example, one account may seem to be a mere imitation of another, or other historical evidence may render that particular supposed miracle improbable, and so on. But the general objection to miracles is not based on anything peculiar to history as such, but on philosophical grounds.

Another objection to miracles is the supposed objection from experience. Most versions of this objection trace back more or less indirectly to a famous objection by David Hume, which goes as follows:

A miracle is a violation of the laws of nature; and as a firm and unalterable experience has established these laws, the proof against a miracle, from the very nature of the fact, is as entire as any argument from experience can possibly be imagined. . . . Nothing is esteemed a miracle, if it ever happens in the common course of nature. It is no miracle that a man, seemingly in good health, should die of a sudden; because such a kind of death, though more unusual than any other, has yet been frequently observed to happen. But it is a miracle that a dead man should come to life; because that has never been observed in any age or country. There must, therefore, be a uniform experience against every miraculous event, otherwise the event would not merit the appellation. And as a uniform experience amounts to a proof, there is here a direct and full proof, from the nature of the fact, against the existence of any miracle; nor can such a proof be destroyed, or the miracle rendered credible, but by an opposite proof, which is superior. ([3] pp. 27f.)

Now obviously we must interpret Hume's objection in such a way that it is not an objection to any unique event. After all, up to a certain date, there was "uniform experience" against a man setting foot on the moon. It must, therefore, be a certain *class* or *kind* of events we are eliminating. But what class? Miracles? But this begs the whole question. As an "argument" against the statement that miracles occur, we have the assertion that there is uniform experience against miracles—in other words, the unsupported assertion that miracles don't happen!

Put in this way the point may seem obvious, but both in Hume's original account and in modern restatements of views like Hume's the point is often concealed. Instead of saying baldly that experience shows that miracles do not occur, which is obviously question-begging in the context of this argument, the class of events which "experience proves don't happen" is described in some other way—as events which "exhibit causal irregularity" or as events which "neither obey known scientific laws nor are taken as refuting alleged scientific laws," or some similar description. But looked at carefully, all such descriptions turn out to be indirect ways of describing miracles. And to argue for the conclusion that miracles do not happen by assuming that miracles, under whatever description, don't happen is just to argue in a circle or beg the question.

This is not to deny that there could be some argument which concludes that miracles don't happen. But whatever that argument is, it must not have as one of its premises an assertion which amounts to saying that miracles don't happen, because that would be assuming what is supposed to be being proved.

Of course defenders of a Humean position would deny that they are arguing in a circle in this way. But to avoid the charge of circularity they must show that the class of events they are claiming experience rules out is not just an indirect description of the class of miracles. So far as I can see neither Hume's own argument or any neo-Humean argument can meet the challenge.

I think that the only respectable way of interpreting what Hume says here is to take him as arguing that past experience gives us some kind of assurance that laws of nature *cannot* be suspended. (If it merely alleges that they *have never been* suspended, it is just "miracles don't happen" in a new guise.) We interpret Hume, then, as saying that experience proves that natural laws are "unsuspendable." But how *could* experience show any such thing? Any such theory must be a philosophical interpretation of experience, not the direct result of experience. So before coming to any decision on this matter, we must look at the philosophical, as well as the historical, pros and cons with regard to the question of miracles. We can distinguish two separable arguments which need to be looked at in turn: the argument *for* (the possibility of) miracles, and the argument *from* miracles (for religious belief).

The argument for miracles consists of two stages—an argument for the general possibility of miracles, and an argument for the historical actuality of certain miracles. The first stage is philosophical and can be developed fairly completely within the limits of this chapter. The second stage is historical and we can only indicate the main lines of the argument. The argument *from* miracles for religious belief also has two stages—the first stage a philosophical consideration of the evidential value of miracles, and the second stage a historical consideration of what specific beliefs the evidence of miracles supports. Again, we will try to cover the philosophical stage as completely as we can and only indicate the general lines of the historical argument.

Let us begin, then, with a definition of miracle. By a miracle we will mean an exception to the natural order of things caused by the power of God. By this we will mean very much what people mean when they define miracle as a suspension or violation of natural law, but for reasons that will become clear "exception" is preferable to the terms "suspension" or "violation," and "natural order of things" is preferable to the term "natural law." Notice that by this definition no event which occurs as part of the natural order of things, no matter how improbable or how faith-inspiring, will count as a miracle. There may be a wider and looser sense of miracle in which striking coincidences which inspire religious belief are called "miracles," but they are not miracles in the stricter and narrower sense in which we are now using that term.

Before we can speak of exceptions to the natural order of things we must believe that there *is* a natural order of things. If anyone holds that there is no natural order, that the universe is chaotic, that the apparent order and understandability of the universe is an illusion, then that person can give no meaning to the idea of miracle, for that idea depends on contrast. Before there can be exceptions there must be rules or patterns for them to be exceptions to. The progress of science gives us an enormously strong argument against the idea that the universe is chaotic and without order and pattern, and we will assume in what follows that we can speak of the universe as genuinely orderly and intelligible. But if anyone really wished to challenge this, we would have to settle that issue before going on to any argument with him either for or from miracles.

Given that the universe is orderly and understandable, however, we can ask whether this order can have exceptions and whether such exceptions could be due to the power of God. The answer to this question depends on the answer to another question. How can we account for the order and understandability of the universe? Ultimately there are only two possible answers to this question. We can account for the order of the universe by saying that the universe was made by a person, by a Being with knowledge and will, by someone who knows what he is doing and what he intends—in other words by God. And we can account for the understandability of the universe by saying that we are made in the image and likeness of the God who made the universe; our minds resemble His, however remotely. *Or* we can account for the order of the universe by saying that there is some inherent principle of order in the fundamental stuff of the universe, and account for our understanding that order by saying that our minds are the outcome of the unfolding of this inherent principle of order.[1]

Either theory, if accepted, would have consequences. If we really accepted the idea that our minds were the accidental result of the workings of mindless forces, we should be haunted by doubts as to whether our apparent understanding of the universe is illusory. Dogmatic confidence of any kind, including dogmatic confidence that certain sorts of events "can't happen" is not what we should logically expect from a Universe Ultimate view. (Of course, insofar as dogmatism is often the outcome of a feeling of uncertainty, we might explain the dogmatism psychologically.) The consequences of the God theory are rather different. Our confidence in the understanding of the universe given to us by science would be considerable, but it would not be absolute. If the natural order is the result of God's action, then sometimes God might act in such a way as to make exceptions to the natural order.

In this view an exception to the natural order would be like the exceptions we sometimes make to established rules and procedures— for example, allowing an exceptionally gifted child to skip grades or enter college without graduating from high school, or declaring a holiday on a day that would normally be a working day. We can often see that not making exceptions to rules would be unreasonable or unkind. Exceptions must, of course, be rare if rules are to be generally relied upon, but we can live perfectly well with a system of rules or procedures which have occasional exceptions. We may or may not think President Ford's pardon of ex-President Nixon wise or fair, but occasional exceptions to legal procedures, such as presidential pardon, do not make our legal system chaotic or unreliable.

Furthermore, provided that God wished to give us strong evidence that a given message has His authority behind it, there would seem to be no better way than a miracle. If I claim to have authority in a certain organization, strong evidence of my authority would be an ability to suspend the rules or make exceptions to usual procedures. You might meditate on the problem of how a God who never interfered with the working of the universe could establish a message from Himself as authoritative.

The scientist, of course, *as* a scientist, ignores the possibility of

1. In Chapter 1 of *Thinking About Religion*, Purtill called this the Universe Ultimate View and discussed its difficulties in detail.

miracles, just as the lawyer, *as* a lawyer, must ignore the possibility of a presidential pardon for his client, since there is nothing he can do *as a lawyer* which will ensure a presidential pardon. A pardon is a free action by the President, which cannot be guaranteed by any legal maneuver; a miracle is a free act by God which the scientist cannot bring within *his* procedures.

A presidential pardon is like a miracle in that though the *origin* of the pardon is outside ordinary legal procedures, a pardon once granted has legal consequences. A miracle, once it has occurred, has consequences which fit into the kind of patterns scientists study: Drinking too much of the wine Christ made from water at Cana in Galilee would make a wedding guest drunk, and if a scientist had been there with his instruments he could verify, though not explain, the change and measure the alcoholic content of the wine made from water.

It is important to note that a presidential pardon is not *il*legal: It does not violate any laws. Furthermore, it does not suspend the laws in the sense that at a given time or place some laws cease to operate in all cases—as if, for example, the laws of libel were suspended in Hannibal, Missouri, on the first Sunday in March, so that no libels in that place or time were punishable. Rather, an individual exception is made to the law, so that of two men convicted of the same crime at the same time, one may be pardoned and the other not. Similarly, a miracle does not *violate* the laws of nature, nor suspend them for all events at a given time or place: The water in one jar might be changed to wine and that in an adjacent jar be unchanged. Lazarus may be raised and a man in an adjacent tomb who died at the same time may remain dead.

A presidential pardon cannot be compelled by any legal means; it can only be asked for. It is a free act of the President. Similarly, a miracle cannot be brought about by scientific means; it can only be prayed for. It is a free act of God. A presidential pardon cannot be predicted from the legal facts and it does not create a precedent: A pardon may be granted in one case, and in precisely similar circumstances another request may be denied. Similarly, a miracle cannot be predicted by scientific means and it gives no scientific grounds for prediction once it has occurred: The miracle at Cana in Galilee does not increase the probability that water will change to wine in similar circumstances.

To sum up: We can imagine a different legal system in which there were no pardons and so no exceptions to the rule of law. However, our system is not such a system but rather one in which certain exceptions to the legal order, called presidential pardons, sometimes occur. Lawyers as such have no concern with presidential pardons, for they cannot predict them, bring them about, or draw any precedents for them. A presidential pardon is, you might say, supralegal and therefore of no *legal* interest. Similarly, it could be that our universe was one in which there were no exceptions to the natural order, but if traditional religious believers are right, our universe is not such a universe, but one in which certain exceptions to the natural order, called miracles, sometimes occur. Scientists, as such, have no concern with miracles, for they cannot predict them, bring them about, or draw any conclusions about the future course of nature from them. A miracle is supernatural, and therefore of no scientific interest.

We could not settle whether presidential pardons are possible by looking at the day-to-day business of the courts; rather, we must ask what kind of legal system we live under. We cannot settle whether miracles occur by looking at the ordinary course of nature; we must ask what kind of universe we live in. This is a philosophical, not a scientific, question, and one very relevant philosophical consideration is that a universe made by God leaves room for confidence in human reason, whereas a universe of natural necessity does not.

If we come to the conclusion that miracles are possible, then we must consider miracle as one possible explanation of certain events recorded in history. Again, because most readers of this book will have been influenced to some extent by Christianity, we will consider Christian claims with regard to miracles. Early Christians claimed that the tomb of Christ was empty and that Christ had risen from the dead. The Roman and Jewish authorities did not refute this claim by producing the body, as they would certainly have done had *they* removed it from the tomb. The Apostles suffered persecution, hardship, and martyrdom to proclaim the message of Christ risen from the dead, which they surely would not have done if *they* had removed and hidden Christ's body. Christians claim that no naturalistic explanation which tries to explain the disappearance of the body and the confidence of the early Christians comes anywhere near accounting for all the facts.

If miracles were impossible, we should have to try to account for the data in some other way; but there is no good argument which shows that miracles are impossible. If miracles were tremendously improbable, many times more improbable than the most farfetched naturalistic explanation of the data, then it might be reasonable to accept an otherwise very implausible naturalistic explanation. But there seems to be no argument to show that miracles are tremendously improbable. It is not enough to say that they are rare and unusual— any event may be rare and unusual but still to be expected in given circumstances. It is rare to have world records in athletic events broken, but it is to be expected at the Olympic Games. President Ford's pardon of ex-President Nixon was a rare and unusual event, but not unexpected in the very unusual circumstances which then prevailed. The Resurrection of Christ was a rare and unusual event, but in the context of His life and teaching, was it unexpected?

It is even possible to give some general idea of the circumstances in which miracles are to be expected. The first is extraordinary goodness or holiness on the part of the miracle worker. As the man born blind said to the Jews, "We know for certain that God does not answer the prayers of sinners." The second circumstance is the need to back up or authenticate a message from God. Christ was as good and holy the year before He began his public ministry as He was after He began it, but He did not begin to work miracles until He began to preach. There is, I think, a third condition: an openness and willingness to learn on the part of the audience. In some places Christ worked few miracles because of the hardness of heart of those in that place. Christ worked no miracles at Herod's request; He cast none of His pearls before that swine.

Let me pause here and make a parenthetical remark which is not directly relevant to my main theme, but has a connection with it. I have been mentioning as examples various miracles attributed to Christ in the Gospels, including the Fourth Gospel. This may seem to some to fly in the face of much recent biblical scholarship, which has argued that the miracles attributed to Christ are additions to the record of His life made by later generations of Christian believers rather than accounts of what actually happened at the time given by eyewitnesses. Now in some cases there may be reasons for doubting on purely textual grounds whether a certain part of the New Testament as we now have it was part of the original record, for example, in the debated case of the "long ending" of Mark's Gospel. But a careful examination of a good deal of "higher" criticism (as opposed to textual criticism) of the New Testament shows that it is not the case that the miraculous element is rejected because the text is doubtful, but rather that the text is regarded as doubtful because of a prior rejection of any miraculous element.

Insofar, then, as we can show by philosophical argument that neither science nor reason requires us to reject the possibility of miracles, we undermine the kind of doubt as to the reliability of our texts which is based on hostility to a miraculous or supernatural element in Scripture. We must entertain the possibility that Luke recounts the Virgin birth of Christ because it actually happened and not because the later Christian community borrowed elements from pagan mythology to enhance the importance of the founder of Christianity. To the unbiased eye the first hypothesis might seem much more plausible than the second. We might even be daring enough to entertain the hypothesis that the Fourth Gospel, which is full of eyewitness detail and local knowledge, was actually written by the Apostle John, and that its theological depth as compared to the other Gospels is due to the fact that John understood his Master better than some of the other disciples, rather than due to later interpretations by second-generation Christians. Plato's picture of Socrates is more profound than Xenophon's, at least partly because Plato was better fitted to understand Socrates than Xenophon was.

Do historical arguments based on the New Testament record, which argue that miracle is the only or best explanation of certain well-attested events amount to a *proof* that miracles have occurred? So long as we understand that the term "proof" means something different in historical studies than it does in mathematics or science or philosophy, it may well be that we do have adequate historical proof of miracles. But to show this in detail would involve getting down to the historical nitty-gritty, and I cannot do that here.

Let me turn, then, to the related question of what miracles prove. If it is granted, at least for the sake of argument, that God exists, that miracles are possible, and that we have good historical evidence that miracles marked the beginning of Christianity, does this prove the Christian claim to the truth of the revelation given to us by Christ? Before we can decide this, we will have to examine three apparent difficulties.

The first difficulty is what we might call the problem of contradictory miracles. If it were the case that genuine miracles were worked
in support of contradictory religious revelations, we would not know
what to think. It would be like a witness whose integrity we were
absolutely sure of giving contradictory testimony for both sides of
a dispute. Something would have to give. We would have to conceive
that the witness was not really honest, or deny that he actually gave
the testimony on both sides, or find some way of showing that the
contradiction was only apparent.

Similarly, if it were claimed that miracles are worked in support
of contradictory religious revelations, we would have to give up the
idea of miracles as proving a system of religion, unless we could show
that the contradiction was only apparent, or that one set of opposed
miracles was not genuine.

In some cases perhaps we can show that there is no genuine conflict. Many religious believers accept both Old Testament and New
Testament miracles, and deny the claim (which has been made) that
Old Testament miracles worked in the name of the One God of
Judaism are in some way incompatible with New Testament miracles
worked in the name of God the Father, God the Son, and God the
Holy Spirit. (This is, of course, because they would deny, on
theological grounds, that Christian belief in the Trinity amounts to
belief in three Gods.)

Many Christian religious believers would not even deny the
possibility that God might have worked miracles for the "virtuous
pagans" before Christ, to encourage them to emphasize those parts
of their religion closest to the truth. If, for instance, God had worked
a miracle for the Egyptian Pharaoh Amenhotep in support of his ef-
forts to establish monotheism and overthrow the dark gods of old
Egypt, they would find in this no challenge to Christianity, even
though Amenhotep's monotheism might have been very crude and
contained elements of untruth.

What would threaten the argument from miracles for the truth
of Christianity would be genuine miracles worked in opposition to
Christian claims or in support of incompatible claims. If, for instance,
a Moslem holy man raised a man from the dead in order to persuade
Christians that Mohammed's revelation had superseded that of Christ,
this would be a case of genuine incompatibility. However, so far from
any case of this kind being established, it is hard to show that any

case of this kind has even been claimed. General statements are often made by opponents of Christianity that miracles are claimed by all religions, but leading cases of these alleged claims are hard to come by.

Certainly fairy-tale-like legends sometimes grow up around a figure like Buddha or Mohammed, but these have certain common characteristics. Such tales arise centuries after the time of their alleged occurrence. They contain strong elements of the fantastic (e.g., Mohammed riding his horse to the moon) and in their manner of telling they reveal their kinship to legend and myth. Compare any of these accounts with the accounts we find in the Gospels and the difference in atmosphere is at once apparent. Either the Gospel accounts are eyewitness accounts of real events occurring in genuine places, or the four writers we call Matthew, Mark, Luke, and John independently invented, out of the clear blue sky, a sort of realistic fantasy or science fiction which has no antecedents and no parallels in ancient literature. Those who have no metaphysical objections to miracles may find the hypothesis that the events really happened as they are related immensely more plausible than the other hypothesis.

It may be worthwhile to take a quick look, for purposes of comparison, at the closest thing we have around the time of the Gospels to an attempt at a realistic fantasy. This is the story of Appollonius of Tyana, written about A.D. 220 by Flavius Philostratus, which is sometimes referred to by controversialists as if it were a serious rival to the Gospel accounts of Christ's ministry and miracles. Penguin Classics publishes an excellent little paperback edition of this story, to which you may go for details, but let me note a few points in passing.

The story concerns a wandering sage who allegedly lived from the early years of the first century until about A.D. 96 or 98. Philostratus mentions some earlier sources for his work but at least some of these sources are probably his own invention. For one thing, Philostratus's account contains serious historical inaccuracies about things like dates of rulers, which seem to rule out reliance on any early source. The work was later used as anti-Christian propaganda, to discredit the uniqueness of Christ's miracles by setting up a rival miracle worker, as Socrates was sometimes set up as a rival to Christ as a martyr and teacher of virtue.

Still, there is some evidence that a neo-Pythagorean sage named Appollonius may really have lived, and thus Philostratus's work is a real example of what some have thought the Gospels to be: a fictionalized account of the life of a real sage and teacher, introducing miraculous events to build up the prestige of the central figure. It thus gives us a good look at what a real example of a fictionalized biography would look like, written at a time and place not too far removed from those in which the Gospels were written.

The first thing we notice is the fairy-tale atmosphere. There is a rather nice little vampire story, which inspired a minor poem by Keats, entitled *Lamia*. There are animal stories about, for instance, snakes in India big enough to drag off and eat an elephant. The sage wanders from country to country and wherever he goes he is likely to be entertained by the king or emperor, who holds long conversations with him and sends him on his way with camels and precious stones.

Interspersed with picturesque adventures there are occasional accounts of miracles, often involving prophecy or mind reading. A ruffian threatens to cut Apollonius's head off and the sage laughs and shouts out the name of a day three days hence; on that day the ruffian is executed for treason. Here is a typical passage about healing miracles:

> There came a man about thirty who was an expert lion-hunter but had been attacked by a lion and dislocated his hip, and so was lame in one leg. But the Wise Man massaged his hip and this restored the man to an upright walk. Someone else who had gone blind went away with his sight fully restored, and another man with a paralysed arm left strong again. A woman too, who had had seven miscarriages was cured through the prayers of her husband as follows. The Wise Man told the husband, when his wife was in labor, to bring a live rabbit under his cloak to the place where she was, walk around her and immediately release the hare: for she would lose her womb as well as the baby if the hare was not immediately driven away (Bk. 3, Sec. 39).

Now the point is not that Apollonius is no serious rival to Christ; no one ever thought he was except perhaps a few anti-Christian polemicists about the time of some of the early persecutions of the Church. The point is that this is what you get when imagination goes to work on a historical figure in classical antiquity; you get miracle stories a little like those in the Gospels, but also snakes big enough to eat elephants, kings and emperors as supporting cast, travelers' tales, ghosts, and vampires. Once the boundaries of fact are crossed we wander into fairyland. And very nice, too, for amusement or recreation. But the Gospels are set firmly in the real Palestine of the first century, and the little details are not picturesque inventions but the real details that only an eyewitness or a skilled realistic novelist can give.

As against this, those who wish to eliminate miracles from the Gospels have not textual evidence, but theories. We do not have any trace of early sober narratives of the life of Christ without miracles and later versions in which miracles are added. What we have is a story with miracles woven into its very texture. Someone once made a shrewd point about this. Christ, say the Gospels, "went about doing good." Fine. But what good did He do? Did He clothe the naked, visit prisoners, counsel people on personal problems? No. He went about making the extravagant claim to forgive sins and backing this up by working miracles, mostly miracles of healing. Eliminate this element and, setting aside His preaching, what good did He go about doing?

The point is that the miraculous is interwoven with the primary story of Christianity in a way in which the miraculous is not interwoven with the primary story of Buddhism or Mohammedanism. Again, however, this is a matter for detailed inquiry into comparative religion and the history of religions.

The second major difficulty as to the evidential value of miracles which we will consider is the objection that what seems to us to be an exception to the natural order may just be the operation of some natural regularities which we do not yet understand. Perhaps, says this objection, Jesus was merely a rare type of charismatic personality who could arouse a faith response in people such that their minds acted on their bodies in a way that freed them from illness. After all, the relation of the mind and body in illness is a mysterious one, and some studies suggest that mental attitude has a great deal to do with illness. Thus we may someday understand scientifically, and even be able to reproduce, some of Christ's apparently miraculous cures.

The first comment to make on this line of objection is that, like any argument which depends on what science *may* be able to discover in the future, it is extremely weak. But we can also ask what range of illnesses and cures this theory is supposed to account for. For example, Christ might have cured a paralytic because the paralysis was hysterical and subject to psychosomatic healing. But what about the cure of leprosy? What about the cure of the man blind from birth? And it is no use saying that psychosomatic illnesses cured by the impact of a charismatic personality account for *some* of Christ's cures and that the rest are fictional, for this would be to pick and choose among the evidence in a blatant way. If I am allowed to pick which of the evidence I will explain and reject the rest, I can make almost any theory look plausible.

But, of course, the cases which are decisive against any theory of psychosomatic cures are the raisings from the dead reported in all four Gospels. A last-ditch attempt to explain these "naturally" might be to allege that the seemingly dead persons were only in a cataleptic state, but cases of this kind are so rare that to allege this as an explanation of the raising of the daughter of the Jairus, *and* of the son of the widow of Nain, *and* Lazarus, brings in coincidence to a fantastic degree. Each of these accounts is highly circumstantial, and none can be plausibly treated as a variation on one of the others.

In others words, the proponent of the view that Christ's cures were psychosomatic—"faith healing" in a limiting sense—must make up his mind whether or not he accepts the written records as factual or fictional, or whether he holds them to be a mixture of fact and fiction. If the records are fictional, no explanation of the cures is necessary. If the account is factual, all of the reported miracles must be accounted for, not just those which can be plausibly accounted for on naturalistic grounds. If it is alleged that there is a mixture of fact and fiction, there must be an independent standard of what is factual in the record and what is fictional. We cannot in logic allow the principle of choice: "What I can explain is fact, the rest is fiction." (Think what ex-President Nixon could have done to the Watergate story using that principle!)

If the proponent of an explanation by so far unknown laws of nature goes so far as to say that even raisings from the dead can be accounted for by these laws, he must again explain a tremendous implausibility: either that these laws operated coincidentally in the neighborhood of Jesus, or that an obscure provincial carpenter somehow was able to discover and make use of natural powers and possibilities that none of the wise sages or deep researchers had ever been able to master or control.

A final difficulty about the evidential value of miracles rests on the fear that some supernatural power less than that of God might account for the wonders worked by Christ—that Jesus did His works, if not by the powers of Beelzebub, then at least by the power of some spiritual being less than God. To say what power this might be, of course, would be in some sense to give a theological account of what powers greater than human there might be, and how they are related to one another.

Consider, however, a line of argument sometimes heard from people influenced by certain sorts of Eastern religions, which goes something like this: Yes, of course Jesus was able to do apparently miraculous things; He was a Master, or Adept, and they can all do things of this sort. Jesus, living at the time and place that He did, tried to teach the Palestinian people a simple religion of love, put in terms of their own religious concepts, and this message has reached us in a distorted form. His real power lay in spiritual enlightenment, which you can learn by practicing Yoga (*or* going to Tibet, *or* studying with Mahatma X, or the like).

Again, there is a large blank check, drawn this time not on science, but on some sort of mystical religion. A friend of mine, arguing religion with opponents who seemed dogmatically sure of what God could or could not create, would challenge them, if they knew so much about creation, to create just one small rabbit—"to establish confidence." A similar challenge might be put to the exponents of "Eastern Wisdom" to duplicate even the least of Christ's miracles, to establish their claims. If they admit their own lack of power but claim others have performed some feats as great as Christ's, the problem simply reduces to one of the evidence for rival miracles discussed earlier.

In addition, there is a theological question as to whether a wise and loving God would allow people to be misled by permitting some lesser being to work apparent miracles. Real raising from the dead, creation of food or wine which is genuine and not illusory—such miracles seem by their nature to be the province of God only. But even if such things as the reading of thoughts or the manipulation of matter in scientifically inexplicable ways were possible to powers less than God, would God permit such occurrences in a context which gave rise to a false belief in men of good will, or seriously challenged the true beliefs of those already on the right path? A priori, it would seem not; and again, it does not seem that there is any reliable record of any such occurrences. (This is not to say that God may not sometimes permit "wonders" of this sort to be worked in order to refute them by His own power—for example, the story in Acts of the girl with the "prophetic spirit.")

The preceding comments, necessarily brief, give some indication of the lines along which the evidential value of miracles must be assessed. Are there indeed rival miracles? Can miracles be explained as due to powers less than God? If the answer to all these questions is no, then we are forced to grant that miracles give a strong argument for the existence of God.

BIBLIOGRAPHY

Items [2] to [16] refer to the extracts presented in this volume.
For further discussion by Christian theologians on the topic of miracles, see

[17] St. Augustine, *De Civitate Dei*, xxi 6–8 and xxxii 8–10.

[18] Pope Benedict XIV, *De Servorum Dei Beatificatione et Beatorum Canonizatione, iv: De Miraculis*, 1738.

For useful historical discussion on the evolution of the Greco-Roman and Christian understandings of miracles, see

[19] Moule, C. F. D., ed. *Miracles*. London, Mowbray, 1965.

[20] Grant, R. M. *Miracle and Natural Law in Graeco-Roman and Early Christian Thought*. Amsterdam, North Holland, 1952.

[21] Hardon, J. A., S.J. "The Concept of Miracle from St. Augustine to Modern Apologetics", *Theological Studies*. 15, 1954.

It is an interesting exercise to read different New Testament commentaries and books about New Testament times, including those listed above, and note how different authors make different background assumptions about whether there is a God capable of intervening in nature and prepared on occasion to do so, and in consequence reach quite different conclusions about whether an apparent miracle really occurred, while using the same detailed historical evidence. This is as it should be, but what is to be regretted is that the different writers do not make explicit how their conclusions are determined largely by background assumptions.

The Roman Catholic Church has some fairly precise criteria for recognizing a miracle. These are outlined, discussed, and illustrated by examples of alleged miracles in

[22] West, D. J. *Eleven Lourdes Miracles*. London, Helix Press, 1957.

For other examples of alleged contemporary miracles, see

[23] Gardiner, Rex. *Healing Miracles*. London, Darton, Longman and Todd, 1986.

Several philosophers and popular writers criticized the belief in miracles during the century preceding Hume's *Inquiry*. Spinoza wrote against miracles in Chapter VI of his *Theological-Political Treatise* (various editions) and Bayle attacked the belief in numerous articles in the *Historical and Critical Dictionary*, an English translation of which was published in four volumes between 1734 and 1738. All of the major deists who wrote on the subject are sympathetically discussed in Vol. 1 of Leslie Stephen's *History of English Thought in the Eighteenth Century* (1872, Harcourt Brace reprint 1962).

For later writing in the Humean tradition and further commentary on Hume, see

[24] Voltaire. "Miracles." *Philosophical Dictionary*, 1764.

[25] Mill, J. S., *A System of Logic*, 1843, 3.25, "Of the Grounds of Disbelief."

[26] Broad, C. D. "Hume's Theory of the Credibility of Miracles," *Proceedings of the Aristotelian Society*, 1916–17, *17*: 77–94.

[27] Nowell-Smith, Patrick. "Miracles," originally published in *Hibbert Journal*, 1950, and republished in *New Essays in Philosophical Theology*, edited by A. Flew and A. MacIntyre. London, SCM Press, 1955.

[28] Flew, Antony. *Hume's Theory of Belief*. London: Routledge and Kegan Paul, 1961, Ch. 8 ([10] is an extract from this chapter.)

For another application of the probability calculus to Hume's argument on the weight of evidence needed to establish a miracle, see

[29] Sobel, Jordan Howard. "On the Evidence of Testimony for Miracles: A Bayesian Interpretation of David Hume's Analysis," *Philosophical Quarterly*, 1987, *37*: 166–86.

For a radical Protestant view, together with a history of development of radical Protestant thinking, see

[30] Keller, E and M-L. *Miracles in Dispute*. London, SCM Press, 1969.

For a well-known modern popular defense of the possibility of miracles, see

[31] Lewis, C. S. *Miracles*, rev. ed. London: Collins Fontana Books, 1960.

For further modern philosophical discussion of miracles, see

[32] Smart, Ninian. "Miracles and David Hume", *Philosophers and Religious Truth*. London, SCM Press, 1964, Ch. 2.

[33] Flew, Antony. *God and Philosophy*. London: Hutchinson, 1966, Ch. 2.

[34] Dietl, Paul. "On Miracles," *American Philosophical Quarterly*, 1968, 5: 130–34.

[35] Ward, Keith. "Miracles and Testimony," *Religious Studies*, 1985, 21: 134–45.

For a standard modern account of the nature of scientific explanation, see

[36] Hempel, C. G. *Philosophy of Natural Science*. Englewood Cliffs, NJ: Prentice-Hall, 1966, Chs. 1–5.

For further modern philosophical writing on whether "agent causality" differs in kind from "scientific causality," see

[37] Davis, L. H. *Theory of Action*. Englewood Cliffs, NJ: Prentice-Hall, 1979, Ch. 1.

[38] Davidson, D. "Actions, Reasons, and Causes," *Essays on Actions and Events*. Oxford, Clarendon Press, 1980.

[39] Chisholm, R. M. "The Agent as Cause" in *Action Theory*, edited by M. Brand and D. Walton. D. Reidel, Boston, 1976.

For petitionary prayer in relation to miracles, see

[40] Young, Robert. "Petitionary Prayer," *American Philosophical Quarterly*, 1974, 11: 193–201.

[41] Brummer, Vincent. *What Do We Do When We Pray?* London, SCM Press, 1984, especially Ch. 5.

For general defense of theistic and atheistic world views, respectively, see

[42] Swinburne, Richard. *The Existence of God*. Oxford, Clarendon Press, 1979.

[43] Mackie, J.L. *The Miracle of Theism*. Oxford, Clarendon Press, 1982.